Advance Praise for *The Secret*

"Where the business climate and the political climate come together, opportunities are to be found—and when the subject is political and economic climate change, James Pinkerton knows which way the winds are blowing."

—Michael Lind, author of *Land of Promise: An Economic History of the United States*

"Jim Pinkerton, widely reputed to be the smartest man in Washington, has always had an uncanny ability to see around corners. Now future-minded readers can profit from Pinkerton's boundless curiosity, voracious reading, brilliant synthesis, and visionary insight. And despite the book's unflinching prediction that Red America and Blue America are becoming opposed and incompatible tribes, there's comfort in the conclusion that the country ultimately can live with its differences—and that wise investors will reap benefits from the new national arrangements."

—Geoffrey Kabaservice, Vice President for Political Studies at the Niskanen Center

"If America remains in a hopelessly polarized Blue State, Red State American condition today, is a rapid destructive decline inevitable? In his new book, *The Secret to Directional Investing*, Jim Pinkerton boldly demonstrates how America remains a land of unique opportunity—as a result of its diverse opinion, population and unique constitutional system. If we direct our divergent perspectives toward more creative entrepreneurial targets. Our differences may actually uncover dramatic, exponential breakthroughs in healthcare, energy, education, longevity and prosperity instead of wasteful destructive debate."

—Clara Del Villar, Founder, CEO Schola Labs

"Drawing from an entertaining mix of popular culture, history, technology, and public policy mayhem, Jim Pinkerton's new book will shock and delight its readers. Pinkerton delivers an insightful, forward-looking view of the forces shaping America and its future. You don't want to be the last person to read this book!"

—Jim Carter, past appointee to senior positions at the White House National Economic Council, the Departments of Treasury and Labor, and the Senate Budget Committee

THE SECRET OF DIRECTIONAL INVESTING

MAKING MONEY
AMIDST THE RED-BLUE RUMBLE

JAMES P. PINKERTON

Post Hill
PRESS

A POST HILL PRESS BOOK
ISBN: 979-8-88845-048-2
ISBN (eBook): 979-8-88845-049-9

The Secret of Directional Investing:
Making Money Amidst the Red-Blue Rumble
© 2024 by James P. Pinkerton
All Rights Reserved

Cover design by Cody Corcoran

Post Hill Press, LLC
New York • Nashville
posthillpress.com

Published in the United States of America
1 2 3 4 5 6 7 8 9 10

To Elizabeth ... and Jan.

CONTENTS

EVERY DOLLAR TELLS A STORY

Big money comes from big things. The bigger the inflection point, the bigger the return. The more delta, the more alpha. Big deltas, and their big alphas, come in two categories: those that can be *observed*, and profited from, and those that can *initiated*, and profited from. Either way, the trend is your friend. The distinction is whether it's a trend one is content to *spot*, or a trend one helps to *shape*. Both modes—passive and active, trend-spotting and trend-shaping—can make money. Yet trend-shaping is potentially more lucrative. There's no better way to get on the ground floor than to *build* the ground floor. And there's no better way to deal with change than to shape it yourself. The Romans weren't kidding when they said, *Audentes Fortuna Iuvat*. Fortune favors the bold.

The first half of this book concerns trend-*spotting*. That is, seeing the cultural and political trends that shape the economy, pointing to opportunities for business and investors. We will include capsulized historical points on how consequential trends came to be, and how they might arise again. Because, after all, no trend involving human beings ever goes away completely. If it happened once with human nature, it will happen again, albeit in some new form. All the more reason to be able to recognize the historical traces, so as to quickly profit from the reemerging pattern.

The second half concerns trend-*shaping*. That is, the political factors that can shape the economy, leading to opportunities for business and investors. Trend-shaping is, of course, more difficult. But just as we most admire that which is hard to do, we most profit from that which is hard to do. The last chapter points to ways of using the political process to put positive investment trends in motion. In fact, the reengineering of American politics is itself an investment opportunity.

Directional Investing is the realization that cultural and political trends drive investments, and that those trends can be shaped, not just spotted.

Yet there's an even larger point to be made. Money is a thing of value, and people care about things of value. Yet because money is all around us, its motion is often as indistinct as water is in water. So if we take time to discern its currents, we see that money has an interesting past, and a compelling future. Some will say, of course, that money is just fiat currency— cheap metal, or paper, or electrons—not in and of itself worth anything. And they're right. But that makes money all the more interesting, because the tale of how something with no intrinsic worth comes to be worth a lot is, by definition, quite a tale. What forces were put in motion, giving force to the fiat? How did people come to accept it? What's the legal and political framework that enables people to invest money to gain wealth, and to enjoy that wealth? The answers to those questions have to be juicy: sagas of ideas and politics, of power and even violence.

What a long strange trip it has been, and will be. How does wealth compound? How do investors plan, and strive, to make their nest egg grow bigger? What has to seem true to give an investor hope? What has to *be* true to make an investment succeed? Every dollar tells a story of great expectations, realized, or not. So we'll examine scenarios—ones that have happened, are happening, and could happen—especially if they were to get a friendly boost. For sure, we'll look at the investment boost that comes from the lift of a driving dream.

As we gaze out at the moneyed horizon, we see how imagining stakes out the future. If we can envision it, we can invest in it. Along the way, we'll gain new perspective on our work, greater purpose for our wealth—and make the world a better, richer, place.

This is Directional Investing.

CHAPTER ONE

ENVISIONING LAS VEGA$

NEVADA, ENTERPRISE ZONE

On March 19, 1931, with the stroke of a gubernatorial pen, Nevada's economic trajectory changed—it moved sharply upward. The state legalized all gambling. Nine decades later, Nevada's population has grown from less than 100,000 to nearly 3.2 million.[1] In 2022, the state boasted gambling revenues of $14.8 billion, up more than 10 percent from the previous year and up from virtually nothing in 1931.[2] In 1930, "160 acres-near town-fronting on Los Angeles highway" sold for $75 per acre.[3] Today that highway is known as the Strip, and a single acre there has sold for as much as $40 million.[4] Great fortunes have been made, including that of the late casino owner Sheldon Adelson, whose wealth peaked at $38.5 billion.[5] In fact, in 2022, an estimated seventeen billionaires lived

[1] Nevada Population 1900-2022, https://bit.ly/3N4vhjM
[2] Stutz, Howard, "Nevada casinos close out 2022 with record gaming revenue figures," *Nevada Independent,* January 31, 2023. https://bit.ly/44pkJBP
[3] Segall, Eli, "Las Vegas' record house prices still below bubble days, in a way," *Las Vegas Review-Journal,* August 14, 2021. https://bit.ly/3Jy9E9R
[4] Segall, Eli, "Land values on Strip can vary greatly—even for same-sized plots," *Las Vegas Review-Journal,* June 11, 2022. https://bit.ly/46v9x8I
[5] "Forbes Profile: Sheldon Adelson," *Forbes,* September 8, 2020. https://bit.ly/3pqtWLu

in Nevada.[6] To be sure, not all those fortunes can be solely attributed to gambling. But most of that wealth comes, directly or indirectly, from "the green felt jungle."[7]

The legal inflection point, back in 1931, was the pen stroke of Nevada's governor, Fred Balzar. Actually, it was *two* strokes of his pen that changed the state's destiny. The governor signed two bills sent to him by the legislature—one to legalize "wide open" gambling, and the other to ease divorce. In the words of historian Michael Green, "The 1931 legislative session proved to be the most important in Nevada's history. Its members passed two laws that…changed Nevada's economy and society."[8] According to another Nevada historian, Russell Elliot, the two acts "were directed, at least in part, toward increasing the state's economic potential." Hmm. There's that word, *directed*, close to *directional*. Elliott continues, "Although gambling was not a large producer of revenue in the 1930s, nevertheless it was in that decade that the foundation was laid for developments which ultimately made gambling the state's prime industry."[9]

Some historians say that Nevada's legislative moves were just in keeping with the libertarian ethos of the frontier. Others say the legislature was bribed by gangsters in Chicago, notably, Al Capone and Murray "The Hump" Humphreys. Of course, both theories can be true. And neither theory argues against a third explanation—that Nevadans had a *vision*. A vision of their state letting the good times roll, making money along the way.

Interestingly, of the two new laws enacted in that hinge year of 1931, the most immediately impactful was the change in divorce laws,

[6] "Richest billionaires in Nevada," *Stacker.com*, April 6, 2023. https://bit.ly/3CMLEfk

[7] Reid, Ed, and Demaris, Ovid, *The Green Felt Jungle: The Truth About Las Vegas Where Organized Crime Controls Gambling—And Everything Else* (Trident Press, 1963).

[8] Green, Michael S., *Nevada: A History of the Silver State* (Reno: University of Nevada Press, 2015), 231.

[9] Elliott, Russell R., *History of Nevada* (Lincoln: University of Nebraska Press, Second edition, 1987), 277, 282.

shortening the residency requirement for a divorce to six weeks. In those days, in much of the country—including the then-largest state, New York—divorce was hard to get, sometimes impossible. And so it often-times made sense for would-be divorcers to establish a legal residence of convenience in a state with laxer laws, such as Nevada, which in 1915 had cut its residency requirement from a year down to six months. Allowing divorce-seekers to end their marriage this way was a tourist-trappy form of economic development.

In fact, in this "divorce-trade war," Nevada found itself in a competi-tion with two other states possessed of the same idea, Arkansas and Idaho. So in 1927, the Nevada legislature cut the state's residency requirement in half again, to a mere three months. A cartoon in the *New York Herald Tribune* that same year captured the dynamic. It shows a prospector exul-tantly throwing gold coins in the air as he stands next to a sign reading "New Divorce Law"; the caption reads "Another Gold Strike in the West."[10] And in 1931, the requirement was cut again. George Cukor's 1939 movie *The Women*, starring Joan Crawford, Joan Fontaine, and Norma Shearer, among other females, tells the tale of would-be divorcees decamping to Reno, spending good money during their six-week stint. Yet Nevada's com-parative advantage as a "divorce enterprise zone" petered out in the middle of the last century, when other states made divorce easier, obviating the need for a Nevada sojourn.

So it's been gambling (Nevada officials prefer to call it "gaming") that has been the longer-lasting economic driver. At the time of that wide-open legalization in 1931, the population of Las Vegas was a mere 5,000. Immediately after the law changed, small gambling hubs opened up (or at least made honest establishments of themselves). But the Depression and World War II got in the way of major development. After the war, in 1946, Los Angeles mobster Bugsy Siegel debuted the Flamingo Hotel. To add to the glamor, Siegel imported Hollywood types such as George Raft. The

---

[10] Reno Divorce History, "Residency Requirements," https://bit.ly/3PyUAwn

Flamingo was a leap far beyond the sawdust of Cowboy Vegas. According to one account, Siegel had a vision.

> *"He would become the greatest impresario of gambling in America. He would erect the largest and most luxurious gambling casino in the world. It would not be just a casino, but a plush hotel as well, with a night club, restaurant, bars, swimming pool, exotically landscaped grounds, and the finest service imaginable. He would, above all else, become legitimate. So legitimate that "no FBI man can ever as much as lay a finger on my shoulder."[11]*

Budgeted at $1.5 million, the Flamingo cost $6 million, and customers valued every penny. Of course, Siegel was still a gangster, and so even if the FBI couldn't touch him, his fellow hoods could. Accused of skimming, he was rubbed out in 1947. Yet even post-Bugsy, the state's course was clear. "The rise of gambling and tourism," historian Green writes, "exploited people's weaknesses and belief in their luck, but also exploited prosperity elsewhere to create wealth for Nevada."[12] We can pause over that point—*exploited prosperity elsewhere to create wealth for Nevada*. That's the business model of any attraction—to entice people and their money.

THE LONG AND WINDING ROAD TO "WIDE OPEN"

By now, Las Vegas is regarded as legit and the casinos are mostly publicly traded corporations. And if there's still a mob vibe, some of that's marketing sizzle. Yet it's useful to take a closer look at the long and winding road to "wide-open" gambling, as it speaks to the Directional theme of this book—legal changes have huge financial consequences.

Long before the White man came to Nevada, Puebloans and other tribes engaged gambling similar to today's bingo. Such traditional play

---

[11] Reid, Ed and Demaris, Ovid, *The Green Felt Jungle*, 20.
[12] Green, Michael S., *Nevada:*, 3.

was little changed by the coming of Europeans. In 1774, a Franciscan missionary, Francisco Garcés, reached the territory of Alta California, and in 1776, Spanish soldiers arrived in Las Vegas, establishing the dominion of King Carlos III. When Mexico won its independence from Spain in 1821, Nevada lands were governed from Mexico City. Then in 1848, after the American military prevailed in the Halls of Montezuma, title to Nevada was transferred to the United States.[13] In the nineteenth century, prospectors combing through the earth of what would come to be known as the Silver State loved to gamble as much or more as the natives. Yet in 1861, President Abraham Lincoln put a shadow on that love, appointing James W. Nye as governor of the Nevada Territory. Nye was a stern opponent of gambling, declaring to the territorial legislature, "I particularly recommend that you pass stringent laws to prevent gambling. Of all the seductive vices extant, I regard that of gambling as the worst." In those days, the main political goal of Nevadans was achieving US statehood. So the legislators, knowing they had to bow down to their federal overseers and their Yankee morals, made gambling a felony.[14]

Yet once Nevada had secured its sovereignty as the thirty-sixth state in 1864, the locals set about reasserting their freewheelin' ways. And in 1931, Governor Balzar clinched the deal. He formalized a protective legal framework around the instinctive impulses of his people. In Directional terms, he *spotted* a trend, and then *shaped* it.

These geopolitical transitions are worth recalling, because each speaks to a turn in Nevada's destiny. After all, whoever is in charge gets to make the laws. Yet there's one thing we can say. Once Nevada *had* become a state, it would enjoy substantial self-determination. And that's because the US Constitution includes a key feature that will loom large in this book—the distribution and compartmentalization of political power, also known as federalism, also known as states' rights. As we shall see, this isn't just arcane history. This is the living, breathing, *investing* stuff of today's America.

---

[13] Ibid., 29-42.
[14] Ibid., 84-100.

Back in 1788, while championing the ratification of the new Constitution, Alexander Hamilton pledged that state power would be protected under the new national document. "The State governments would clearly retain all the rights of sovereignty which they before had, and which were not, by that act, EXCLUSIVELY delegated to the United States."[15] In other words, the states retain their right to do as they please, unless that right was explicitly surrendered to federal authority—and there's no mention of gambling in the Constitution.

Thus Nevada was armored up, legally, to chart its own course on gambling. So when *The Chicago Tribune* thundered, "Cancel Nevada's Statehood!"[16] Nevadans could shrug. Being secure in their state's constitutional rights, they didn't have to worry about a newspaper's opinion. Indeed, in 1971, Nevada went further in its pursuit of profitable sin. It legalized prostitution in some parts of the state. So the famous wink of an ad campaign made all the more sense—"What happens here, stays here."[17]

As a US state, Nevada has been able to participate in national projects vital to its well-being, including water projects. Nevada is literally the driest state in the union, and it gets the most of its water from the Colorado River, which it must share with a half-dozen other states, as well as Mexico. Without that water, the growth of Nevada, gambling or no gambling, would simply not have happened. (We'll have much more to say about water in Chapter Twelve.) So we can see, Nevada's prosperity has been due, first and foremost, to the vision of its entrepreneurs, and yet the state's success has also been a function of politics. It was *intra*-state politics that that gave

---

[15] Hamilton, Alexander, *The Federalist Papers: No. 32*, National Archives, Founders Online, 1788. https://bit.ly/43cmNMC

[16] Green, Michael S., *Nevada*, 233.

[17] The ad campaign, frequently recalled as "What happens in Vegas, stays in Vegas," became a 2008 Hollywood movie starring Cameron Diaz and Ashton Kutcher.

Nevada its libertarian policies.[18] And it was *inter*-state politics that made it effective on such matters as water and, crucially, lenient federal tax rules on casino transactions.[19] And yet it was muscular geopolitics that made Nevada a US state, and not a state in Mexico, or potentially a vassal of some other country. For instance, in the popular counterfactual novel-turned-TV series, *The Man in the High Castle*, Nevada is controlled by imperial Japan, while most of North America is controlled by Nazi Germany. Not a good look for investment, or any other form of freedom.

DIFFERENT STROKES FOR DIFFERENT STATES

Here we might pause to observe that gambling is hardly the only route to riches—and perhaps far from the best. It's noteworthy, for example, that three neighboring states (California, Oregon, and Utah) have higher per capita incomes.[20] Most notably, California, has had its own growth industries, and some of them benefited, too, from a freebooting mentality, involving the *de facto* legalization of an activity that was closely regulated elsewhere. As Harvard Law School's Lawrence Lessig recalls, "The

---

[18] Many of the early pioneers to Nevada were Southerners, often ex-Confederate soldiers, seeking the opportunity that couldn't be found in devastated Dixie. Hence, for instance, Virginia City, Nevada. The most famous Western novel, *The Virginian*, from 1902, captures this phenomenon. Once these transplanted Southerners gained a foothold, they could use politics to find a peaceful and prosperous way to express their hostility to central authority.

[19] As historian Jerome E. Edwards writes in his 1982 book, *Pat McCarran: Political Boss of Nevada*, major issues concerning McCarran, a US senator from 1933 until his death in 1954, included the protection of gambling from the threat of federal interstate taxation. Writes Edwards, "gambling became the state's largest industry by 1955, and Nevada was increasingly dependent upon it. And Nevada gambling cannot flourish without federal acquiescence. Even though legalization may be purely a state matter, gambling could be terminated rather quickly by imposition of a federal tax on gambling transactions." Until 2021, the major airport in Las Vegas was named after him.

[20] "Per Capita Income by State 2023," World Population Review, https://bit.ly/3X-rQuYG. To be sure, these statistics can be analyzed, massaged, even "tortured," to prove various points.

Hollywood film industry was built by fleeing pirates. Creators and directors migrated from the East Coast to California in the early twentieth century in part to escape controls that film patents granted the inventor Thomas Edison…California was remote enough from Edison's reach that filmmakers like Fox and Paramount could move there and, without fear of the law, pirate his inventions."[21] So is this an argument for breaking the law? No. And in any case, the law soon changed. In 1915, the courts ruled against Edison and his camera trust. But by then, the movie biz was anchored in Southern California.

To be sure, in recent years, Nevada's growth as a gambling destination has decelerated, as other states have legalized at least some form of gambling. Today, some forty-five states have lotteries, and twenty-nine states host some 474 tribal casinos.[22] There have even been plans to put a casino in Manhattan.[23] In fact, Las Vegas is now home to just 20 percent of the nation's casino industry. As one observer puts it, "[C]asino gambling has evolved into a downscale business. Affluent and educated people visit casinos less often than poorer people do.…"[24] So it's no wonder the casinos are working hard to redefine themselves as entertainment destinations. In 2023, The Sphere, a 366-foot high "eyeball," made its debut. Boasting mesmerizing digital displays on its exterior, its interior seats 20,000.

In the meantime, Nevada is hardly giving up on its old core business. Mindful that geography can determine prosperity, the state's casinos have staunchly opposed online gambling; they were happy in November 2022, when the voters of California rejected, overwhelmingly, internet-based betting. As the Vegas newspaper put it, "Nevada will be watching intently

[21] Lessig, Lawrence, "Some Like It Hot," *Wired*, March 1, 2004. https://bit.ly/3XrLqng

[22] Meyersohn, Nathaniel, "Why these five states don't sell lottery tickets," CNN, November 9, 2022. https://bit.ly/3XuSxLN. See also: List of Casinos State-by-State, *500 Nations*. https://bit.ly/44cRH8C

[23] Hong, Nicole, et al., "Where Could a Casino Be Built in New York City? What We Know," *New York Times*, September 13, 2023. https://bit.ly/3XvaQjL

[24] Frum, David, "A Good Way to Wreck a Local Economy: Build Casinos," *The Atlantic*, August 7, 2014. https://bit.ly/3NPtuQb

to see whether it will continue to draw customers away from California who enjoy betting on games."[25]

Yet just as it had to look beyond the economic value of lax divorce laws, Nevada must look beyond gambling and entertainment. And here it has another economic strength connected to its libertarian culture— its tax differential with other states. Most glaringly, California, just to the west, has the nation's highest state income tax rate, 13.3 percent—and *The Wall Street Journal* editorial page argues that it's even higher than that.[26] In competitive contrast, Nevada has no state income tax, including no tax on investment income; it's one of just eight states in that ultra-low tax category. So heck yeah, Nevada is encouraging people and firms to move across the state line, whether or not they have any interest in gambling. For instance, from 2013 to 2023, manufacturing jobs in Nevada surged by 70 percent, while at the same time, manufacturing jobs in California grew a mere six percent.[27] Speaking of California refugees in Nevada, in 2023, movie star Mark Wahlberg announced plans to build a "Hollywood 2.0" in Las Vegas, pledging to create 10,000 jobs. "There's lots of opportunity for growth here," the actor said. "And the government, especially our new governor, is really looking for opportunities to create jobs outside of gaming."[28]

Indeed, in May 2023, Nevada reasserted its libertarian stance while at the same time burnishing its status as a lifestyle refuge. The state's Repub-

---

[25] Velotta, Richard N., "How long will it take for California sports betting to regroup?" *The Las Vegas Review-Journal*, November 20, 2022. https://bit. ly/3PyTDnV

[26] Luhby, Tami, "Californians approve massive tax hike on the wealthy," CNN, November 7, 2012. https://bit.ly/3XqylL4. See also: "Gavin Newsom's Stealth Tax Increase," *The Wall Street Journal*, October 5, 2022. https://bit.ly/44naVIP. The *Journal* argued that removing the $145,600 wage ceiling on the state's 1.1% employee payroll tax means that California's top marginal income tax rate increases to 14.4 percent.

[27] Data from US Bureau of Labor Statistics, November 2023 https://bit.ly/ 3QQ8jOo and https://bit.ly/3GjW4or

[28] Hume, Ashley, and Fink, Larry, "Mark Wahlberg's mission to turn Las Vegas into 'Hollywood 2.0' with 10,000 new jobs," Fox Business, March 31, 2023. https:// bit.ly/42X3M0J

lican governor, Joe Lombardo, who counts himself as pro-life (that is, anti-abortion), nevertheless signed legislation assuring that his state's authorities would not cooperate with other states that have outlawed abortion and who might be pursuing women who received an abortion in Nevada.[29] We can see that across the centuries, Nevada has shown that a free and easy approach to morals brings with it plenty of money. To be sure, other states have done it differently, but this is the life Nevada has chosen.

INVESTMENT TAKEAWAYS

- At the end of each chapter, we will summarize some key investment points. This book doesn't attempt to figure out exactly which company, or stock, is going to do well. Instead, it offers examples of phenomena and trends that have made money, eyeing lessons about making money in the future. If you can *spot* the trend, you can follow the trend to success. And if you can help *shape* the trend, all the better. To those good ends, this author particularly admires the investment-relevant acuity found in three books from the last century: Peter Lynch's *One Up on Wall Street* (1989), Alvin Toffler's *The Third Wave* (1980), and Daniel Bell's *The Cultural Contradictions of Capitalism* (1976).

- Peter Lynch stands as one of the most successful money managers of modern times. When he took over the Fidelity Magellan fund in 1977, its assets were $18 million; when he retired in 1990, the amount was $14 *billion*. Anyone who stayed with Lynch for all those thirteen years enjoyed a 29.2 percent annual return.[30] In picking investments, he emphasized the power of direct personal observation. Lynch was a great trend-spotters—and then, of course, he

---

29 Stern, Gabe, "Nevada Republican governor approves abortion protections in cross-party move," Associated Press, May 31, 2023. https://bit.ly/3JteDs3

30 Hannon, Kerry, "Fidelity legend Peter Lynch: 'I never said to invest in the stock market,'" Yahoo News, June 20, 2023. https://bit.ly/3XI9AKk

put his money where his eyes were. At the same time, Lynch counseled readers to ignore "hot tips" and "can't miss" touts—including those from investors such as himself—and instead focus on noticing. "Buyers and sellers of any product notice shortages and gluts, price changes and shifts in demand," he wrote. "If you stay half-alert, you can pick the spectacular performers right from your place of business or out of the neighborhood shopping mall, and long before Wall Street discovers them."[31] Using this approach, he one-upped his money-managing competition. For instance, Lynch invested in Hanes, maker of L'eggs pantyhose, for the simple reason that women he knew loved the product. He made similar first-hand observations about Apple and Dunkin' Donuts. It's hard to beat the insight that comes from actually watching how something operates, year in and year out.

- *The Third Wave*, from Alvin Toffler, was journalistically textured and data-rich—more than 500 pages of interviews, anecdotes, and statistics—and yet it was also deeply perspectival. Toffler was a trend-spotter; he spotted the biggest trends. *The Third Wave* argued that civilization had moved in three waves. The first was agriculture; the second, industry; and now, the third, information. Any reader paying close attention four decades ago would have known much about spotting emerging trends. For instance, Toffler foresaw work from home, in what he called the "electronic cottage," thereby "telecommuting" to work. As he wrote, "To suggest that millions of us may soon spend our time at home, instead of going out to an office or factory, is to unleash an immediate shower of objections." And yet, Toffler prophesied, "by the 1990s, two-way communications capability [will have been] enhanced sufficiently to encourage a widespread practice of working at home." So it was. Furthermore, "[A]s environmentalists and conservation-minded citizens groups battle against the destructive

---

[31] Lynch, Peter, *One Up On Wall Street* (New York: Simon & Schuster, 1989). 14, 90.

effects of the auto, and oppose road and highway construction, or succeed in banning cars from certain districts, they unwittingly support the transfer of work." So we would see the "building [of] an intelligent environment, thus revolutionizing the *info-sphere* as well."[32] Info-sphere, of course, sounds a lot like cyberspace, and the internet. Any investor following the trail of those digital bread crumbs was likely to reap a reward.

- The third book, *The Cultural Contradictions of Capitalism*, from Daniel Bell, was a more scholarly tome, befitting a Harvard professor. It described how capitalist abundance was inadvertently subsidizing, and even encouraging, attacks on capitalism and on cultural conservatism. A half-century later, we can see that Bell's was trend-spotting on a grand historical scale. He anticipated wokeness. And yet to observe the woke trend in the light of Bell's wisdom, we realize that it is anything but a passing fad. It's a deep current, akin to past religious and moral movements that convulsed societies and civilizations. And so of course the new thinking will carry some corporations with it, even as other companies array against it. Out of this cultural conflict—a new kind of creative destruction—we've already seen winners and losers, with more winning, and more losing, to come. So now to some useful takeaways from this chapter:

- For those who skipped the Introduction, it bears repeating: *Directional Investing is the realization that cultural and political trends drive investments, and that those trends can be shaped, not just spotted.* In Nevada, there was a trend to spotted, namely, the innate libertarianism of the population. And then there was a trend to be shaped, the shaping of that libertarianism into an enduring legal and political framework.

- Liberty is energy. It's an economic bazooka. Freedom-enhanced geography equals prosperity. At one time or another, jurisdictions

---

[32] Toffler, Alvin, *The Third Wave* (William Morrow, 1980), 211-14.

as varied as Venice, Luxembourg, Switzerland, Hong Kong, Panama, the Grand Caymans, American Indian reservations, and many others have found some lucrative loophole of liberty—and profitability. The challenge, of course, is to keep it.

- The corporation, too, is an economic bazooka. While companies operate best in a free environment, firms themselves tend to be tightly structured—that's how they stay efficient and effective. Even the "loosest" company is still mindful of the bottom line, otherwise, it doesn't last long. So we see a paradox: *freedom flourishes with taut organizations.* Anyone familiar with how the gambling industry operates sees this paradox. The casinos are tight as ticks, security-wise. Nobody is more surveilled than a customer, or a worker, on the floor. Indeed, the whole commercial district of Las Vegas is carefully, even zealously, policed. Panhandlers don't last long near the casinos, and as for homeless tents, *fuhgeddaboudit.* So the unstructuredness of the state's laissez-faire approach to good times is, in fact, a purposeful artifact of premeditated legal contrivance. Having fun is safe and easy in Vegas, but that's because the security guards and cops are so tough. (And yes that's a lesson for other cities, whether or not they have gambling.)

- No US state, whatever its economic model, is safe if the larger American nation-state isn't safe. Nevada has been part of the federal union for more than a century and a half, and that has left it free to prosper. Yet as other, weaker, countries have learned to their sorrow, there's always a predator lurking nearby, hungry like the wolf. So we might pause over the fate of such formerly free places as Hong Kong and Macau. They might still be rich, but they're not free, and that has eroded, and will continue to erode, their riches. Hard-nosed international politics also explains why various attempts to carve out an independent country based on libertarian principles have not worked. It's been tried with Vanuatu in the South Pacific, and in various other islands, oil platforms, forts and sea-steading places.[33] So far at least, these tax-haven strategies haven't been successful. All the more reason to admire Nevada, preserving its independence as a US state, while still enjoying safety within the American nation-state.

- The experience of Nevada—and every other place where capital has landed, and new wealth has been created—shows that capital, and talent, are always watching, waiting for opportunities to make their move. That's the near-unlimited economic energy that an investor-friendly polity can harness. Let's keep some numbers in mind. First, the United States GDP nears $30 trillion. World GDP, $105 trillion. Assets of the US, 150 trillion. Assets of the world, ten times that.[34] Big liquidity, bigger leverage potential, and biggest of all is the future potential of properly structured freedom.

---

[33] "History of a Nation," Principality of Sealand, https://sealandgov.org/the-story/

[34] "Global gross domestic product (GDP) at current prices from 1985 to 2028," Statista, https://bit.ly/44Dqa0l. See also: "Financial Accounts of the United States," Federal Reserve, March 31, 2023. https://bit.ly/3XIYHrV. And "The rise and rise of the global balance sheet: How productively are we using our wealth?", McKinsey & Company, November 15, 2021. https://bit.ly/3rhldvG

CHAPTER TWO

LOOKING FOR LUCK IN ALL THE RIGHT PLACES

WHERE THE BLACK SWANS ARE

We've seen the positive economic impact of a political vision leading to private sector prosperity. Legalize something customers want, build a sturdy framework around it—and watch the profits roll in. That's not the only way to make money, but it's worked for Nevada.

But okay, not everyone can live in a place where the legislature passes a law that permits a gold rush. Yet still, the Nevada example gets us thinking about the value of being in the right place at the right time. And so if the alpha seeker can't change the surrounding legal environment, perhaps he or she can change his or her location—move to a better place, with more delta. Go across the ocean, go west. It's a proven approach. In 1925, movie screenwriter Herman Mankiewicz telegrammed his fellow writer Ben Hecht, then still living in New York City, urging him to come out to Hollywood. Surveying the windfall profits being reaped in the young movie business, Mankiewicz wrote, "Millions are to be grabbed out here and your only competition is idiots."[35]

---

[35] Hecht, Ben, *A Child of the Century* (New York: Simon and Schuster, 1954), 466. Mankiewicz added a closing adjuration: "Don't let this get around."

Of course, the move to a better place doesn't have to be physical. It can be virtual. In any place, there are clusters of different activity. Some are more lucrative than others. As investors say, *the trend is your friend*. So it helps to know the trend, and to be where the action is. This idea was expressed by investor/author Nassim Nicholas Taleb in his book, *The Black Swan: The Impact of the Highly Improbable*. Taleb's Black Swan is an unpredictable large event—a big delta, up or down. "It is an *outlier*, as it lies outside the realm of regular expectations," he writes. "It carries an extreme impact." Impact, of course, is another way of saying *delta*, and, hopefully, *alpha*. Taleb suggests getting close to "some domains—such as scientific discovery and venture capital investments [where] there is a disproportionate payoff from the unknown." That makes sense, since there's so much potential energy in science, technology, and venture capital. "The strategy for the discoverers and entrepreneurs is to rely less on top-down planning and focus on maximum tinkering and recognizing opportunities when they present themselves," Taleb writes. And so, "Try to collect as many Black Swan opportunities as you can." He concludes, "The reason free markets work is because they allow people to be lucky, thanks to aggressive trial and error."[36] That's a plan for intentionality within the free market: Be where the Black Swans are. Or, to put it another way, *plan to get lucky*. And yet with the Nevada precedent in mind, we should realize that arranging for good fortune can take many different forms.

PLANNING FOR LUCK

In his 1944 book, *The Great Transformation*, a history of capitalist economic development since the Middle Ages, Karl Polanyi was blunt about the beginnings of the economic takeoff, a thousand years prior, writing,

---

[36] Taleb, Nassim Nicholas, *The Black Swan: The Impact of the Highly Improbable* (New York: Random House, 2007), 20-24. https://bit.ly/46gscF8

"Laissez-faire was planned...the product of deliberate state action."[37] Hmm. To the contemporary ear, planning might sound like bureaucrats and socialism, but then we remember that everyone is in favor of some kind of planning—even if it's just a plan to mingle with Black Swans.

The planning that Polanyi described was, as he put it, "embedding" entrepreneurial vitality into medieval realms. Rulers designated *fairs*, where markets were both legal and protected. Once again, to the contemporary ear, the need to legalize markets might seem strange, because we're so used to the idea of capitalism. But it wasn't always this way. During the European Dark Ages, roughly 500 CE to 1000 CE, there was so little safety or order that there wasn't much travel and commerce—it was simply too danger- ous to go beyond one's hovel or village. In the absence of trade, there was no comparative advantage, not much innovation, unprotected property rights—and so, according to economic historian Angus Maddison, the European standard of living fell sharply.[38] Polanyi evokes the spirit of those murky times. "Traditionally, land and labor are not separated; labor forms part of life, land remains part of nature, life and nature form an articulate whole." Indeed, there was an onus—and likely a hex—on whoever messed with hoary norms. In such a stultifying environment, were a Black Swan to emerge, he or she would likely be regarded as a witch—and we know what happened to witches in ye olden days. Polanyi continues, "Land is thus tied up with the organizations of kinship, neighborhood, craft, and creed—with tribe and temple, village, gild, and church."[39] In that knotted and clotted tangle of reaction and conservatism, there's not much room for freedom, or for free enterprise.

Yet then the Dark Ages began to give way to the relative enlightenment of the Middle Ages. Medieval leaders were not exactly libertarians, but many of them came to understand the value of merchants and commerce.

---

[37] Polanyi, Karl, *The Great Transformation* (New York: Farrar & Rinehart, 1944), 81. https://bit.ly/3NNNxP5

[38] Maddison Database, Groningen Growth and Development Centre, University of Groningen, accessed July 1, 2023. https://bit.ly/3Kkj34W

[39] Polanyi, Karl, *Transformation*, 103.

And so they carved out space for proto-capitalism. They established, for instance, rules by which itinerant peddlers could operate, being allowed to visit the town, say, once a year. Furthermore, towns could get a charter from the prince to establish a fair. "Scarborough Fair" was made into a hit single by Simon & Garfunkel in 1968, and yet it's actually a traditional English song bespeaking this economic development. Scarborough Fair received its charter from King Henry III on January 22, 1253. It reads, "The Burgesses and their heirs forever may have a yearly fayre in the Borough, to continue from the Feast of the Assumption of the Blessed Virgin Mary until the Feast of St. Michael." That is, forty-five days in August and September, a good run for a laissez-faire fair. Strangers were welcome to the town, invited to sell goods "of true worth," including, of course, as the lyrics go, "parsley, sage, rosemary, and thyme." Everyone was invited to "sport and play" and to "do all things."[40]

Hmm—"sport and play"…"do all things." That sounds a bit like Vega$. But just as the casinos of Las Vegas were planned—or, if one prefers, intentioned—by the legalization in 1931, so, too, the good times of medieval fairs were foreordained. "There was nothing natural about laissez-faire," Polanyi writes, "free markets could never have come into being merely by allowing things to take their course…laissez-faire itself was enforced by the state."[41] One key aspect of enforcement was the simple protection of markets and market-players—no spiteful calling out of the successful for witchcraft. A prosperous economy requires not only the enforcement of contracts, but the literal protection of persons and property. States have hardly been perfect at such legal shielding, of course, but they are usually better than rumormongers and bandits. Over time, helpful legal structures developed, allowing for larger enterprises and even for-profit corporations. This was Polanyi's *Great Transformation*, and it was, indeed, great.

Indeed, once markets are protected, we see the emergence of specialization. Which, as Adam Smith would point out, is the key to surging

---

[40] "Scarborough Fair," Scarborough Maritime Heritage Center, accessed November 25, 2022. https://bit.ly/3PuYrdI
[41] Polanyi, Karl, *Transformation*, 80.

productivity.[42] Yet there was a fateful development here. The emergence of a distinct capitalist class meant splits in the old ways, and that hurt feelings. Some of this hurt is called alienation, as the ancient collective oneness—to be sure, a oneness of poverty—gave way to a new sense of distance, even rivalry. A rivalry that is, pitting the rising bourgeoisie against the old guard of aristocrats, clergymen, and warlords. Later, as capitalism continued to evolve, we saw a new form of alienation—the peasantry becoming the proletariat.

We can add that around the same time that Smith was arguing for specialization, or separation, as the way to the wealth of nations, the French political philosopher Montesquieu was arguing that separation was the way to the liberty of nations. In *The Spirit of the Laws*, he wrote that if there is not separation of the executive, legislative, and judicial functions "there is no liberty."[43] We can observe that the American Founders understood that the economic specialization championed by Smith had to be joined with the political separation championed by Montesquieu. Otherwise, unitary tyranny would impose itself. So we can see, the freedom to start a business is linked to the political freedom that comes when power is separated. Indeed, the US Constitution greatly separated power—not just between the three branches of the federal government, but also to the now fifty states. And that's why Americans are prosperous. And yet as we think about becoming even more prosperous, we see obstacles, including ever-mutating alienation. So if we want to move ahead with greater Directionality, it behooves us to understand these roots of what we will call Anti-Directionality.

---

[42] As Smith wrote, "The greatest improvement in the productive powers of labour, and the greater part of skill, dexterity, and judgement with which it is anywhere directed, or applied, seem to have been the effects of the division of labour." Smith, Adam, *An Inquiry Into the Nature and Causes of the Wealth of Nations*, 1776, Chapter One. https://bit.ly/3JxV6XQ

[43] Montesquieu, *The Spirt of the Laws*, ed. Franz Neumann (New York: Hafner, 1949), 152.

OCCAM'S KILLJOY AND THE ANTI-DIRECTIONALISTS

The standard of living in the West today is over 1,000 times higher than it was in the Dark Ages.[44] Around the world, the percentage of people living in what the World Bank calls "extreme poverty" has fallen from around 70 percent in 1900 to less than 10 percent today.[45] Yet even so, not everyone loves markets and capitalism. Some of that hostility comes from the alienation that arose from the splits championed by Smith and Montesquieu. That is, the sense of difference, mixed in, of course, with jealousy. In the 1936 novel *Gone With the Wind*, Rhett Butler warns the entrepreneurial Scarlett O'Hara, "All you've done is to be different from other women and you've made a little success at it...That is the one unforgivable sin in any society. Be different and be damned!"[46]

We can also observe that capitalism encourages the sort of careful calculation that critics will dub "cold-hearted," even "ruthless." In fact, in the long climb up from pre-modern magical thinking, all climbers owe a debt to the English monk William of Ockham (1287-1347). He put forth a new way of thinking that was simultaneously obvious, radical, and far-reaching. Occam's Razor tells us, *Everything else being equal, choose the simplest explanation.* Ever since, the Razor has been used to slice away mental frippery and sentimentality, including unprovable dogma and superstition. It's that sort of impatient, bottom-line approach that makes the Razor so valuable to business people and investors. Even if they've never heard of Occam, they know to chop inefficiency and b.s. in pursuit of the bottom line. Yet the Razor is definitely doubled-edged, because plenty of people

---

[44] Maddison Database, https://bit.ly/3Kkj34W
[45] Hasell, Joe, and Roser, Max, "How do we know the history of extreme poverty?", Our World in Data, February 5, 2019. https://bit.ly/3Nt7Hwp
[46] Mitchell, Margaret, *Gone With the Wind* (New York: The MacMillan Company, 1936), 899. https://bit.ly/3JxvOny

like frippery, sentimentality, dogma, superstition—and even inefficiency and b.s. They are offended, even angered, when it's taken away.[47]

Back in 1976, Harvard's Daniel Bell warned that capitalism, in its efficiency—critics called it ruthlessness—would make enemies. As he wrote, "bourgeois society introduced a radical individualism in economics, and a willingness to tear up all traditional social relations in the process."[48] So now we can better see the backlash against capitalism and freedom. We can add that the backlashers are on both the right and the left. On the right, defenders of cultural tradition, however idealized, romanticized, and Tolkeinized. On the left, defenders of economic tradition (the old ways), including Luddism, NIMBYism, and certain retro-socialisms and communisms. Sometimes these backlashers even blend into one another. In 1848, the first Communist, Karl Marx, invoked nostalgia as he sniped at the bourgeoisie, "It has drowned the most heavenly ecstasies of religious fervor, of chivalrous enthusiasm, of philistine sentimentalism, in the icy water of egotistical calculation."[49] Today, it's sometimes impossible to thresh out the ideologies of the various reactionaries.

So here we are, enjoying prosperity and liberty both—and yet alienation, even paranoia, strikes deep. So popular culture has produced an endless number of capitalists-as-villains, from Scrooge to Charles Foster Kane to Mr. Potter to Goldfinger to the Ferengi to Gordon Gekko. And the news media, of course, has emerged from popular culture. To be sure, negative images and bad press haven't stopped capitalists from being capitalists, but it does mean that Oscar Wilde's jibe, about knowing "the price of everything and the value of nothing," will be hurled in their face.[50] Yes, prosperity breeds its own kind of discontent. People like the money, but

---

[47] In his 1948 book, *Ideas Have Consequences*, Richard M. Weaver, a patron saint of traditionalist conservatism, decried Occam's Razor as the cutting rupture threatening the mystical-spiritual understanding of the world. He was right!

[48] Bell, Daniel, *The Cultural Contradictions of Capitalism* (New York: Basic Books, 1976), 18.

[49] Marx, Karl, *The Communist Manifesto*, 1848. https://bit.ly/3Jz3JB9

[50] Wilde, Oscar, *The Picture of Dorian Gray*, 1890. https://bit.ly/3Py1a69

they don't love money-*makers* (unless, of course, it's themselves, in which case, it's completely different).

Not so long ago, this sort of free-floating hostility to markets and private property manifested itself as socialism or communism. These days, there aren't many reds around, but oppositional and mutant isms abound, including Anti-Directionalism. These people are numerous and, since, they are, as Bell observes, the fruit of capitalism, they are well-fed, well-educated, and well-placed. They have proven that they can wear down, distort, and even block progress—including the best investments. In the chapters to come, as we describe Directional Investing, we must keep in mind that Anti-Directionalists are always lurking. Finally, in Chapter Sixteen, we'll consider ways to defeat them.

LAST POINT ON SWANS

Good investment advice, according to Taleb, is to be near a Black Swan, because perhaps it will turn into a unicorn. And since we can't all move to Silicon Valley, or to some other high-delta, high-alpha innovation cluster, the question arises, is it possible to attract Black Swans? Is it possible, even to breed them? Or to clone or otherwise manufacture them? The answer is, yes! We can point to history and see where groups consciously set themselves to crank out—breed, one might say—Black Swans. Back in 1626 came the publication of Sir Francis Bacon's *New Atlantis*. His was an allegorical tale of a society in which people use their brains to prosper. Bacon envisioned "Salomon's House," a permanent laboratory of innovation and application. It was to be, Bacon wrote, "the very eye of this kingdom." Yet

Bacon was no mere fantasist. He was hard-nosed, and compelling, when he wrote "knowledge is power."[51]

Duly inspired by Bacon, the British government established The Royal Society of London for Improving Natural Knowledge. The idea of institutionalizing advancement and prosperity was taking hold, and not just in Britain. As the mathematician-philosopher Alfred North Whitehead put it, "The greatest invention of the 19th century was the invention of the method of invention."[52] In that century, research institutes were created across the world to advance science, not just for the joy of knowing but as conscious instruments of national wealth and military might. One apostle of innovation was Bradley Fiske, who served in the US Navy from 1874 to 1916, rising to the rank of rear admiral. Fiske's many inventions, not surprisingly, were focused on naval warfare. Some might say, okay, that's just military stuff. Yet of course, the military is also an industry producing jobs and profits. Moreover, from a macro-investment point of view, we can say it's a lot better to win wars than to lose them. And in fact, Fiske was a macro-historian. In 1921 he published *Invention, the Master-Key to Progress*. "Let us therefore utilize all means possible to develop this Godgiven faculty, the chiefest of the talents committed to our keeping," he wrote. "That way lie[s] progress, prosperity and happiness. How far and how high it may lead us, God only knows; for the resources of invention are infinite."[53] Amen!

---

[51] The exact quote from Bacon is "knowledge itself is power." It was shortened and clarified by his onetime secretary, Thomas Hobbes. At around the same time, in 1637, the Frenchman Rene Descartes published *Discourse on the Method*, asserting, "Practical philosophy... would show us the energy and action of fire, air, and stars, the heavens, and all other bodies in our environment, as distinctly as we know the various crafts of our artisans, and could apply them in the same way to all appropriate uses and thus make ourselves the masters and owners of nature."

[52] Whitehead, Alfred North, *Science and the Modern World* (The MacMillan Company 1925), Chapter VI. https://bit.ly/3XrWeSh

[53] Fiske, Bradley, *Invention, the Master-Key to Progress* (New York: E.P Dutton, 1921). https://bit.ly/3NvNINK

INVESTMENT TAKEAWAYS

- Across the past four centuries since Bacon's *New Atlantis,* we have seen many different models for Black Swan-making, some public, some private, some in-between. For instance, there was Bell Labs, which flourished from the 1920s to the 1980s. During those decades, it supported the work of eleven Nobel laureates and countless additional geniuses who might have contributed even more. For instance, Claude Shannon, "the father of information theory"—not a bad way to be remembered in this, the Information Age.[54] In its glory days, the lab was supported by the profits of monopolistic AT&T, this being the era of Ma Bell. And yet it was more than the pursuit of profit that made Bell a font of tech. Its leaders, corporate as well as scientific, had a sense of mission— the advancement of science, of course, but also the well-being of the US, including American victory in World War II and the Cold War. And yet over the years, appreciation of that mission faded, such that few worried about the lab when AT&T's monopoly was broken up in 1984. In the aftermath, Bell Labs was downsized and dissipated; in 2007, its last vestige disappeared. There's no need to overly lament the demise of any one institution. But what *is* needed, always, is what Whitehead outlined—the permanent idea of invention. That idea needs to be actively fostered. Farsighted investors, contemplating their own future security, as well as prosperity, will wish to replenish the wells of innovation.

- It's easy to understand why an investor or entrepreneur would wish to be near a Black Swan, but the larger society needs to be persuaded that the commonweal, too, will benefit from the prevalence of the "Ebon Cygnus." That takes a political vision embracing

---

[54] Georgescu, Iulia, "Bringing back the golden days of Bell Labs," *Nature Portfolio,* January 27, 2022. https://bit.ly/3JBRe87. See also: "Claude Shannon: The Father of Information Theory," *History of Data Science,* June 5, 2021. https://bit. ly/44giKAf

the laissez-faire transformation of Polanyi, the scientific vision of Bacon, the economic specialization of Smith, the political separation of Montesquieu, and the intentional invention of Whitehead. If we can put all that together, we'll have a lot of Black Swans.

CHAPTER THREE

PARADIGMS OF PROSPERITY

THE STRUCTURE OF ECONOMIC EVOLUTIONS

I n the previous two chapters, we've considered historical examples of economic development—and profitability. Since their common theme is the power of free markets in a protected setting, let's connect the two. Let's recognize that we have identified a paradigm, a mental model—free markets within a framework—of how the world works. A paradigm can be a passive observation or an active creation. Either way, paradigms can be powerful tools for wealth creation.

The "p" word was popularized by Thomas Kuhn in his 1962 book, *The Structure of Scientific Revolutions*. In that volume, Kuhn considered past scientific controversies, such as astronomy's evolving understanding of the solar system. And yet along the way, Kuhn makes the canny—and to this day, somewhat unsettling—point that paradigms can be powerful, even when they are wrong. That is, any paradigm organizes thinking into a framework, and that framework can be positive or negative, depending on the eye of the beholder.

Kuhn's point is that while science is "true," human understanding of science can be as variable as, well, human nature. Happily, in science, the truth eventually sets us free. So we now know, for example, that the earth revolves around the sun. Yet as Kuhn chronicles, the discovery of the truth—the shift from the geocentric (Sun revolves around the Earth) paradigm of the ancient astronomer Ptolemy to the heliocentric (Earth revolves around the Sun) paradigm of Copernicus was not easy. The process was, in fact, intensely political. In Kuhn's words, the scientific world "is divided into competing camps or parties, one seeking to defend the old institutional constellation, the others seeking to institute some new one." Kuhn specifically recalls of the sixteenth century: "The state of Ptolemaic astronomy was a scandal before Copernicus' announcement." Yes, clinging to the geocentric paradigm, in the face of overwhelming evidence for heliocentrism—that was scandalous intellectual corruption. And that corruption was made all the worse when old-paradigm dogmatists invoked the Inquisition to terrorize "heretics"—such as Galileo, a higher-profile follower of Copernicus—into submission. Yet because astronomy *is* science, truth wins in the end. By the seventeenth century, the accumulated proof of heliocentrism made geocentrism look ridiculous. That "sense of malfunction," Kuhn writes, was the "prerequisite to revolution." Thus the Copernican truth prevailed in one of the scientific revolutions in Kuhn's title. He wrote, "When paradigms change, the world itself changes with them. Led by a new paradigm, scientists adopt new instruments and look in new places."[55] With its paradigmatic foundation finally set in empirical truth, modern astronomy took flight. Four centuries later, we are still reaping the benefits.

Yet what happens to paradigms that cannot be proven or disproven? What about those idea systems that are matters of opinion? And those in which one proponent can pick selected facts, or factoids, and another proponent can graze completely different facts—or even fables? In science, the key term is *falsifiable*. That is, can a statement proven to be false? If it can be proven false, then it's not going to survive as science, although the idea could survive as a non-scientific belief system, in the way that astrology has spun off from astronomy.

---

[55] Kuhn, Thomas S., *The Structure of Scientific Revolutions* (Chicago: University of Chicago Press, second edition, 1970), 93, 67, 92, 111. https://bit.ly/3XnFMCN

But we're not just talking about fads or fancies here. We're talking about ideas of political and economic organization—written down in briefs and books—including business and investment. As we all know, there are myriad schools of thought as to how firms, economies, and societies operate, or should operate. Indeed, whenever we use concepts such as "system," or "six sigma," or "standard operating procedure," we are speaking in paradigmatic terms. We can quickly see that one school of thought can collide with another.

To cite another area where schools of thought clash, we can look to relatively recent tendency within the business world—ESG. That stands, of course, for Environmental, Social, and Governance. It's also become a political football, left v. right. According to a 2022 article in *Review of Finance*, the opposing players can't even agree on the benchmark statistics. "Our findings demonstrate that ESG rating divergence is not merely a matter of varying definitions but a fundamental disagreement about the underlying data."[56] If there's a fog of war, there's also a fog of numbers, all part of the fog of life. And in that haze, disputants will grope toward their version of the truth, their thinking guided, most likely, by a paradigm. We'll deal more with ESG in later chapters, but for the moment we can see, if the issue is not clear-cut—as is, say, the question of whether or not Earth revolves around the Sun—then it is unlikely to ever be fully resolved. Indeed, once we're outside the realm of science, we confront the reality that different cultural, social, intellectual, and even technological paradigms can coexist forever. For instance, in aviation, jet engines go fastest, but there're still plenty of propeller aircraft (including the most popular drones) and gliders. Each paradigm of flight abides because it fills a niche. And come to think of it, people still walk because they want to, even as faster modes of transport exist. The point is, if a paradigm, a way of thinking, can't be definitively discredited, it can linger, even flourish. People might stick with a paradigm,

---

[56] Berg, Florian, et al., "Aggregate Confusion: The Divergence of ESG Ratings," *Review of Finance*, May 23, 2022. https://bit.ly/43etmhP

seek to advance it—and even to crush rival paradigms—for all the myriad human motivations.

Now here we can add another point. The coexistence of multiple paradigms adds energy. We might compare the pluralistic environment to a bag of marbles, always bouncing into each other. The process is noisy and messy, and yet there's excitement. There's more action in a bag of marbles than from a monolith. To put that yet another way, if everybody thinks the same, things get dull fast. So within reason—all things in reference in proportion—we should celebrate difference as the giver of life and vitality. In *The Federalist Papers*, the documents written to encourage ratification of the US Constitution, James Madison pointed to the upside of carefully frameworked freedom. Asserting that liberty would reveal the "diversity in the faculties of men" he posited that limited government would be necessary to protect both liberty and property. There's that idea again— celebrate freedom, but also safeguard freedom.[57] Because we are, indeed, diverse. And as with anything dynamic, diversity can cut both ways. Around the world, we see all manner of political and economic paradigms, from communism in North Korea to chaos in Somalia. Fortunately, the US has been spared the worst of paradigmatic extremism and calamity, and for that we owe much to our Constitution. In fact, a look back at American history tells us that two politico-economic paradigms have predominated. As shall see, the interplay, even competition, between the two models has been stimulating, even thrilling.

THE PROMISE OF AMERICA: IN STEREO

In 1909, the American journalist Herbert Croly published *The Promise of American Life*, casting the nation's history as the rivalry between the political and economic traditions of Thomas Jefferson, on the one hand, and Alexander Hamilton, on the other. In a nutshell, Jeffersonianism was

---

57 Madison, James, *The Federalist Papers: No. 32*, National Archives, Founders Online, 1787. https://bit.ly/3XCxneC

decentralized and put liberty first, while Hamiltonianism was centralized and business-minded. In Croly's reckoning, Jeffersonianism was good for personal freedom, but lacked the economic muscle of Hamiltonianism, which was needed to build America into a world power. That is, Hamiltonian mojo was required to assure that canals, railroads and highways—what Hamilton, back in his day, called "internal improvements"—were built, these being sinews of industry and prosperity. Croly was on the side of Hamilton, and yet he recognized that Jeffersonianism was central to American life. The challenge—synthesize the best of both isms.

Hence Croly's "stereo" approach. We would work with both visions. Indeed, both were necessary. "It is very generally understood," he wrote, "that neither the Jeffersonian nor the Hamiltonian doctrine was entirely adequate…a combination must be made of both." And here, Croly makes a key point—with such a combination, the nation could enjoy "a wholly unaccustomed energy."[58] Croly's book proved to be deeply influential. It was embraced, most notably, by two US presidents, Republican Theodore Roosevelt and Democrat Franklin D. Roosevelt. Indeed, across American history, the two ideas have contended, mixed, unmixed, and contended. We can go further and say that the two visions have improved each other. The more spiritual-minded Jeffersonian can say, "Man does not live by bread alone," and be correct. Yet the Hamiltonian could say, "Yes, but he does have to eat." And they'd both be right.

Jefferson himself embodies this toggling back and forth. He is best remembered for his championing of liberty—for example, his authorship of the Declaration of Independence. And yet he was much less of a libertarian later, when serving as third president of the United States. In 1803, he borrowed money—some of it from Great Britain—to fund the Louisiana Purchase, 530 million acres of land, some or all of fifteen future US states. To guide the defense of this enormous acquisition, Jefferson established the military academy at West Point. And to help make sure American

---

[58] Croly, Herbert, *The Promise of American Life* (New York: The MacMillan Company, 1909), Chapters I, II, and VII. https://bit.ly/3JxP3lV

soldiers could actually march or ride to defend the far-flung realm, he initiated the National Road. That early venture into infrastructure is now US 40, stretching from New Jersey to Utah. We can add that such infrastructure is not just for the benefit of military movement; it's a vital piece of economic development. As they say, trade follows the flag—or, in this case, the road sign. So we can see that Jefferson's oft-used phrase, "empire of liberty," was itself a well-crafted duality, communicating empire, as well as liberty.[59] A nation-state benefits from both strength and freedom.

For his part, Hamilton was never president, and yet his influence, too, endures, based on his pro-business activism and his faith in American greatness. In 1787, he argued that only a strong America, boasting a robust navy, could adequately defend its commercial interests: "Under a vigorous national government, the natural strength and resources of the country, directed to a common interest, would baffle all the combinations of European jealousy." Continuing in that vein, "an active commerce, an extensive navigation, and a flourishing marine would then be the inevitable offspring."[60] So we can say that Hamilton envisioned the full use of Adam Smith's "invisible hand" (market forces) but he also didn't hesitate to use the visible hand of state power to build a pro-business framework. The idea wasn't so much insurance as assurance—to make sure the invisible hand could never be chopped off.

We might pause to note a useful saying: There aren't thirty-eight ways to do one thing. There can be thirty-eight *names* for one thing, or 380 names, but the thing itself is finite. And so if we want to attract capital, get people to build things, inspire them to innovate, then we have to build a structure that makes them feel safe to do. Safe in their persons, obviously, but also safe in their property and their investments. And so there's a certain sameness, even oneness, to such systems. Call it a "fair," or an "enterprise zone," or a "special economic zone," or "freedom with the rule of law." Call it anything you wish. But in its essence, it will be *assurance*.

---

59 "Empire of Liberty (quotation)," monticello.org, https://bit.ly/44gKSTt

60 Hamilton, Alexander, *The Federalist Papers: No. 11,* National Archives, Founders Online, 1787. https://bit.ly/3Py6yXg

By whatever name, entrepreneurs will know opportunity when they see it—and they will flock to it.

The canonical Hamiltonian text is his *Final Version of the Report on Manufactures*, published when he served as the nation's first Secretary of the Treasury. His ostensible main focus was on strong national defense. He recalled that the Thirteen Colonies had nearly lost the American Revolution because of inadequate access to the industrial wares needed for war. So the young republic must strive to "render the United States independent on foreign nations for military and other essential supplies." To that end, the US should embrace the "Means proper" for industrialization. Hamilton discoursed about the merits of "bounties" (subsidies for production) "protecting duties," and the cultivation of a skilled workforce, including from immigration. Mindful, too, of "the prosperity of manufactures," he urged help for "infant manufactures" that would grow up to make the country not just militarily strong, but economically rich. "It may be inferred... [t]hat manufacturing establishments not only occasion a positive augmentation of the Produce and Revenue of the Society, but that they contribute essentially to rendering them greater than they could possibly be, without such establish-ments."[61] That same year, Hamilton established the quasi-private Society for Establishing Useful Manufactures in Paterson, New Jersey, there to tap the energy of the seventy-seven-foot waterfall of the Passaic River. The area was an industrial hub for the next two centuries. The rate of return on that investment has been enormous. We can add that Hamilton was also an apostle of high finance. Even before his *Report on Manufactures*, he had founded the Bank of New York (now BNY Mellon) and published tracts on national credit and banking. Those efforts led to the creation of the Bank of the United States, a proto-Federal Reserve, in 1791.

Sadly, Hamilton was killed in a duel in 1804, thus snuffing out whatever political future he might have claimed for himself. Yet after his death,

---

[61] Hamilton, Alexander, *Final Version of the Report on the Subject of Manufactures*, National Archives, Founders Online, 1791. https://bit.ly/3PxZhX5

some of his bitterest rivals came around to his ideas. For instance, Jefferson, by then retired in Monticello, conceded the value of his rival's vision. "Experience has taught me that manufactures are now as necessary to our independence as to our comfort."[62] So Hamilton's legacy lives on, bigly. To this day, activist economic development is dubbed *Hamiltonian*.

JEFFERSONIAN LIBERTY AND THE HAMILTONIAN FRAMEWORK

We can think of Jeffersonianism and Hamiltonianism as respective paradigms. It's easy to see the Jeffersonian paradigm in Nevada. And yet Nevada would never have become a gambling destination had not Hamiltonians built railroads, highways, and airports to connect the state to its customers, as well as water pipelines and other utilities. And, of course, it's the Hamiltonian paradigm, writ large, that has defended Nevada, and all of the United States, from various foes and potential foes.

But let's get off this "p" word, paradigm. Let's speak, instead, more naturally. Let's speak of Jeffersonian Liberty and the Hamiltonian Framework. As American history has demonstrated, the two concepts do, indeed, make a great combination. Moreover, we could say that each man, in his own way, was planning for free enterprise—Jefferson focusing on "free," and Hamilton focusing on "enterprise." So in some ultimate sense, the two are one. Freedom needs enterprise, and enterprise needs freedom. Indeed, back in the 1950s, the distinguished American historian Louis Hartz noted "the silent unity of Hamilton and Jefferson."[63]

Still, when there's something that absolutely positively needs to get built, the Hamiltonian Framework is more essential. In Hamilton's era, the hot infrastructure idea was waterways. The most famous of these being the 362-mile Erie Canal. Completed in 1825, it connected the Hudson River to

---

[62] Jefferson, Thomas to Austin, Benjamin, January 9, 1816, National Archives, Founders Online https://bit.ly/46rktV1

[63] Hartz, Louis, *The Liberal Tradition in America* (New York: Harcourt, Brace, 1955), 146.

the Great Lakes, cementing New York as the Empire State. Yet the following year, 1826, something better than canals began to emerge—the first three miles of railroad track were laid down in Quincy, Massachusetts. That was the start of something big. During the nineteenth century, Americans laid down some 215,000 miles of rail.[64] Let steel magnate Andrew Carnegie describe the efficient and prosperity-making result: "Two pounds of iron stone mined upon Lake Superior and transported nine hundred miles to Pittsburgh; one pound and one-half of coal mined and manufactured into coke, and transported to Pittsburgh; a small amount of manganese ore mined in Virginia and brought to Pittsburgh—and these four pounds of materials manufactured into one pound of steel, for which the consumer pays one cent."[65]

Their good effects notwithstanding, railroads were never without controversy. Native Americans didn't like the Iron Horse, of course, and securing rights of way was sometimes problematic, even in the era before environmental impact statements. And there were liability issues, too, to be resolved, such as what happened when farm animals were killed by locomotives, or if sparks from the smokestack started fires. (In keeping with the pro-rail spirit of the age, these fights were typically resolved in favor of the railroads.) Moreover, once the rails were built, farmers and others who depended on them to move their goods were furious over freight rates. In response to the ensuing political pressure, in 1887, the first federal regulatory body, the Interstate Commerce Commission, was tasked with monitoring prices. Yet even so, the can-do consensus on behalf of railroads was both national and bipartisan. No major political figure ran for election opposing the railroads; everyone regarded them, warts and all, as a vital aspect of American life. With such broad support—the trend is your

[64] "Railroads in the Late 19th Century," Library of Congress. https://bit.ly/3NPRXVQ

[65] Lind, Michael, *Land of Promise: An Economic History of the United States* (New York: Harper, 2012), 163.

friend—the Pennsylvania Railroad emerged in the nineteenth century as the largest corporation in the world.[66]

What was the larger economic impact of the railroads? Well, that's hard to say, because it's hard to count that high. By a crude measure, one could take the net worth of the United States, measure in the hundreds of trillions, and say that it would be much less had the railroads not happened. For instance, the Transcontinental Railroad, completed in 1869, helped connect the country at a time when other countries were sniffing around for new colonies. Without a troop moving network, it's possible that, say, Britain or Japan or Russia might have grabbed off the West Coast. What would the US be worth without California? What would be the condition of American finances if Uncle Sam was bearing the burden of big border armies, and perhaps border wars, on North American territory?

However, in the twentieth century, enthusiasm for railroads ebbed. The once robust Hamiltonian Framework faded, even the once world leading Pennsy went bankrupt in 1970. Yes, the twentieth century brought a new kind of transportation—roads and highways for automobiles and trucks. Once again, the developmental can-do spirit of Hamilton kicked in. Today America has some 2.6 million miles of paved roads.[67]

Yet just as the railroads eventually met a kind of nemesis, so, too, have roads. One indicator is the fate of the Embarcadero Freeway in San Francisco. Opened in 1959, at the high tide of the highway Framework, it was a double-decker part of the Interstate system that traced along the waterfront of the city. Yes, in the middle of the last century, authorities actually thought it was a good idea to put a freeway in front of views of the San Francisco Bay. The Embarcadero collapsed in a 1989 earthquake, and the city wisely chose not to rebuild it, opening up the waterfront to

---

[66] Churella, Albert J., *The Pennsylvania Railroad, Volume 1: Building an Empire, 1846-1917* (Philadelphia: University of Pennsylvania Press, 2013), ix. https://bit.ly/46ldSeH

[67] Cielic, Lynn, "How Many Miles Of Roads Are There in the U.S.?", Midwest Industrial Supply, December 28, 2015. https://bit.ly/44e63p2. Speaking of Frameworks and their features, estimates of the number of parking spaces in the US vary widely, some up to two billion.

touristy as well as swanky development. Indeed, in many places today, it's probably impossible to build a new road, and certainly not a new highway. We can see that once again, the Hamiltonian Framework has eroded.[68] Why it's now even federal policy that some roads, particularly highways, must be removed, as they are seen by some as not only environmentally destructive, but outright racist. The 2021 infrastructure bill, for example, contains $1 billion for highway removal.[69] A 2023 poll found that just eight percent of Americans supported new highway construction. By contrast, the poll showed higher numbers for road repairs, mass transit, sidewalks, and bicycle lanes.[70] If democracy matters—and it does, and it should—it's the end of an era of new highway construction.

Yet Hamiltonianism springs eternal. In the late twentieth and early twenty-first century, a new kind of network emerged—the internet. Interestingly, the internet was pioneered by the military-industrial complex, which counts as Hamiltonian, and yet it was Jeffersonian entrepreneurs who took the net and ran with it. And yet at the same time, the net has benefited from its Hamiltonian Framework, including behind-the-scenes maneuvering. Reed Hundt, chairman of the Federal Communications Commission during the Clinton administration, takes credit for some of that, recalling the FCC's decision "to allow the computers to use the telephone network to connect to the Internet...and to do it for free." He

---

[68] Another elevated highway still disfigures a valuable American waterfront. That's the Whitehurst Freeway, running alongside the Potomac River in the ritzy Georgetown section of Washington, DC. Whitehurst was completed in 1949, amazingly, as part of a master plan for DC developed by the US Commission of Fine Arts. Yes, in the middle of the last century, highways were art—such was the power of a dominant automotive paradigm. Whitehurst, will eventually be de-motored; perhaps it will be a Manhattan-style Highline, and/or a bicycle path. Or perhaps it will be torn down completely. When and if any of that happens, views and property values will soar.

[69] Epstein, Jennifer, and Wingrove, Josh, "Buttigieg Says U.S. Will Use Infrastructure Bill to Address Racist Highway Design," Bloomberg News, November 8, 2021. https://bit.ly/3XsPtQj

[70] "New survey: 82 percent of voters don't believe highway expansions are the best solution for reducing congestion," Transportation for America, June 29, 2023. https://bit.ly/3D5aXt3

added, "In other words we stole the value of the telephone network…
and gave it to society." It was, he added with a chuckle, "a little naughty."[71]
Whether or not one approves of this giant transfer, it happened, and investors back then who were paying attention, and drawing the correct conclusion, were rewarded.

Yet today, the most obvious expression of the Framework is Section
230 of the Communications Decency Act of 1996. That provision provides
a sweeping liability shield for digital companies that no other industry possesses. Yet in testament to the power of a Framework at its high point, back
in 1996, the bill passed the Senate with a vote of 91 to 5, and the House,
414 to 16.[72] The vote today on 230, of course, would be nothing like that—
it might not even pass at all. The argument was made, of course, that without Section 230, the digital biz would have been throttled, and that's probably true. The industry would not have grown had it been shadowed with
all the civil and criminal liability of various kinds of trafficking. But every
industry makes an argument that it needs to be shielded for the sake of
growth, and yet few have been blessed with such a liability shield. And the
differential—the blessed and the unblessed—makes a multi-trillion-dollar
difference as it vectors out over the decades. As we all know, the digital
has advanced much more rapidly than the physical (analog). We can recall
Peter Thiel's quote from 2011, "We wanted flying cars, instead we got 140

---

71   Flint, Joe, "Former FCC Chairman Reed Hundt says he favored broadband over
     broadcast," *Los Angeles Times*, April 2, 2010. https://bit.ly/46JbPkU In fact,
     the favoritism for the internet goes back further. In his memoir, Hundt recalls a
     "far-sighted, or accidentally smart" ruling by the Reagan-era FCC that prohibited
     phone companies from levying "access charges" on data (as distinct from voice)
     transmissions. "In the absence of the FCC's decision," Hundt writes, "the Internet
     would have been so expensive that [founder Marc] Andreessen's Netscape would
     not have been a hiccup, much less one of the first bubble stocks of the Internet."
     In other words, it was actually the Reagan-era FCC, under Chairman Mark
     Fowler, that shifted the value. Hundt, Reed, *You Say You Want a Revolution: A
     Story of Information Age Politics.* (New Haven: Yale University Press, 2000), 133.
72   "All Actions: S.652—104th Congress (1995-1996)," Congress.gov. https://
     bit.ly/3NM1nSa. The legislative language declared, "It is the policy of the
     United States to promote the continued development of the Internet and other
     interactive computer services and other interactive media."

characters."[73] The 140 characters (now more) on the social media platform once known as Twitter (now X) are nice, but it also would've been nice to have flying cars.

Still, thanks to the Framework around digital, a full 43 million miles of fiber optic cable have been laid in the US, and more than 142,000 cell towers built, as well as nearly a million cell sites and small cell nodes. All this action, of course, is up from virtually zero three decades earlier.[74] Perhaps most pertinently to an investor, one recent estimate concluded that the internet was worth $30 trillion.[75] In other words, a lot of Black Swans to get to know. We can step back and see, this endless braiding of Jeffersonianism and Hamiltonianism has once again led to a Croly-esque unaccustomed surge in energy. Today, tech isn't just Big Tech, it's Huge Tech—proof that a Framework gets the job done. When the Framework is on your side, the trend is your friend, so you can happily go with the flow. So even if an investor hadn't known which Silicon Valley stock to pick in the 1990s, he or she could've done fine with a basket, or just by investing in local real estate.

To be sure, the list of concerns about the internet—privacy, censorship, algorithmic alienation—is long and growing. So we're seeing indicators that perhaps echo the sort of swelling concerns that buffeted, and then blocked, first, the rails, and then the highways. We can think of Framework as a series of mounds, or bell curves, one succeeding the other, while still overlapping. The railroads rose and fell, then highways, and now, we have to figure out where we are now on the S-Curve of internet growth—the

[73] Gobry, Pascal-Emmanuel, "Facebook Investor Wants Flying Cars, Not 140 Characters," *Business Insider*, July 30, 2011. https://bit.ly/3Ntcxtp

[74] Interestingly, most of that fiber-optic mileage is "dark," that is, unused, which only speaks to the ability of a Framework to build, even if overbuild. See Kushnick, Bruce, "How Did America Lose Over 41 Million Miles of Fiber Optics Since 2007?", Medium, May 27, 2020. https://bit.ly/3JDcAlp. See also: Dano, Mike, "US cell towers and small cells: By the numbers," *LightReading*, March 21, 2023. https://bit.ly/3NS4196. And "Internet Traffic Volume," *Ibis World*, August 31, 2023. https://bit.ly/3NOfeam

[75] Islam, Ariful, "How much is the Internet Worth?", Medium, May 13, 2020. https://bit.ly/3O3Ri30

steep part or the flat part? It's possible that the Framework around the internet will go the way of the Frameworks around rails and roads. Obviously the internet is not going away, but then, neither have the railroad or the automobile. They're both still big, even if they have been demoted. But of course, it's more likely that the internet will get folded into the next net-based thing, artificial intelligence. Will AI be Frameworked? Or, in some way we have yet to fathom, will it Framework us? We'll ponder all that in Chapter Fourteen.

POLITICAL ECONOMY AND REALITY

As we consider Jeffersonian Liberty and the Hamiltonian Framework, we come to the topic of *political economy*. That's a phrase worth pausing over. Political economy simply describes the way of the world. That is, the economy—here, there, and everywhere—will always exist within a political construct of law, taxation, and regulation. It seems naive to think that will change, absent some shift that eliminates, for instance, the value of humans writing and reading books, or investing, or doing anything else. And whereas intellectuals and ideologues can afford to be naive (there's something charming about passionate innocence) investors cannot afford to be naive. Joe Lonsdale, a co-founder of Palantir and now a prominent venture capitalist, wrote knowingly in 2020, "At least since the New Deal, the political reality is that government involvement in our lives has increased in irreversible ways." And so, he continued, "The duty of the modern libertarian is to stop grousing about American government and start fixing it. If we remain true to the principle of LIBERTY and sustain a healthy respect for the creative energies of free people, we can transform our government and improve the lives of Americans across the country."[76] Lonsdale's own career shows the productive interplay of Hamiltonianism and Jeffersonianism. He was born in California, went to Stanford, and

---

[76] Lonsdale, Joe, "Libertarianism is Dysfunctional, But Liberty is Great," JoeLonsdale.com, February 4, 2020. https://bit.ly/3qT0lKX

founded his first companies in that blue state—all of which vindicates the Hamiltonian Framework. And yet then in 2020, he moved to Jeffersonian Texas, penning a stinging op-ed explaining why. He wrote, "It's tragic that California is no longer hospitable…but beautiful that Texas is. Our job as entrepreneurs and investors is to build the future, and I know of no better place to do so than Texas."[77] The Framework lives, too, in the Lone Star State.

INVESTMENT TAKEAWAYS

- *Structure of Scientific Revolutions* author Kuhn sticks to science, even as his insights about human nature leave the reader scribbling excited sidenotes in the margins. "The study of paradigms," Kuhn writes, "is what mainly prepares the student for membership in the particular scientific community with which he will later practice."[78] We can see that the presumption, here, is, "go along, get along." In Kuhn's schema, most scientists are content to operate within the intellectual confines of a paradigm, making only incremental refinements as they can. Kuhn calls this rote task "solving puzzles," and we could add other familiar phrases that get the same thought across, such as "staying in your lane" or "sticking to your knitting." He emphasizes the dogged power of conventional wisdom and orthodoxy. These are the prerequisites, for what he calls "normal science." That is, getting through a normal career. And yet a key Kuhnian point is that normal is not the same thing as correct, or true. So as we veer away from hard science, we can observe that for hard science, and related technology, it's impossible to fake it. If you don't believe in electricity, you don't have a future in electronics. But in other fields, the closer you get to humans

---

[77] Lonsdale, Joe, "California, Love It and Leave It," *The Wall Street Journal*, November 15, 2020. https://bit.ly/3pfKxBO
[78] Kuhn, *Structure of Scientific Revolutions*, 11.

and human nature—and human flesh—the more room there is for debate. And so that includes just about every aspect of health and medicine. There's plenty of science there to be sure—and that science makes plenty of disparate points about health, wellness, and treatment. Diversity of thought allows for different lessons being learned by divergent schools of thought. We can step back and see, even people who might be deemed as under-informed, wrong-headed, and even ill-willed can still be regarded as good customers. In anything to do with human nature, there's simply no one right answer. But then, mystery isn't so bad. Investor Ed Butowsky likes to say, "Uncertainty creates opportunity."

- Decades before Kuhn and his study of paradigm shifts, George Bernard Shaw declared, "The reasonable man adapts himself to the world: the unreasonable one persists in trying to adapt the world to himself. Therefore all progress depends on the unreasonable man." That emphasis on the unreasonable man anticipated the Kuhnian paradigm-shifter, the Promethean romantic figure who breaks with the old orthodoxy to bring forth a new vision. For the strong of will, it is, of course, a flattering self-conception. That's why so many entrepreneurs speak in terms of paradigms and their disruption. In fact, it's rather Nietzschean. The idea of the *Übermensch* is bad-boy catnip to a certain turn of mind. So sure, it's fun to think about being Henry Ford, or Steve Jobs—or the young James T. Kirk solving the *Kobayashi Maru* puzzle in *Star Trek*—and it's often good to invest with them. But Byronic adventures don't always end well. One virtue of Frameworks is that they offer the non-Byronic a comforting degree of predictability. And if we think about it, civilization is tolerable when most things, at least, are predictable.

- Paradigms are paradoxical. On the one hand, the contrarian seeks to bet against the dominant paradigm, and the other hand, once the contrarian case is made, the paradigm shifts and the contrarian becomes the majoritarian. The investor can flourish either way—by index-ily going with the flow, or by zigging when others are zagging. How to keep one's edge? Same way that Peter Lynch advised us about staying one up on Wall Street. Pay attention. Notice things.

- When things grow fast, they often take the form of an S-Curve—steep for awhile, and then they flatten out. So the challenge to an investor, of course, is to figure out where he or she is on the S-Curve—or if it's an S-Curve at all. That takes situational awareness, of course, and historical perspective, too, is useful. Nothing steep stays steep forever.

- The Hamiltonian Framework can be an accelerant for certain modes or technologies. From canals to railroads to roads, the Framework rose and fell, even as elements will last perhaps forever. It's been a long time since anyone thought of canals as a hot new thing, and yet they are still in wide use, from Panama to Suez, and many points in between. So even if the transportation mode is eclipsed, it still generates value. In the meantime, a more virtualized network, the internet, is still going strong.

- We can add another regulatory framework that has collapsed: the once-sturdy carapace around the taxi industry. Plenty of opportunity-seekers had taken note of the overpriced cartel of taxis, and yet nobody thought it could be broken—until Uber, along with Lyft, broke it.

- Interestingly, one subset of automotive transportation still enjoys substantial regulatory Frameworking. That's automated vehicles, aka driverless cars. In California, home to so much powerful Big Tech, pro-industry state authorities have overridden local authorities to advance the new technology. Accidents and fatalities have not stopped this Hamiltonianian process. The lesson: If the product can be successfully pitched as "the wave of the future," it will wash forward.[79]

---

[79] La, Lynn, "San Francisco seeks stop sign on driverless cars," *Cal Matters*, August 18, 2023. https://tinyurl.com/56xdhmua

- There's another physical transportation modality that's booming—bicycles. Even though bicycles have been around for a century-and-a-half, in their mass application as a commuter vehicle, they rate as a paradigm shift. Away from automobiles, of course, but also away from mass transit. Of course, these various transport paradigms can coexist. It's estimated that more than 50 million Americans ride bicycles; in 2023 the industry was valued at $6.5 billion—and projected to grow fast.[80] Yet eager Jeffersonian passion for exercise and independence in the open air isn't enough. To be fully successful, including being safe on the road, bicyclists need a Hamiltonian Framework—which they are creating. Some of the most organized and committed people in America are focused on bicycling, involved as well in the closely related concerns of building curbed bike lanes and designated routes, as well as boosting other benefits, such as commuter tax breaks for cyclists.

- The U.S. Bicycle Route System (USBRS) was established in 1978 by the American Association of State Highway and Transportation Officials. The plan is to use government funds to build long distance bike trails. As of 2022, USBRS could point to fifty-three designated routes, encompassing thirty-four states and the District of Columbia, totaling nearly 19,000 miles.[81] The goal is a full-fledged interstate bikeway system. And there's more. As anyone can notice in the cities, bike lanes are everywhere, with plans to build more. The long-term vision, of course, is to substantially displace autos, making American cities look more like, say, Amsterdam. Which is to say, trillions of dollars will be riding on the outcome of this cultural movement, which will be punctuated, of course, by political struggles over everything from curb cuts to separated bike

---

[80] "Bicycle market size in the U.S. in 2021, with a forecast from 2022 to 2027," Statista, accessed July 7, 2023. https://bit.ly/3PJZgj2

[81] "A new state joins the USBRS!" American Cycling Association, November 30, 2022. https://bit.ly/3rhd9Lp

lanes to congestion pricing. Investors could calculate, how much concrete needs to be poured to provide a safety barrier for every bike lane in America? Familiar infrastructure construction companies could find that they have a whole new gig. And the decay of the automotive lifestyle opens up new vistas for apps. To sum up, given the élan of bicyclists, their Jeffersonian passion and their demonstrated capacity for Hamiltonian Frameworking, bikes are an investment trend to befriend.

- In the meantime new kinds of micro-mobility, including e-bikes and scooters, enrich and complicate the picture, bringing up new opportunities and liabilities. Tiny-motored vehicles are popular, and yet they are a challenge to charge. Many people charge them at home, or in their apartment, and this can stress wiring, which can lead to fires, or else the batteries themselves can catch fire or explode. In 2022, hundreds of battery-related fires, some of them fatal, erupted just in New York City.[82] So we can look ahead, Directionally, and see, there's going to be a good market for better wiring for homes, as well as for fire extinguishers—and most of all, a premium for better batteries.

- There's also an overlapping movement for hiking and walking trails, which also, not surprisingly, is big in Blue.[83]

- Taking all these transportation trends together, as well as working from home—we see another clear trend: the decay of mass transit. Every trend points toward "particle-ized transit" that focuses on point-to-point, as opposed to the older hub-and-spoke model. In fact, sometimes even mass transit itself chooses to go "particle."[84]

---

[82] Ferrechio, Susan, "Faulty batteries in popular e-bikes causing significant rise in deadly fires," *Washington Times*, July 10, 2023. https://bit.ly/46FyGO9
[83] Guffey, Alysa, "A 27-mile community-made trail brings urban hiking to Boston," *The Boston Globe*, July 24, 2023. https://bit.ly/46Z8mil
[84] Repko, Melissa, "DART hires Uber to give Dallas-area customers free, discounted rides," *Dallas Morning News*, March 12, 2019. https://bit.ly/3NJywh4

Bodes poorly for anything else to do with the mass-transit "mainframe."

- If US history is the interplay of the Jeffersonian and Hamiltonian visions, we should always be on the lookout for their next jag. These days, the free-trade thinking that dominated from the Reagan to Obama presidencies—which we might consider Jeffersonian—has been eclipsed by a Hamiltonian emphasis on domestic manufacturing.

- Investors should realize that *both* Hamiltonianism and Jeffersonianism are important. While it may seem tempting to think that the bulldozer of Hamilton is good, in terms of clearing away obstacles to enterprise, overdoing *anything* is bad. China, for example, is all Hamilton and no Jefferson. Lots of capitalist economic development, but little personal freedom. That "market-Leninist" model worked to propel the economy forward, greatly, from the 1980s to the 2010s. Yet by now it's clear that systemic assaults on human liberty and dignity—including lack of due process, arbitrary arrests, seizure of property, and hideously excessive COVID lockdowns—have deeply cut into China's growth prospects. Indeed, the mysterious disappearances and deaths of billionaires, generals, foreign ministers and many others have led to fears of a return to totalitarianism. In the words of *Politico.eu*, "a Stalin-like purge is sweeping through China's ultra-secretive political system."[85] For Westerners, including businesspeople, travel to China is scary.[86] Revealingly, in the first quarter of 2023, just 52,000 people arrived to mainland China from overseas on trips organized by travel agencies—an astonishing 98 percent drop from the first quarter of 2019.[87] In the words of conservative pundit David Frum, "Security

---

[85] "China's paranoid purge," *Politico.eu*, December 6, 2023. https://bit.ly/3RvJ0CX
[86] Hemmings, John, "China is taking US citizens hostage," *Telegraph*, July 5, 2023. https://bit.ly/3NVrrZP
[87] Fan, Wenxin, "China's Latest Problem: People Don't Want to Go There," *The Wall Street Journal*, August 23, 2023. https://tinyurl.com/mr2vy52m

of investment is a national super power. Western democracies offer it. Russia, China etc. cannot."[88] The cost to the Chinese (and Russian) economy will be enormous. If investors are personally afraid to go there, they're less likely to put their money there. At the same time, the collapse of Chinese "soft power"—its cultural attraction and role-modeling power—is thoroughly bearish for the People's Republic. Nimble Chinese companies are getting the message. In 2023, *The Wall Street Journal* reported of the "fast fashion" company Shein, " In recent years, Shein has sought to build a non-Chinese identity. It has moved headquarters to Singapore and has been building supply chains outside China."[89]

[88] Frum, David (@davidfrum) "Security of investment is a national super power," X, July 17, 2023. https://bit.ly/3XWep2H

[89] Lu, Shen, "The World's Most Anonymous CEO Is About to Take Center Stage," *The Wall Street Journal*, December 8, 2023. https://tinyurl.com/5n6pnb8u.

CHAPTER FOUR

BLUE HAMILTONIANISM

FROM DROPPING OUT TO CASHING IN

In the 1960s, the hippie counter-culture seemed anti-capitalist, even if much more energy was devoted to being pro-drugs, sex, and rock 'n' roll. A common catchphrase had it, "turn on, tune in, drop out"—and that was taken to be a slap at the free market, even if market, back then, for love and other pleasures was free, indeed. Amidst the libertinism of the Age of Aquarius, many thought they detected a Jeffersonian strain—contemplative, back to the land, soft energy paths—in this Woodstock Nation. As for the original Jefferson, he certainly believed in personal freedom, but he was never a dropout. Indeed, he regarded liberty as "the great parent of science & of virtue," blending in no-nonsense nationalism: "a nation will be great in both always in proportion as it is free."[90]

In any case, this being America, Hamiltonianism was never far. We can see this in the life of Stewart Brand. Back in 1968, Brand published the *Whole Earth Catalog*, which seemed fully counter-culture-ish, chock full of hippy-dippy references and New Age nuggets. And yet the catalog was essentially a sales document—a granola Sears Catalog, hawking tools, gadgets and even the pop-futuristic technology of Buckminster Fuller. Brand

---

[90] "Extract from Thomas Jefferson to Joseph Willard," Jefferson Quotes & Family Letters, March 24, 1789. https://bit.ly/3XyTumf

made millions. He was, in fact, a thoroughgoing entrepreneur, and if he seemed like a hippie, well, that was fine with him, because it disarmed potential critics on the left, many of whom were going through their Maoist phase. Indeed, Brand was actually Promethean in the scale of his ambition. As he wrote in his catalogue, "We are as gods and might as well get used at it."[91] By that he meant that since human beings had developed the power to change the world, best to figure out how to change it for the better. That's the sort of vaulting ambition we have come to see in Silicon Valley, and it's been noted that many hippies, including the Steves—Jobs and Wozniak— became epic techies. Indeed, it's arguable that the '60s generation, or the Baby Boomers, rates as one of the most energetic and dynamic—albeit, many would say obnoxious—cohorts in American history. So there we have it, once again—the helixing of Jefferson and Hamilton. The great Hamilton was after all, Promethean, too. Americans should, he declared, "cherish and stimulate the activity of the human mind, by multiplying the objects of enterprise … by which the wealth of a nation may be promoted."[92]

As is the case with any historical figure, Hamilton's star has risen and fallen over the centuries, although he has never been totally eclipsed. And these days, he's back, bigly—among Democrats. In 2006 the left-of-center Brookings Institution launched its Hamilton Project, aiming to "advance America's promise of opportunity, prosperity, and growth."[93] And in 2015 came the admiring Broadway musical *Hamilton*, written from a perspective that was simultaneously multiethnic and capitalistic. In 2020, left-wing academic Christian Parenti published *Radical Hamilton: Economic Lessons from a Misunderstood Founder*. In 2021, Democrat Joe Biden moved into the Oval Office and put up oil portraits of six Americans on the wall: Four were presidents: Washington, Jefferson, Lincoln, and Franklin D.

---

[91] *Whole Earth Catalog*, 1968. Accessed, March 11, 2023. https://bit.ly/46BcGEa
[92] Hamilton, *Report*, 1791. https://bit.ly/3PxZhX5
[93] "The Hamilton Project," brookings.edu. https://www.brookings.edu/
wp-content/uploads/2016/06/200604hamilton_1.pdf

Roosevelt. The other two were Hamilton and Ben Franklin, another symbol of capitalist enterprise.[94]

Indeed, some might say that as Democrats have embraced Hamilton, American capitalism itself moved left—all that green spiel, all that diversity, all that wokeness. Daniel Bell, and others since, have argued that this shift comes from rising secular cosmopolitanism, which leaves businesspeople hostile to old conservative verities. Others put forth a more instrumental argument—that, in the wake of the 2008 meltdown and Occupy Wall Street, the leftward lurch of business was a cynical strategy of adaptation, even preemption.[95] These questions will come up again in later chapters; for now, suffice it to say that American capitalism finds itself in a sweet spot. It's moved left enough to be popular with progressives (not many advocate seizing the means of production, they'd rather be funded by it) while still keeping good with the right. In this context, wokeism, in some form or fashion, might last forever.

So now, as we consider the Hamiltonian Framework, let's add a partisan element. The places that were once the citadels of Hamilton's Federalist Party—New York City, Philadelphia, and Boston—are now heavily Democratic. And we can add, to the Democratic column, the big cities on the other coast. So let's give this blue bicoastal phenomenon a name: Blue Hamiltonianism. It's capitalist, for sure, and yet it also includes an activist government. And while blue government is much more activist than Hamilton favored in his life, the Hamiltonian spirit abides today, most notably in the knowledge economy and high finance.

---

[94] Katkov, Mark, "PHOTOS: President Biden's Redecorated Oval Office," NPR, January 21, 2021. https://bit.ly/440mlCf

[95] Ramaswamy, Vivek. *Woke, Inc.: Inside Corporate America's Social Justice Scam* (New York: Center Street, 2021)

BLUE CAP MASS

Let's consider one very blue state with more than its share of progressives *and* Prometheans: Massachusetts. Boasting the third-highest per capita income in the nation, the Bay State offers long-running testimony to the power of innovation. That is to say, to the power of Black Swans. As we have seen, it was host to the first American railroad. It powered itself to further prosperity with textile mills, and it stayed prosperous even after the mills left New England for Dixie in the twentieth century. After all, Massachusetts still had all those good schools, and white-collar companies, as economic engines. Brainwork has, for sure, proven to be the best path for wealth generation.

For all its on-the-sleeve liberalism, the state is mindful wherefrom its money comes. In fact, few big-city newspapers devote as much attention to the entrepreneurial economy as *The Boston Globe*. In 2021, when most newspapers were shrinking, the *Globe* launched a new daily feature, Innovation Beat, boasting a five-reporter team. "Our goal is to cover—on a daily basis and with a critical eye—the people, companies, and ideas that are driving growth and new trends, and to highlight this key pillar of the local economy and everyday life."[96] It's fair to say that the tone is more deal-booking than muckraking. The *Globe's* overall wokeness is not an impediment to business development-friendliness.

For instance, in 2023, the *Globe* cheered Lego's decision to move its Americas headquarters from Connecticut to Boston. The newspaper observed, "Being just a mile down Mass. Ave. from the Massachusetts Institute of Technology was also a plus. The toymaker has partnered with MIT for nearly 40 years, sponsoring the MIT Media Lab and collaborating on robotics and automation, and the LEGO Foundation in 2017 endowed a graduate student fellowship program at the Media Lab."[97]

---

[96] Huang, Gregory, "The Globe launches a new expanded section and newsletter on technology," *The Boston Globe*, September 23, 2021. https://bit.ly/3PyVqJx

[97] Carlock, Catherine, "Lego reveals location of its new Boston headquarters," *The Boston Globe*, August 21, 2023, https://tinyurl.com/s8nnvwu7

For its part, MIT is liberal, but not woke. In the 2020 presidential election, Joe Biden carried the student body over Donald Trump by a vote of 11:1, and yet the school's commitment to hard-nosed excellence wavered for only a brief moment in response to Black Lives Matter-type activism.[98] In 2022, after a brief detour away from standardized testing, the school announced its return to rigor, reinstating its SAT/ACT requirement. Dean of Admissions Stuart Schmill was blunt. "There is no pathway through MIT that does not include a rigorous foundation in mathematics, mediated by many quantitative exams along the way."[99] No wonder MIT is pulling away in mathematics.[100] We know that it's rigor that generates technological innovation, and from there, startups, and from there, riches. (So if there's wokeness in the picture, it's a garnish, an add-on.) Revealingly, MIT students with bachelor's degrees make more money than bachelor degree grads from any other college in the country.[101] A 2015 study found that MIT alumni-founded companies have created 4.6 million jobs, generating $2 trillion in annual revenues.[102] To put this in a Taleb-ian way, MIT is educating and incubating Black Swans. So if the investment-minded can't visit them in person on their Cambridge turf, they can at least look them up on LinkedIn.

Brainy work is going in fascinating, as well as remunerative, directions, including toward brains. Headline in the *Globe*: "Can light reset brainwaves to treat Alzheimer's? This Boston startup has $73 million to find out." A new company, Cognito Therapeutics, relying on optogenetic research

[98] Yglesias, Matt, "Education polarization is only growing," Slow Boring Substack, September 27, 2021. https://bit.ly/3Nq3MR3

[99] Wren, Kathy, "Q&A: Stuart Schmill on MIT's decision to reinstate the SAT/ACT requirement," *MIT News*, March 28, 2022. https://bit.ly/446VEfy

[100] Miller, Sandi, "MIT wins 83rd Putnam Mathematical Competition, sweeps top five spots for third consecutive year," *MIT News*, February 23, 2023. https://bit.ly/3ptV0cD. "In total, a striking 70 out of this year's top 100 test-takers were MIT students, including 21 of the top 25."

[101] "MIT Students after Graduation," MIT Facts, accessed February 24, 2023. https://facts.mit.edu/alumni/.

[102] Matheson, Rob, "New report outlines MIT's global entrepreneurial impact," *MIT News*, December 9, 2015. https://bit.ly/3PKmQw4

from two scientists at—wait for it—MIT, has raised eight figures to test the theory that gamma wave therapy can clear away amyloid plaques, the lumps of unwanted protein associated with Alzheimer's Disease. Cognito's backer, FoundersX Fund Ventures, operates from nearby Cambridge.[103] In other words, a blue ecosystem. There are thousands more startups in Massachusetts. The power of brains to command that kind of capital puts the state, well, light years ahead of low-tech competition.

As an aside, this IQ-driven phenomenon is larger than Massachusetts. Colorado State University has spawned its own startup ecology in the Fort Collins area, focused heavily on agricultural tech.[104] The resulting "techonomic" transformation, *Politico* reports, has flipped surrounding Larimer County from red to blue.[105] To further illustrate Blue's powers of wealth-summoning, we might consider the diabetes drug-turned-diet drug Ozempic. Approved in the US in 2017, its sales have surged to $12.5 billion.[106] The maker, Novo Nordisk, is headquartered in Denmark, and so most of the company's fifty-fold increase in value over the past two decades has presumably accrued over there. But plenty of wealth has been shared with folks in its main US office, in Plainsboro, New Jersey. All this is a formula for prosperous Democrats. Critics on their left, such as Sen. Bernie Sanders of Vermont, might deride them as "corporate Democrats," but for many affluent blues, that's not an insult, but rather, a lived reality.

Interestingly, two economists of very different ideological orientations reached overlapping conclusions about the money-power of knowledge.

---

[103] Cross, Ryan, "Can light reset brainwaves to treat Alzheimer's? This Boston startup has $73 million to find out," *The Boston Globe*, March 22, 2023. https://bit.ly/3NvF8ym. Cognito also believes its technology could work against Parkinson's, MS, and ischemic strokes.

[104] "Meet Our Startups," Colorado State University. https://bit.ly/43zf1ga

[105] Mahtesian, Charlie, and Alexander, Madi, "'This Is a Really Big Deal': How College Towns Are Decimating the GOP," *Politico*, July 21, 2023. https://bit.ly/44zHbsq

[106] "Novo Nordisk's blockbuster Ozempic sales to surge by 23% in 2023, forecasts GlobalData," MarketScreener, May 16, 2023. https://bit.ly/43g947m. Other companies marketing semaglutide, under their own trade names, have also made big money.

MIT's Robert Solow was on the left, and the University of Chicago's Gary Becker was on the right, and yet they converged around ideas of innovation and human capital—to make productive machines, you need smart people. Solow was awarded the Nobel Prize for economics in 1987, and Becker received his in 1992. Human capital makes intellectual property (IP), which the US Patent and Trademark Office (PTO) says accounts for 41 percent of American GDP. And where is most of this IP? According to PTO, "States in the Northeast, Mid-Atlantic, Upper Midwest, and West Coast regions generally have the highest concentrations of workers in IP-intensive industries."[107] We can add that back in the '90s, the Clinton administration was notable for its blue-business orientation, focused heavily on protecting the IP of Hollywood, Silicon Valley, and Wall Street.[108] As we know, those sectors returned the affection for the Democrats. And Massachusetts has been part of the upswell. In 2023, a 3.5 acre compound on Nantucket Island—where three years earlier, the Biden-Harris ticket won 71 percent of the vote—sold for a $38.1 million.[109]

But what about the rap of "Taxachusetts"? According to the Tax Foundation, the Bay State has the thirteenth-heaviest tax burden, (New York State, of course, has the highest).[110] And in fact, pro-business Democrats in the state are in a permanent tussle with their left-wing,

[107] Toole, Andrew A., et al., "Intellectual property and the U.S. economy: Third edition," United States Patent and Trademark Office, 2019. https://bit.ly/46mxG1c

[108] "The Clinton Presidency: Unleashing the New Economy—Expanding Access to Technology," Welcome to The White House, accessed April 17, 2023. https://bit.ly/44mBPk6; see also, "Oct. 28, 1998: President Signs New Copyright Law," *Wired* https://bit.ly/3uBemPr; "Financial Services Modernization Act of 1999 (Gramm-Leach-Bliley)" U.S. Federal Reserve, accessed November 28, 2023. https://bit.ly/3T4hEVG

[109] Solomont, E.B., "A $38.1 Million Nantucket Home Sale Sets Massachusetts Record," *The Wall Street Journal*, June 30, 2023. https://bit.ly/3NwVJ56

[110] "State and Local Tax Burdens, Calendar Year 2022," Tax Foundation. https://bit.ly/3PxNMzd

tax-hiking comrades.[111] If the progressives win, as they sometimes have, it's possible there will be a flow of rich people out of the state. And yet it's also the case that when some people get rich enough, they worry less about tax rates, and more about, say, mindfulness. This is an especially comfortable state of mind for those sitting on unrealized capital gains and so aren't paying much in the way of income taxes. Moreover, life for the Blue Hamiltonian is good when the state's Democratic power structure is so assiduous about providing certain kinds of NIMBY-ish services. For instance, the state is notable for making sure that migrants—including those sent up from Florida—do not stay long in Martha's Vineyard, or in any of the state's affluent enclaves.[112] So while hate has no home in Massachusetts, don't expect to see many Guatemalans or Kenyans at home in Brookline or Newton.

In fact, the state's economic history suggests that the Blue Hamiltonian model can create wealth faster than taxes can chase it away. Over the past two decades, jet traffic at the Boston area's largest private aviation airport, Hanscom Field, has quadrupled. Looking ahead to still more growth, in 2023 Hanscom applied to build twenty-seven new hangars.[113] One might wonder, how does private aviation square with concerns about climate change? For sure, polls show that Bay Staters are concerned. A 2022 poll found that 77 percent are either "somewhat" or "very" worried about climate change. And yet at the same time, solid majorities support mitigation efforts, including solar power, energy efficiency measures—and crucially, tax credits.[114] So we can see, combating climate change becomes its own

[111] Gross, Samantha, and Stout, Matt, "Months in, Healey is scoring wins with a Democrat-led Legislature in the very places her GOP predecessor failed," *The Boston Globe*, April 17, 2023. https://bit.ly/3XudxT2

[112] Carr, Howie, "Lucky 28 towns get migrants…guess who doesn't?" *Boston Herald*, July 12, 2023. https://bit.ly/3JSKx1G

[113] Abel, David, "Plan to expand hangar space for private jets at Hanscom sparks concerns about a surge in climate pollution," *The Boston Globe*, May 20, 2023. https://bit.ly/3NkcYGA

[114] "Poll: Massachusetts residents see climate change as a serious problem for state," MassINC Polling Group, 2022. https://bit.ly/450NqWh

kind of Hamiltonianism. These efforts will mean, inevitably, innovation. And Massachusetts is all about innovation.

Nationwide, Blue is generating plenty of money with ideas. When it comes to the next gusher of human capital, blue states tend to have better education. For instance, of the top ten colleges as rated by *US News*, nine are in blue states.[115] To be sure, these rankings can be argued and counter-argued every which way, but as the income statistics show, the economic impact can't be disputed. To this variable of human capital, we can add the impact of skilled immigration, on the theory that the most "valuable" immigrants are those coming with skills, to gain more skills—and they often end up in Blue. To name one, Sundar Pichai, CEO of California-based Alphabet Inc., was born in India, and then earned his graduate degrees in blue territory: at Stanford and Penn's Wharton School. In fact, according to one study, "almost 44 percent of 2018's Fortune 500 companies were founded by immigrants or their children. Among these are some of the largest and most successful companies in the world, including Apple, Amazon, Costco, and Bank of America. Together, these companies employ 13 million people worldwide."[116] Once again, the greatest wealth comes from the smartest people. And where they cluster, wealth accumulates. So far at least, that's mostly in Blue.

THE BIG BLUE BAILOUT

As Hamilton would have been the first to say, the lifeblood of any capitalist economy is credit. If credit is easy, times tend to be good, albeit bubbly.

---

[115] "Best National University Rankings," *US News*, accessed June 14, 2023. https://bit.ly/43YcAo9. The nine "blues" are, in order, Princeton, MIT, Harvard, Stanford, Yale, University of Chicago, Johns Hopkins, and the University of Pennsylvania. The one "red," listed tenth, is Duke, tied with Northwestern (blue). We could point to similar blue-tilted rankings for medical schools and hospitals.

[116] "Almost 44 Percent of All U.S. Fortune 500 Companies in 2018 Were Founded by Immigrants or Their Children, New Research Shows," New American Economy, October 10, 2018. https://bit.ly/3Jt1jEo

Back in the nineteenth century, US railroads were chronically a bubble. The technology of transportation was fine, but railroad men, having fun with other people's money, frequently overbuilt. In fact, the bubble was most often inflated by European investors, mostly British, eager to get in on American growth, not realizing that they were playing the role of greater fool. So American railroads frequently went bankrupt. This liquidated the holdings of the overseas shareholders, but left the actual railroad intact. As for rail executives, they could keep whatever they could hide. So Britain got hurt, while America was fine, benefiting from the economic activity of construction, keeping the miles of new track.[117] If we step back a bit, we see that economic history is oftentimes just the history of bubbles, in one year or another, in one sector or another. And yet when the many bubbles are all beaded together, they start to look like…economic growth. As Keynes said, the long run is a series of short runs.

Finance is a mostly blue industry. Democrats know that, of course, and they take care of their own. That was evident in the wake of the 2008 financial crisis, when the $498 billion bailout went mostly to Blue. According to one study, "The main winners were the large, unsecured creditors of large financial institutions. While their exact identities have not been made public, most are likely to have been large institutional investors such as banks, pension and mutual funds, insurance companies, and sovereigns."[118] These are now the citadels of—and piggy banks for—Blue.

In addition, blue California is conscious that tech can be *fintech*. And so the state renamed its bank regulator the Department of Financial Protection and Innovation. Yet who can know what kind of innovation works best. For instance, in 2023, Bloomberg News reported on insider dealing by blue banks, including Silicon Valley Bank and First Republic Bank, headquartered in San Francisco. It seems they had extended $10 billion in low-interest-rate loans to "well connected people…

---

[117] Fulfer, Johnny, "Panic of 1857," *The Economic Historian*, January 6, 2022. https://bit.ly/3rp6zT1. See also: "Railway Mania," Wikipedia, https://bit.ly/3NJnjMp
[118] Harbert, Tam, "Here's how much the 2008 bailouts really cost," *MIT Management*, February 21, 2019. https://bit.ly/3NQ0Oa0

insiders," defined as "their own directors, officers and major shareholders." Bloomberg added, "Wealthy homebuyers and property investors with high incomes...could get a mortgage from First Republic Bank with a rock-bottom rate for several years. Better yet, they didn't have to start repaying the principal for a decade." The article continued, "Across Manhattan, the San Francisco Bay area and Southern California, Atherton, the Hamptons, Beverly Hills, those terms attracted legions of wealthy clients—including executives from other banks—as interest rates sank during the pandemic. The loans left borrowers with more cash to invest and spend than if they financed their properties with more conventional mortgages. Demand was so strong that it helped First Republic double its assets in four years, while deposits surged." In other words, a big boost—more like a bubble—for Blue. Crucially, these low-rate loans were issued before the big interest rate increases of 2023.[119] And with those higher interest rates, of course, came the crunch. Yet here's where the closerthanthis relationship between blue business and blue politics paid off. After Silicon Valley Bank went under in 2023, depositors were all bailed out, way past the statutory limit on deposit insurance, $250,000 per account. We learned that ten depositors—including Sequoia Capital and a Chinese firm, Kanzhun, Ltd.—with deposits totaling $13.3 billion were fully covered. This seemingly extralegal ladling proved easy. All a federal official had to do was say the magic words, "systemic risk exception."[120] But then, what are friends for, if not to get special treatment? Indeed, the friendship seems destined to be long-lasting. In March 2023, the Treasury Department announced a $25 billion

---

[119] Buhayar, Noah, and Brush, Silla, "Insider Loans Surged Ahead of Turmoil at US Regional Banks," Bloomberg News, April 14, 2023. https://bit.ly/3Py0JsH. See also: Buhayar, Noah, et al., "First Republic Worked Hard to Woo Rich Clients. It Was the Bank's Undoing," Bloomberg News, April 16, 2023. https://bit.ly/440ypU9

[120] Cox, Chelsey, "Warren, AOC press top Silicon Valley Bank depositors about any cushy treatment they received," CNBC, April 10, 2023. https://bit.ly/3piH59w. See also: Chapman, Lizette, and Leopold, Jason, "The Big Names That Got Backstop for Billions in Uninsured SVB Deposits," Bloomberg News, June 23, 2023. https://bit.ly/3Py06PF

program to cover big blue bank losses, and yet as of June 2023, Treasury had combined with the Federal Reserve to bail banks out to the tune of $153 billion—six times the amount originally stated.[121] A lot of Blue can be made happy this way—and a lot of blue politicians, too. Yet even after its billion-dollar bailouts to free lending institutions, the Federal Deposit Insurance Corporation has been exploring additional ways to increase deposit insurance for big business. As yet another Bloomberg story said of FDIC, "The regulator highlighted the impact of technological changes and high concentrations of uninsured depositors in pockets of the banking system as reasons for a possible overhaul."[122] We can say, "pockets of the banking system" is code for blue zip codes. Blue has deep pockets, fully able to hold more money. In the words of tech critic Ben Tarnoff, "The swiftness with which Biden rescued the depositors of Silicon Valley Bank is a testament to the clout that valley elites continue to hold at the highest levels of the Democratic Party."[123] Some might say this is *corruption*. Others might say it's a *business model*.

Speaking of blue-philic regulatory chumminess, *The Wall Street Journal* reports that Manhattan-based JP Morgan Chase has grown into a colossus, boasting 4800 branches across forty-eight states, holding more than 13 percent of the nation's deposits and 21 percent of all credit-card spending. The *Journal* adds that the implicit assurance of FDIC—there's now seemingly no limit to the size of the account protection, statutory cap be damned—is helping Chase, and other big banks, to grow bigger. "That implicit guarantee encourages people and businesses to move their money

---

[121] Balaji, "No Cap," Balaji.com, June 23, 2023. https://balajis.com/p/the-feds-self-bailout-is-25b. See also: "The BTFP makes funding available to eligible depository institutions to help ensure that banks have the ability to meet the needs of all their depositors." "Periodic Report: Update on Bank Term Funding Program," Federal Reserve System, June 12, 2023. https://bit.ly/3XtETbV. There have been efforts to claw back some of these bailouts, but it's a safe bet that the clawbacks will always be smaller than the payouts.

[122] Johnson, Katanga, "US Weighs More Business Deposit Insurance After Banks Fail," Bloomberg, May 1, 2023. https://bit.ly/42UCube

[123] Tarnoff, Ben, "Better, Faster, Stronger," *New York Review of Books*, September 21, 2023. https://tinyurl.com/ybxpzjf6

to them in times of stress creating a feedback loop that makes big banks bigger at the expense of their smaller peers."[124] Gee, it's almost as if there's a plan to engorge big banks in New York City while thinning out smaller banks, thus putting red states at the mercy of Big Blue.[125] And did we mention that Chase is spending $12 billion on fin-tech-y, AI-y, computer technology?[126] That money will be spent mostly, of course, to improve the UX—user experience—for Chase customers. And while frictionlessness is certainly a good thing, we are beginning to see how Blue—including blue Massachusetts—continues to thrive. There's more money in fintech than in farming or fracking, especially if the most favored Hamiltonians have that pipeline to federal bailouts. Not everyone will like that approach. But like it or not, we are reminded, Blue Hamiltonians are rich for a reason.

BLUE MONEY, BLUE POWER

Blue Hamiltonianism has political implications. For instance, Blue has mostly made its peace with bigness, in part because that's what capital wants, and in part, too, because big allows for more specialization within the company. And it's that specialization that creates departments of communications, community relations, and human resources—and those units, of course, are reliably blue, maybe even woke. Moreover, blueness begets big money in politics. In 2020, Joe Biden raised more than a billion dollars for his presidential campaign, outspending incumbent president Donald Trump by a 4 to 3 ratio. Indeed, Democrats overall outspent

---

[124] Benoit, David, "America's Biggest Bank Is Everywhere—and It Isn't Done Growing," *The Wall Street Journal*, May 21, 2023. https://bit.ly/3r3871B

[125] And while JP Morgan Chase CEO Jamie Dimon has been regarded as a moderate, "flexible" is probably a better word. In 2020, Dimon had himself photographed taking a knee, and committed $30 billion of shareholder money to "racial equity." In 2023, the conservative watchdog 2nd Vote, which rates companies on a one-to-five scale, with one being most left, gave the company a rating of 1.26—which is to say, pretty far over. https://bit.ly/46BcvbS

[126] "This $12 Billion Tech Investment Could Disrupt Banking," JP Morgan Chase., accessed June 15, 2023. https://bit.ly/3NN7yp4

Republicans by billions.[127] Interestingly, "money in politics" doesn't seem to be quite the journalistic concern that it once was. In the meantime, the Democratic National Committee's finance committee—a socialist-free zone—helps Blue Hamiltonians mingle with the politicians who join them in playing the bailout game.

Inevitably, this much money spills across national borders. Blue tends to be more internationalist—or, if one prefers, globalist—in outlook. And so we're starting to see a new phenomenon—left-leaning capital reaching around the country and around the world, seeking to "discipline" right-leaning politics. To put that another way, market forces are being joined by non-market factors. One way or another, personal and institutional opinions—likes and dislikes—have always affected fiscal flows. Yet the gushing of postindustrial wealth means that blue influence floods all the more visibly. For instance, since its Brexit vote, much loathed by blue capital, the United Kingdom has been made to suffer. That is, the organs of international finance have been judging Britain harshly, with vehemence, even vengeance.[128] The point here isn't to argue the merits of Brexit. Instead, we can just observe that the campaign to undo the vote has been about as top-down as anything since Zeus rained lightning bolts down on the Greeks. This incandescence has zapped all Brexit governments since 2016, and it absolutely fried the short-lived government of Liz Truss.[129]

---

[127] Evers-Hillstrom, Karl, "Most expensive ever: 2020 election cost $14.4 billion," Open Secrets, February 11, 2021. https://bit.ly/3CVe06V

[128] See, for example, Berthelsen, Derrick, "The Financial Times has a Brexit problem," The Critic, August 20, 2022. https://bit.ly/3Oxtkxn

[129] Brexit reminds us that not every attempt at firing a geography-based economic bazooka, as discussed in Chapter One, is a success. Brexit advocates insisted that the UK would do better, economically, if it were free of the EU's onerous regulations. British voters endorsed Brexit, and yet British leaders *increased* regulation, notably on climate matters. Thus the UK got the worst of both worlds; it was outside of the EU free trade zone, but inside its own red-tape hellscape. No wonder the country has stagnated. Still, as the EU moves to regulate artificial intelligence into non-existence within its 27-country domain, the independent UK has another chance to do better way—to be an AI enterprise zone, a "NevAIda."

THE SECRET OF DIRECTIONAL INVESTING

We can observe a similarly successful effort against Jair Bolsonaro in Brazil, and also, much less successfully, against Narendra Modi in India.

Israel makes for another case study. In 2022, prime minister Benjamin Netanyahu was elected to a sixth term atop a right-wing coalition aimin to change the liberal judicial status quo. Peaceful opposition erupted immediately; the business-minded center joined the left in opposition. Israel's status as "Startup Nation" was at risk. In *Foreign Policy*, David E. Rosenberg wrote, "Intentionally or not, the judicial revolution will bring about a state and society antithetical to the liberal values that serve as the foundation of Israel's high-tech economy and military. As another slogan popular with the opposition warns, 'No democracy, no high-tech.'"[130] Hebrew Blue Hamiltonianism had asserted itself. In mid-2023, *Calcalist*, an Israeli tech-business site, reported that startup activity had fallen by 75 percent, adding "India, France, Germany and Canada have overtaken Israel in the amounts invested."[131] Such drastic numbers suggest that Israel has been suffering from—to dig up a phrase from the Depression—a capital strike. To be sure, much changed after the Hamas attack on Israel on October 7, 2023. Military aid from the US poured in, but tech investment is a subtler, albeit still profound, category.

Finally, we can take note that blue investment giant BlackRock has gotten the lead on the reconstruction of Ukraine, sure to be a trillion-dollar project in the years to come. BlackRock is helping to design the country's "investment framework." Very Hamiltonian. Since then, other blue pillars, including JP Morgan Chase and McKinsey & Company, have gained pole positions.[132] We can already see, much of the aid and investment money will be flowing through New York City. Indeed, it's worth noting that the whole of the European Union—of which Ukraine will likely be at least a de

---

130 Rosenberg, David E., "Why Israel's Establishment Is Revolting," *Foreign Policy*, March 1, 2023. https://bit.ly/44fkHgs

131 Calcalist (@Calcalist), X, July 3, 2023. https://bit.ly/446D9HP

132 "BlackRock Financial Markets Advisory to advise Ministry of Economy of Ukraine," BlackRock, November 19, 2022. https://bit.ly/3rtop7n. See also: AFP, "BlackRock Chief Says Investors Ready To 'Flood' Ukraine," *Barron's*, January 19, 2023. https://bit.ly/44cHWra

facto member—is more tied to Blue than to Red. The accession of Ukraine to Blue will be a big boost to the prestige and scale of transatlantic Blue.

INVESTMENT TAKEAWAYS

- Blue knows one big thing—there's more to economic development than just cutting taxes. That is, there's making sales in the first place. As Keynes wrote in 1930, "The engine which drives Enterprise is not Thrift but Profit."[133] Yes, pinching pennies is always a good idea, but the greatest driver of profitability is innovation. So innovative Blue will flourish. But non-innovative Blue? Not so much.

- Perhaps the easiest driver of profitability is getting money from the government, and as we have seen, blue banks have gotten good at that. If this trend continues, investors will have to factor in that, thanks to the solicitous FDIC, investments in Blue will have more access to capital. And if the need arises, access to bailouts. But if Red were to wake up and force changes in the system, then the trend could change.[134]

- Still, by many measures, Blue is losing ground, at least on a relative basis. According to Bloomberg in 2023, "For the first time, six fast-growing states in the South—Florida, Texas, Georgia, the Carolinas and Tennessee—are contributing more to the national GDP than the Northeast, with its Washington-New York-Boston corridor, in government figures going back to the 1990s.

---

[133] Keynes, John Maynard, *A Treatise on Money*, (London: MacMillan and Co., 1930), 149.

[134] To be sure, critics of the banking status quo abound, including in blue states. One such is Sen. Elizabeth Warren (D-MA). Born in Oklahoma, Warren retains an old-line populist disdain for big banks; she is particularly eager to restrict, even claw back, their funny-money gains. She has teamed up with Sen. J.D. Vance (R-OH), a Trumpy conservative mindful that red states have been getting the short end. See: Mueller, Eleanor, "The new power couple taking on Wall Street: J.D. Vance and Elizabeth Warren," *Politico*, July 6, 2023. https://bit.ly/43uPKnn

The switch happened during the pandemic and shows no signs of reverting." Some in the Northeast will find this news disconcerting, but most likely it will cause no great ripple, because rich blues aren't much subject to those sorts of aggregate statistics. That growth is faster in Florida is not a great source of concern to the person who paid $38 million for a place in Nantucket. Indeed, when Bloomberg further reports that the Southeast was home to ten of the fifteen fastest-growing American large cities, that's a sure signal to many Northeasterners that they are better off doing it their way.[135] In point of fact, the population of Massachusetts has risen, albeit at a much slower pace than the country, such that the Bay State has actually lost seven Congressional districts over the last century, shrinking from sixteen representatives to nine. But does that mean that the quality of life for those who stayed has gotten worse? One thing it *has* meant is that Massachusetts is now greener. For the first time in a long time, it's possible to swim in the Charles River. Given such pastoral priorities, Blues do not worry overmuch that the Redbelt is growing faster.

[135] Sasso, Michael, and Tanzi, Alexandre, "A $100 Billion Wealth Migration Tilts US Economy's Center of Gravity South," Bloomberg News, June 29, 2023. https://bit.ly/44wyHSF

CHAPTER FIVE

RED JEFFERSONIANISM

Blue is richer than Red. Of the ten states boasting the highest per capita income, nine voted for Joe Biden in 2020. Of the ten states with the lowest per capital incomes, nine voted for Donald Trump.[136] Yet there's plenty of evidence that riches are moving toward Red, and lower taxes have a lot to do with it. In 2021, the American Enterprise Institute's Mark Perry found that of the top ten states for inbound migration in the previous year, eight had Republican governors, and of the top ten states for outbound migration, eight also had Democratic governors. He further noted that the average top individual income tax rate in the top ten inbound states was 3.8 percent, compared to an average top tax rate of more than 8 percent for the top outbound states.[137]

Speaking of state taxes, seven states—including Florida and Texas—have no state income tax, and as anti-tax activist Grover Norquist cheerfully noted in 2023, a number of red states are actively exploring getting rid

---

[136] "2022 Per Capita Personal Income," Economic Development Administration, https://bit.ly/3O241mS

[137] Perry, Mark J., "Top 10 Inbound Vs. Top 10 Outbound US States in 2021," American Enterprise Institute, December 29, 2021. https://bit.ly/46nvxCs. There has been some attempt at culture-based pushback. For instance, this *Washington Post* opinion headline from 2023: "Florida might pay for MAGA cruelty and know-nothingism." Might happen, but hasn't happened yet.

of theirs.[138] By contrast, California and New Jersey have raised their state income tax rates.[139] We can add that there's also a skew in state corporate income tax rates, which in 2023 ranged from 2.5 percent in North Carolina to 11.5 percent in New Jersey.[140] So if tax competition among the states is a thing, and it is, we'll see more shifts.

To bring this competition into focus, we can recall that in 2013, Texas began running ads in California, urging Golden Staters to move to the Lone Star.[141] Elon Musk has referred to California as "the land of sort of overregulation, overlitigation, overtaxation"—and then he hied himself off to Texas.[142] In the decade of the 2010s, the Texas labor force grew more than three times faster than the national average.[143] In fact, between 2010 and 2020, four million people relocated to Texas, including 700,000 Californians.[144]

It's still the case, as noted in the previous chapter, that Blue brain-power is the better engine for creating wealth. But once it's created, wealth often seeks, er, redder pastures. Bloomberg News reported in 2023 that the wealthy are making a "broader shift" to lower-tax states. "Their moves, away from places like New York's Upper East Side and San Francisco's Nob Hill to warmer, less-dense regions of Florida and Texas have lifted real estate prices … And as wealthy executives bring their businesses along with

---

[138] Norquist, Grover, "Red States Accelerate Push for No Income Tax," *Townhall*, July 29, 2023. https://bit.ly/3qaFXVK

[139] "New Jersey increases tax rate on millionaires," Grant Thornton, October 28, 2020. https://bit.ly/3rUlC7J

[140] Fritts, Janelle, "State Corporate Income Tax Rates and Brackets for 2023," Tax Foundation. https://bit.ly/3CL5fwt

[141] Chammah, Maurice, "In Radio Ads, Perry Reaches Out to California Businesses," *Texas Tribune*, February 4, 2013. https://bit.ly/3XGX3Hj

[142] Reuters, "Tesla's Musk says he sold 'enough stock'; slams California for 'overtaxation,'" CNBC, December 22, 2021. https://bit.ly/3XpFb3e

[143] Schnurman, Mitchell, "Texas' economy keeps its edge by importing talent from other states and countries," *Dallas Morning News*, December 16, 2022. https://bit.ly/46mUMVr

[144] Li, Roland, and Sumida, Nami, "Texas' population grew more than twice as fast as California's. Experts say there's still no Golden State exodus," *San Francisco Chronicle*, April 26, 2021. https://bit.ly/3Pv6ur2

them, the merely affluent follow, too." Bloomberg noted that zero-state-income tax Florida is "home to 38 of the 50 million-dollar US neighborhoods with the largest price gains by percentage over the past three years... Those areas have all seen home values more than double."[145] Anecdotally, in 2022, National Football League wide receiver Tyreek Hill had a $120 million offer from the New York Jets. Yet when he figured out that if he accepted the New York deal, he'd liable for some $10.8 million in state and local taxes. So he signed instead with the Miami Dolphins, saying, "Those state taxes, man."[146] The shift is happening, too, with regular salaried workers, or at least their employers. "We now have more employees in Texas than in New York state," says JP Morgan Chase CEO Jamie Dimon. "It shouldn't have been that way but Texas loves you being there."[147]

By now we can see a pattern. An industry emerges in one place—textiles in New England a century ago, tech in California more recently—and then the production end of the industry finds itself migrating to another state, even another country, seeking lower costs. Hence Apple's sly locution, "Designed by Apple in California. Assembled in China." We can see the game here—searching for lower costs, seeking tax avoidance, and then adding some nice-sounding words. From the point of view of the wealthy, including top execs and shareholders of Apple all this shifting is not a bad outcome. The money savings aside, from a personal green point of view, it's better that the actual work of production—including the negative externalities of prole-y workers and pollution—is far away. Call it NIMS: Not In My State.

---

[145] Tanzi, Alexandre, et al., "America's Priciest Neighborhoods Are Changing as the Ultra-Rich Move to Florida," Bloomberg News, February 14, 2023. bit.ly/3Y9CLET. Florida has the second-lowest mean elevation (100 feet above sea level) of any state; still, big money is migrating there, including to oceanfront real estate with de minimis elevation. What about climate change? Seems that people with real money aren't worried, or think it's an issue that will be resolved.

[146] Walczak, Jared, "Tyreek Hill Moved to Lower His State Taxes, and He's Not Alone," Bloomberg Tax, October 12, 2022. https://bit.ly/43QIQcV

[147] Zilber, Ari, "JPMorgan CEO Jamie Dimon praises 'pro-America, pro-business' Texas, Florida," New York Post, March 7, 2023. https://bit.ly/46pZLVy

To be sure, factories are good, and a nation needs them, but they are now mostly in Red Jeffersonia. According to *The Economist*, "It is the South—a region running from Texas to Virginia—that is fast becoming America's new industrial heartland."[148] A big selling point, the magazine notes, is energy costs—which are substantially cheaper in the South. In fact, the East South Central region has the least expensive power in the US. That inexpensiveness is, of course, substantially a tribute to the hydropower of the New Deal-era Tennessee Valley Authority, that most Hamiltonian of economic development projects. Although of course, today's Democrats see hydropower, reliant on hulking dams, as not "green."[149] And yet *The Economist* notes that Kentucky, soon to be a hub for green-battery manufacturing, generates some 70 percent of its electricity from coal.[150] To put that another way, none of the South's energy-cost advantage is attributable to the most-favored green energies, solar and wind. It's Blue (trying to incorporate solar and wind into its grid) that tends to have the highest energy costs, and Red (happy with carbon fuels) that usually has the lowest.[151] So yes, it's mordantly funny to think that Kentuckians will be burning coal to make batteries for Californians.

Still, it's nice to think that Red Jeffersonia and Blue Hamiltonia need each other. As Hamilton himself wrote, the various sectors of an economy should enjoy symbiosis. While it might seem that agriculture and industry are in conflict, Hamilton allowed, in reality "their interests are intimately blended and interwoven." He added that cultivation of the land increases the "quantity of money in a state," thus increasing commerce, which in turn

---

[148] "The South is fast becoming America's industrial heartland," *The Economist*, June 12, 2023. https://bit.ly/3JxfQPp

[149] Catenacci, Thomas, "Biden considering tearing down key green energy source over eco concerns," Fox News, March 24, 2023. https://bit.ly/3QbEU2t

[150] "The South is fast becoming America's industrial heartland," *The Economist*, June 12, 2023. https://bit.ly/3JxfQPp

[151] In 2023, the three states with the highest electricity rates were blue Hawaii, Connecticut, and Massachusetts, while the three states with the lowest electricity rates were Louisiana and Idaho, both red, along with hydropower-blessed Washington, blue. "Electricity Rates by State," Choose Energy, accessed June 14, 2023. https://bit.ly/431OmIz

increases land values.[152] So today, are Red and Blue happy together? Not quite, but maybe they should be happier than they are.

FINANCE

As detailed in the previous chapter, Blue has the more sophisticated financial system—boosted, of course, by its politically powered proximity to the federal bailout pipeline. However, given the tax differentials among the states, and given that capital is mobile, it seems likely that Red will develop its own finance ecosystem. We've already seen some of this happening. Big financial players—including Ken Griffin, Carl Icahn, and Paul Singer—have moved not only their personal fortunes, but their operations, to Florida. Even BlackRock is big in West Palm Beach. In late 2023, *The New York Post* reported $1 trillion fleeing Gotham.[153]

Meanwhile, on the other coast, a sharp note was heard in March 2023, when Fisher Investments, located in Washington State, reacted to the imposition of a new capital gains tax with a one-sentence statement. It was moving to Texas.[154] Whereupon Texas governor Greg Abbott, bragging on his state's "zero income taxes," tweeted, "Ken Fisher Boosts Wall Street West With $197 Billion Texas Shift."[155] Now there's a phrase to track: *Wall Street West.* Yet at the same time, Griffin speaks of Florida as "Wall Street South."[156] So will it be Wall Street West or Wall Street South?

---

[152] Hamilton, Alexander, *The Federalist Papers: No. 12*, 1787 Hamilton, Alexander, *The Federalist Papers: No. 11*, Yale Law School, 1787. https://bit.ly/3NsbolZ. The American economist Henry Carey developed this theme in his 1851 work, *The Harmony of Interests: Agricultural, Manufacturing, and Commercial.*

[153] Thaler, Shannon, "New York loses $1 trillion in Wall Street business as firms flee the city," *The New York Post*, August 21, 2023, https://tinyurl.com/a5hyz5a9

[154] "Fisher Investments moving Camas headquarters to Texas after tax ruling," KGW8 News, March 27, 2023. https://bit.ly/3XqDl28

[155] Abbott. Greg (@GregAbbott). "Ken Fisher Boosts Wall Street West," X, March 28, 2023. bit.ly/40PLv4V

[156] Smith, Michael, and Basak, Sonali, "Ken Griffin Sees Miami Possibly Replacing NYC as Finance Capital," Bloomberg News, November 14, 2023. https://bit.ly/4aibzLs

Either way, it seems a cinch that rivals will emerge to BlackRock, which is better described as *Blue*Rock. So let's call the future challenger *Red*Rock. Looking ahead, if finance bifurcates, legacy blue finance will shrink, while startup red finance will rise.

In the meantime, the "red-ification" of finance proceeds in fits and starts. In 2022, an avowedly conservative financial institution, GloriFi, having raised $50 million from right-leaning investors, opened its doors— or, more precisely, debuted its app. It pledged to "celebrate your love of God and country." Yet amidst accusations of mismanagement, GloriFi shut down just two months later.[157] In 2023, another right-leaning financial institution, the former First State Bank in Elmore City, Oklahoma, opened its doors as the renamed Old Glory Bank.

Yet to the extent that banking needs scale—the sort of scale that allows for giant spending on fintech IT, and that convinces national regulators that the bank is too big to fail—a RedRock wannabe will have to confront a persistent characteristic of Red. Namely, its instinctive opposition to centralization. It was, after all, Hamilton, the icon of Blue, who wanted a national bank. By contrast, the patron saint of Red, Thomas Jefferson, was never a fan. But happily for Red, banks aren't the only way to make a buck.

THE WEALTH POTENTIAL OF JEFFERSONIANISM

The true spirit of Red is Jeffersonianism is decentralization. Decentralization may pose a challenge to national or even regional banking, but it allows for in-state experimentation, and that can be valuable in other ways. The decentralizing idea is, in fact, woven into the constitutional fabric of our history. Back in 1799, while serving as vice president of the United States, Thomas Jefferson argued for upholding the power of the states against the federal government. As he wrote in the Second Kentucky Resolution,

---

[157] Andriotis, AnnaMaria, and Ensign, Rachel Louise, "Anti-Woke Bank GloriFi to Shut Down," *The Wall Street Journal*, November 21, 2022. https://bit. ly/431TX1B

"The several states who formed that instrument [the Constitution], being sovereign and independent, have the unquestionable right to judge of its infraction; and that a nullification, by those [states], of all unauthorized acts…is the rightful remedy."[158] That word, "nullification," is powerful. Alongside decentralization, nullification explains much of our economic history. That is, it's the nullification (even if that word wasn't used) of limiting laws that, in turn, offers the *unlimiting* of economic activity. As we saw in Chapter One, the Jeffersonians of Nevada nullified the rules against gambling, and so got rich. Interestingly, in a pinch, even not-quite Jeffersonians agree. The founders of the Hollywood movie industry made a similar nullification play, escaping from Thomas Edison on the East Coast. And then, as we saw in Chapter Three, Silicon Valley used Section 230 to nullify normal liability laws.

A second aspect of the Jeffersonian tradition, of course, is small government. As the man himself said in his first inaugural address, the goal should be "A wise and frugal government, which shall restrain men from injuring one another, shall leave them otherwise free to regulate their own pursuits of industry and improvement, and shall not take from the mouth of labor the bread it has earned. This is the sum of good government."[159] Two centuries later, Red has smaller government and lower taxes. The decentralizing red worldview does, indeed, oppose Big Government. Interestingly, that anti-Big spirit sometimes spills over into anti-Big Business, and not just anti-Big Bank. To be sure, plenty of companies in Red are big, and yet the red populist style favors the "little guy"—and that can have economic implications. In 2021, Missouri's Republican senator Josh Hawley published *The Tyranny of Big Tech*, in which he called for antitrust enforcement, as well as other regulatory measures, against "monopolistic" tech companies—which are, of course, mostly blue.

---

[158] Jefferson, Thomas, "Second Kentucky Resolution," Yale Law School, December 3, 1799. https://bit.ly/3XpFlHS

[159] Jefferson, Thomas, "First Inaugural Address," The Jefferson Monticello, March 4, 1801. https://tjrs.monticello.org/letter/1330

As we think about the red economic model, we can see that, to a great extent, it's the cheaper alternative to Blue. That is, in Red, both people and their money enjoy a lower cost of living, as well as less hassle on land use, recycling, and pronouns. Yet in one area, Red is carving out not just an alternative, but a whole new thing, offering the prospect of a whole new kind of decentralization.

CRYPTOCURRENCY

If the internet was pioneered by libertarians, cryptocurrency has been pioneered by hardcore libertarians, who probably mostly, if they have to, identify as Red. If the internet is now supervised by Blue, then crypto hardcore warriors similarly find themselves confronting Blue.

Crypto traces back to 2008, when Hamiltonian high finance failed so badly in the "Great Meltdown." In that year, "Satoshi Nakamoto" released a treatise on Bitcoin, sketching a new system that "would allow online payments to be sent directly from one party to another without going through a financial institution."[160] Bitcoin offered independence from big banks, and not so coincidentally, it also offered independence from regulators and tax collectors. Yet perhaps just as importantly, it offered the prospect of a fresh way of thinking about finance, politics, and society. In the arcane language of the paper—"a peer-to-peer distributed timestamp server to generate computational proof of the chronological order of transactions"—cryptopians could see an opportunity to build a new libertarian world out of the statist shambles of the old. It might even be a cyber Galt's Gulch.

Perhaps the most original thinker on the future of crypto-politics is Vitalik Buterin, creator of Etherium. He has published numerous essays advancing his own vision of "economic democracy"—which, we should hasten to say, has nothing to do with the economic democracy preached by socialists. Buterin's idea is completely different—using crypto to facilitate

---

[160] Nakamoto, Satoshi, "Bitcoin: A Peer-to-Peer Electronic Cash System," Bitcoin. org, 2008. https://bitcoin.org/bitcoin.pdf "Nakamoto" is a pseudonym.

people "voting" with their asset to incentivize certain outcomes. "It is possible," he wrote in 2014, "to set up currencies whose seignorage, or issuance, goes to support certain causes, and people can vote for those causes by accepting certain currencies at their businesses. If one does not have a business one can participate in the marketing effort and lobby other businesses to accept the currency instead." Critics will dismiss this as timocracy, rule by the rich, and others might see it as simply a new kind of crowdsourcing, but Buterin envisions "a more decentralized, and democratic, way to pool together our money and support public projects and activities that help create the society we want to see."[161]

Buterin, boasting five million X followers, offers a new political science, a fresh synthesis of liberty and structure. In that sense, he echoes Herbert Croly, who a century ago had the idea of synthesizing Jeffersonianism and Hamiltonianism to unleash "wholly unaccustomed energy." So now today we have ideas including "smart contracts" and "decentralized autonomous organizations" to achieve goals. Love it or hate it, it's potentially a paradigm shift, directing toward a new legal, technological, and political constellation. Maybe even a Framework.

Indeed, crypto has been so exciting, for so many reasons, that it has gained adherents all over, including in Blue. One convert to crypto was Silicon Valley's Sequoia Capital. The VC giant took the pre-scandalous Sam Bankman-Fried under its wing, touting him as possibly the world's first trillionaire.[162] Pre-scandal, Andrew Ross Sorkin of the *New York Times* referred to Bankman-Fried as the "J.P. Morgan of crypto," specifically recalling the moment in 1907 when Morgan stepped in to stop a financial

---

[161] Buterin, Vitalik, "Markets, Institutions, and Currencies—A New Method of Social Incentivization," *Bitcoin Magazine*, January 10, 2014. https://bit.ly/3rhRAKw

[162] Fisher, Adam, "Sam Bankman-Fried Has a Savior Complex—And Maybe You Should Too," Sequoiacap.com, September 22, 2022. Pulled from the firm's website, but archived here: https://archive.ph/qFJJN#selection-163.0-163.63

panic.[163] Yet even post-Bankman-Fried, crypto is thought to have crossed the $2 trillion threshold.[164]

Others, of course, are having none of it. Speaking for the establishment, here's Warren Buffett's business partner, Charlie Munger, not long before he died: "A cryptocurrency is not a currency, not a commodity, and not a security. It is an investment in nothing."[165] Advocating for the politico-regulatory wing of Team Blue, Sen. Elizabeth Warren (D-MA) declares, "Crypto needs to be subject to the same money laundering rules that banks, credit unions, gold traders, stockbrokers, credit card issuers and the Western Union have to meet every single day." The Bay State lawmaker added, "Crypto has become the payment of choice for 90 Chinese companies that are supplying the precursor drugs to Mexico so that they can mix up enough fentanyl to kill billions of people."[166] These concerns took on greater saliency after the 10/7 terrorist attack on Israel; reportedly, Hamas had used crypto to move money. In the words of Senate Banking Committee chair Sherrod Brown, Democrat of Ohio, crypto "clearly had a role in terrorism."[167] It's hard to square the circle on crypto: On the one hand, it was designed to facilitate secrecy, and on the other hand, some who seek to use its secrecy are too awful to be tolerated. In any case, blue federal entities, including the Securities and Exchange Commission, are on the hunt, targeting crypto.

Still, crypto endures, even flourishes, as a favorite of Team Red, hubbed in no-state-income-tax enclaves such as Florida and Wyoming. In fact, Wyoming, mostly ignored by the rest of the country, has worked hard on innovations that are, in fact, a new kind of nullification. The legislature

[163] "Transcript of Sam Bankman-Fried's Interview at the DealBook Summit," *New York Times*, December 1, 2022. https://bit.ly/44rKh1K

[164] Golubev, Sergey, "How Cryptocurrency Is Reshaping the Global Trade Landscape," *Payments Journal*, July 28, 2023. https://bit.ly/3qkBJe9

[165] Charlie Munger Fan, (@CharlieMunger00), X, March 3, 2023. https://bit.ly/43dT6dX

[166] "Warren's bipartisan banking moves," *Punchbowl News*, June 28, 2023. https://bit.ly/3JB61j8

[167] *Punchbowl News*, October 31, 2023, https://bit.ly/41cGTqS

in Cheyenne has voted to assure that assets within the Cowboy State are insulated from taxes by concealed ownership trusts known as the "Cowboy Cocktail." As the *Washington Post* reports, "Millionaires and billionaires around the world have taken note. In recent years, families from India to Italy to Venezuela have abandoned international financial centers for law firms in Wyoming's ski resorts and mining towns, helping to turn the state into one of the world's top tax havens."[168] We can see that Wyoming is aiming to do for saving what Nevada did for gambling.

Crypto champions see their product as a steady store of value pitted against inevitably inflating fiat currency. Not to put too fine a point on it, Red sees crypto as insurance against Blue mooching and looting. And if there are crypto bubbles and bankruptcies along the way? Well, the thinking goes, that's the story of everything. And besides, Red insists, the *real* scam is the Federal Reserve. The lesson here is that Red doesn't trust Blue, just as Blue doesn't trust Red—and why should they? So what's emerging is dueling loyalty, each side favoring its own.[169] Out of that rivalry should come yet more of Croly's wholly unaccustomed energy. It's quite likely that there will be dueling crypto regulatory regimes, a federal system, and then, as well, state systems—which some state, perhaps Wyoming, will see as an opportunity to make further Nevada-type deregulatory plays.

It should be noted that many other countries have expressed enthusiasm for crypto, and so even if the industry were somehow to be chased offshore, it's never going to die.[170] Indeed, many rivals of the US, including China, see crypto as part of an overall de-dollarization strategy. To be sure, crypto is so complicated—and so full of future political, as well as economic permutations—that nobody knows where it will end up. That's what makes it so interesting.

---

[168] Cenziper, Debbie, and Fitzgibbon, Will, "The 'Cowboy Cocktail': How Wyoming Became One of the World's Top Tax Havens." *Washington Post*, December 20, 2021. https://bit.ly/43l7hhE

[169] Digital Innovation for America, accessed July 1, 2023. https://digitalinnovation-foramerica.com/

[170] Saacks, Bradley, "Foreign doors open for crypto as US cracks down," *Semafor*, March 10, 2023. https://bit.ly/3pjuqDi

INVESTMENT TAKEAWAYS

- If it needs to be invented, it's more likely to be invented in a high-education blue state, which is also, of course, a high-tax state. But if it *has* been invented, it's portable. That's Blue's vulnerability, and Red's opportunity. To put it another way, Blue is the first mover, and Red is the fast follower. From an investment point of view, first mover is typically the greatest opportunity, and yet plenty of first-mover companies (Ford, Polaroid, Xerox) fade. And of course, sometimes faded companies (Marvel, Apple, Microsoft) recover and get a new burst.

- Half the states (red) are jockeying to cut taxes to entice development, while the other half (blue and purple) are more likely looking to spending plans to create jobs and wealth. Depending on the precise circumstances, and the quality of targeting, both approaches can work. Investors must notice the details and make their own assessment.

- On the whole, Democrats recognize that blue-to-red shifting isn't helping them. So if Democrats were to gain large majorities in Washington—the kind that could allow for real changes in national policy—they will look to squeeze down the ability of red states to make themselves business-friendlier. For example, they could do that by piling on national imposts of taxation and regulation that would lessen or eliminate the power of a red state to magnetize blue wealth. If Democrats were to gain that power, then no state would be able to think about relaxing—to say nothing of nullifying—federal law. This would be the negation of Jeffersonian federalism and states' rights. Of course, the more Red realizes that's what Blue has in mind, the less likely that Red will vote for Blue.

- Conversely, if Republicans are in charge nationwide, they will likely encourage the states to experiment on cutting taxes. But it's an open question whether they'll be okay with states' rights when it comes to, say, legalizing abortion and restricting guns. Recalling the power of Blue Hamiltonians, an investor can ponder these and other "social issues," knowing that they carry a heavy freight of economic consequences, both first-order effects on people and their businesses, and second-order effects on the overall economic development vibe.

- In general, Red favors physical can-do—mining, drilling, farming, manufacturing—while Blue is more amenable to digital can-do.

- So geography is a clear economic development play. For instance, Blue is happy shutting down red industry, delighting in the vision of Red as a giant nature preserve for blue sightseers and good-thinkers.[171]

- Crypto is bringing with it new paradigms of politics and governance. These new models won't necessarily replace the old models, but they could be a supplement. Most likely, recalling Kuhn, different systems will coexist.

---

[171] Beauge, John, "Decision to discontinue plans for $1B gas-fired power plant 'killed us,' mayor of Pa. town says," *PennLive*, April 16, 2023. https://bit.ly/44HmISK. See also: Jones, Mark, "Activists weaponize Endangered Species Act to oppose hunting grizzly bears," *Washington Times*, April 17, 2023. https://bit.ly/3YbpKvS

CHAPTER SIX

THE UNITED STATES OF ARBITRAGE

ONE SIZE DOES NOT FIT ALL

"*E*pluribus unum*" means "Out of many, one." But back in 1994, then-vice president Al Gore mistranslated America's motto as "Out of one, many." Gore was much mocked.[172] However, he was sort of onto something. These days, one size is *not* fitting all. The *one* is, in fact, becoming the *many*. We will recognize this, of course, as diversity, and it's only accelerated since the '90s. For sure, a trend to spot.

True diversity is the diversity of everything. Of course, "everything" is too much for the mind to manage, and so, as Thomas Kuhn explained, we organize our ideas into paradigms, as guides for thought and action. Some of these mental models, such as Jeffersonian Liberty and the Hamiltonian Framework, have been highly successful, and so as we think about investment, we think about them. And yet new ideas are always bubbling up, both variations on themes and new themes altogether. And the lesson of history, as well as real-time observation, is that these ideas and schools of thought can exist at the same time. Sometimes they fight, of course, but most often they peacefully compete and interact. We can all judge this multitude of

---

[172] Kamen, Al, "For Gore, it's all in the translation," *Washington Post*, January 10, 1994. https://bit.ly/3NvFKnO

models however we wish, but that's the point—we can all judge them. So with the input of all, we see the coexistence of many models.

Yet the models reveal, as James Madison put it, "diversity in the faculties of men." And out of that diversity comes opportunity, including the moneymaking opportunity of arbitrage. Investopedia defines arbitrage as "the simultaneous purchase and sale of the same or similar asset in different markets in order to profit from tiny differences in the asset's listed price."[173] The site adds, "Arbitrage exists as a result of market inefficiencies, and it both exploits those inefficiencies and resolves them." So we can see right away that arbitrage is an opportunistic play by the quick-witted. It exploits slower-moving weakness. It can be argued that it's good when inefficiencies are resolved, although, of course, that depends on what's being made more efficient. Arbitrageurs are not often known for making moral judgments. This chapter starts with the reality that Blue Hamiltonianism and Red Jeffersonianism are different—and becoming more different. As we've already seen, states are avidly competing with each other, often on the simple metric of lower taxes. Indeed, across these semi-United States, greater differences among the states open up greater opportunities for arbitrage. If arbitrage is an amoral concept, then this chapter touches on amorality. There will never be a shortage of opinions and judgment on the ideas and policies mentioned herein—from the reader, or from the author. And yet the arbitrageur suspends judgment, because there's money to be made.

LABORATORIES OF PROSPERITY

We can start by asserting that the logical subunit of the United States is the states. It is they, after all, who have their own chief executive (a governor), their own legislature, and their own constitutions. Indeed, James Madison,

---

[173] Fernando, Jason, "Arbitrage: How Arbitraging Works in Investing, With Examples," Investopedia, updated March 20, 2023. https://www.investopedia.com/terms/a/arbitrage.asp#:~:text=Arbitrage%20is%20the%20simultaneous%20purchase,in%20the%20asset%27s%20listed%20price.

principal author of the US Constitution, wrote that the states were more important than the Union. He went so far as to proclaim, "Were the Union itself inconsistent with the public happiness, it would be, Abolish the Union."[174] Madison never said the states could be abolished. Some say that the Civil War did away with the notion of states' rights. Yet here's Salmon P. Chase, Chief Justice of the United States, a strong opponent of slavery, appointed by President Lincoln, writing for the Supreme Court in 1868. "The Constitution, in all its provisions, looks to an *indestructible* Union composed of *indestructible* States."[175] [Emphasis added.] We're thus left with a legal and political puzzle. The union is indestructible, and so are the states. So how do the permanent states interact with the permanent union? The answer we've come up with is that the United States is compartmentalized into fifty states. Federalism is the modern word for this compartmentalization, although states' rights seems to work well. But by whatever term, each generation must sort out the power of the respective governments. To be sure, central federal power has been on the upswing for the past century. But past doesn't have to be prologue. Indeed, as we have seen, Nevada has long been able to chart its own course. And as we shall see, that centralizing upswing is now being reversed. The "unum" is, in fact, getting more "pluribus"-y. So now we come to the twentieth century's most articulate champion of federalism, Louis Brandeis. In the 1932 Supreme Court case of *New State Ice Co. v. Liebmann*, his resonant phrase, remembered for all time as "laboratories of democracy," still excites the imagination ninety years later:

> *"The advances in the exact sciences and the achievements in invention remind us that the seemingly impossible sometimes happens.... The discoveries in physical science, the triumphs in invention, attest the value of the process of trial and error. In large measure, these advances have been due to*

---

[174] Madison, James, *The Federalist Papers: No. 45*, Yale Law School, 1788. https://bit. ly/3PwPpgg
[175] *Texas v. White*, 74 U.S. 700 (1868)

experimentation. In those fields experimentation has, for two centuries, been not only free but encouraged.... There must be power in the States and the nation to remould, through experimentation, our economic practices and institutions to meet changing social and economic needs."[176]

Brandeis continued, his enthusiasm for political and technological innovation bubbling.

"Denial of the right to experiment may be fraught with serious consequences to the nation. It is one of the happy incidents of the federal system that a single courageous State may, if its citizens choose, serve as a laboratory; and try novel social and economic experiments without risk to the rest of the country.... If we would guide by the light of reason, we must let our minds be bold."[177]

Those last words, "we must let our minds be bold." How could an investor not like that? The states must be free to experiment, just like Nevada, and, in their various ways, all the states. Out of those state based experiments will come different policies. We can further assert that all this diversity will lead to opportunity—the opportunity to succeed, and, of course, the opportunity to fail. Indeed, out of the flux will come boundless opportunities for arbitrage. Yet before we consider the possibilities of simultaneously buying low and selling high, let's examine the degree to which the states are growing apart. Then the implications for arbitrage and investment will be all the more manifest.

LABORATORIES OF LIFESTYLE

Back in the 1940s, the American psychologist Abraham Maslow argued that human needs march up a hierarchy, a pyramid, with basic survival at

---

[176] *New State Ice Co. v. Liebmann,* 285 U.S. 262 (1932).
[177] Ibid.

the bottom and "self-actualization"—defined as the fulfillment of one's full potential—at the top.[178] This is a key point, because even as the country grows less religious in the traditional sense, new faiths and creeds become loom larger.[179] Yet whatever the belief system, it's always been true, and always will be true, that man, and woman, does not live by bread alone. People will always quest for self-actualization, even if few questers would use that exact term. So one key aspect of today's arbitrage is that it is not always dependent on economic variables such as profits and taxes. Other goals are worthy of shopping and swapping.

This was a key lesson of a 2008 book by journalist Bill Bishop, *The Big Sort: Why the Clustering of Like-Minded America is Tearing Us Apart*. Bishop assembled a mass of data, showing that "red" and "blue" Americans (a concept that had only recently gained traction) were increasingly moving to like-minded communities and like-minded states. Bishop linked this Big Sort to prosperity, applying the Maslowian point that people were using their affluence as a springboard, making geographic location choices based on lifestyle. Bishop described "a cultural shift powered by prosperity and economic security." He added, "Freed from want and worry, people were reordering their lives around their values, their tastes, and their beliefs.... They were clustering in communities of like-mindedness, and not just in terms of where they lived, geographically, but also, where they dined, worshiped. Churches grew more politically homogeneous during this time, and so did civic clubs, volunteer organizations, and, dramatically, political parties." So yes, birds of a feather were happier as they flocked together. And yet at the same time, hostility to the out-group—those with different feathers—was increasing. In Bishop's words, America was becoming "The United States of 'Those People.'"[180]

---

178 McLeod, Saul, "Maslow's hierarchy of needs," *Simply Psychology*, updated October 24, 2023. https://bit.ly/3D7J3wN

179 Burge, Ryan, "Gen Z and Religion in 2022," Religion in Public. https://bit.ly/3NP0h80

180 Bishop, Bill, with Cushing, Robert G., *The Big Sort: Why the Clustering of Like-Minded American is Tearing Us Apart* (Boston: Houghton Mifflin Harcourt, 2008), 12, 37.

In fact, partially in pursuit of the right in-group, Americans are moving around, a lot. According to one estimate, 7.5 million Americans move across state lines every year.[181] Citing conservatives fleeing California for Idaho, and liberals fleeing Texas for Colorado, the Associated Press reported in 2023, "Americans are segregating by their politics at a rapid clip, helping fuel the greatest divide between the states in modern history."[182] On the right and left, political figures are urging more movement. In 2021, Josh Hammer urged his fellow conservatives, "Relocate as much as possible to safe red states, such as Texas, Florida, and Tennessee, where the arm of the ruling class' Leviathan is less likely to pose an existential danger."[183] And liberal messaging is a mirror. In 2022, New York's Democratic governor, Kathy Hochul, said to Republican opponents, "Just jump on a bus and head down to Florida where you belong. OK? Get out of town. Because you don't represent our values."[184] Perhaps getting the hint, a recent poll found that 27 percent of New Yorkers said they want to leave in the next five years, and 31 percent said that they plan to retire elsewhere.[185] Political analyst Amy Walter summed up the partisan implications of the Big Sort. "At the beginning of this century, 13% lived in a deep red or blue county. Now, almost 30% of us do. Another 8% live in a county that gave

[181] Supan, Joe, "Moving Trends: What the Data Says About How Americans Are Moving," Mymove.com, December 6, 2022. https://bit.ly/3NRUU8o

[182] Riccardi, Nicholas, "Conservatives go to red states and liberals go to blue as the country grows more polarized," Associated Press, July 5, 2023. https://bit.ly/44eBu30

[183] Hammer, Josh, "The Subjugation of the Deplorables," *American Mind*, September 29, 2021. https://bit.ly/46q9jQ5

[184] Williams, Zach, "'You're not New Yorkers': Hochul says political rivals like Zeldin ought to move to Florida," *New York Post*, August 22, 2022. https://bit.ly/42tOAIH

[185] Dilworth, Miles, "New York exodus continues: Staggering 10,000 people fled to Florida in the first quarter of 2023 as almost a third plan to leave in the next five years after being pushed out by high housing prices, taxes and crime," *Daily Mail*, April 13, 2023. https://bit.ly/3NLUpws

80% or more of the vote to a presidential candidate; 30 years ago, just 2% of us did."[186]

Of course, the politics of "Those People" will have business implications. Democrats are now more the party of the affluent, and that shows up when we lay voting data on top of consumer purchases, seeing what sells where. For example, in 2020, Joe Biden won 85 percent of counties with a Whole Foods and just 32 percent of counties with a Cracker Barrel.[187] Indeed, consumer buying power is also expressing itself in less familiar ways. For instance, Oregon counts as a laboratory of experimentation on psychoactive drugs. In 2020, with 58 percent of the vote, the Beaver State passed Measure 110, a referendum de-criminalizing the possession of drugs in small quantities, including methamphetamine, LSD, oxyco-done—even heroin. The penalty for possession is now reduced to the equivalent of a parking ticket. Yet given the political climate in the state, law enforcement has, understandably, given up. In 2023, *New York Times* columnist Nicholas Kristof, a resident of Oregon, described the situation on the streets of Portland. "The cops leave at 5pm and the open-air drug market opens at 6pm -- and overdoses start." Overdose deaths had, in fact, doubled in just three years.[188] Is this progress? Is this progressive? The people of Oregon seem to think so. In the 2022 gubernatorial election, the Democrat who supported Measure 110 was elected, defeating a Republican who pledged to seek its repeal.[189] Yes, it's true that as of 2022, Oregon was losing population, and yet the people remaining seem happy,

---

[186] Walter, Amy, "America on Trial Separation," *Cook Political Report,* March 30, 2023. https://bit.ly/432AMoj

[187] Wasserman, Dave (@Redistrict), X, December 8, 2020. https://bit.ly/42XRYLG

[188] Kristof, Nicholas (@NickKristof), X, July 26, 2023. https://bit.ly/47aQO2M

[189] VanderHart, Dirk, "In their words: How Oregon's governor candidates would handle Measure 110," Oregon Public Broadcasting, October 3, 2022. https://bit.ly/44lJyyv

maybe even high. Indeed, it's likely that for some living outside of Oregon, easy drugs could be a lure to move there.[190]

On a larger scale, it can be argued that drugs are a form of economic development. As of 2023, a total of twenty-four states, two territories and the District of Columbia—representing well more than half the nation's population—have enacted measures to permit cannabis for adult "non-medical use."[191] For clarity we can say that "non-medical" means recreational. To many, druggy capitalism is horrible; they can point to data showing that drug use shrinks the overall economy. Yet to others, it's freedom, and oftentimes, too, it's business. The overall North American market for legal cannabis is expected to grow 15 percent a year.[192]

Yet here's an interesting legal and constitutional wrinkle. Marijuana is mostly legal at the state level and yet it's *il*legal at the federal level. Evidently, the Madisonian-Jeffersonian concept of states' rights is prevailing in the minds of left-leaning drug-deregulating proponents. The left and states' rights. That's a thought to hang on to.

To cite another example of the states making their own choices, we can point to school choice, also known as scholarships or vouchers. The injection of market forces into the schools is full of implications for the schools—and for all their employees, vendors, and contractors. In 2023, public K-12 education spending, nationwide, totaled $794.7 billion. To look at the total a different way, for 49.4 million students, that sum worked out to more than $16,000 per pupil.[193] So even a few students in motion

---

[190] Effinger, Anthony, "Oregon Population Declines for First Time Since 1983, When Timber Was Ailing," *Willamette Week*, December 24, 2022. https://bit.ly/44kEgDK

[191] Meko, Tim, and Blanco, Adrian, "More than half of Americans live in places where recreational marijuana is legal," *The Washington Post*, November 8, 2023. https://bit.ly/40YeDrR

[192] "North America Legal Cannabis Market Size, Share & Trends Analysis Report By Source (Marijuana, Hemp), By End-use (Recreational, Industrial, Medical Uses), By Derivative (CBD, THC), And Segment Forecasts, 2023 – 2030," Grand View Research. https://bit.ly/440mWUB

[193] Hanson, Melanie, "U.S. Public Education Spending Statistics," Education Data Initiative, updated September 8, 2023. https://bit.ly/46qjJz8

puts a lot of money in motion. In fact, the school choice idea has spread fast in the wake of parental frustration over COVID lockdowns, concerns about curriculum, and the general feeling that the schools aren't educating. Of course, the perceived failure of some is an opportunity for someone else. More than thirty states have at least some sort of school choice program. Most are small, but some states, such as Florida, have gone all the way to statewide school choice.[194] Over time, these choice programs will put hundreds of billions of dollars in play, potentially to be snapped up by newcomers, including religious, charter, for-profit, and anything else schools and teaching systems. In the meantime, Alabama is targeting woke textbooks, while Illinois is targeting those who target woke books.[195] So what's an investor to do? As always, notice. To be sure, any political trend can be stopped, even reversed, so investors will have to ponder whether or not the trend today will be their friend tomorrow.

We can also look to another cultural issue with money implications: LGBTQ. In 2023, news accounts identified LGBTQ people who were leaving Florida for other states.[196] Equality Florida "warn[ed] of the risks posed to the health, safety, and freedom of those considering short or long term travel, or relocation to the state."[197] Will this fear of Florida prove to be an economic trend of consequence? Already, blue states see an economic development angle in counter-programming red states. In Los Angeles, for example, DragCon has become a significant economic engine. "DragCon is the mecca of a political statement when it comes to showcasing trans, queer, and drag joy," said Kerri Colby, an L.A.-based performer and *RuPaul's*

---

194 "2023-24 Trends." National School Choice Week, accessed November 29, 2023. https://bit.ly/47vmmQu.

195 "Alabama education director ousted over 'woke' training book," *Politico*, April 22, 2023. https://bit.ly/3Juh9OU. See also: Kapos, Shia, "Preckwinkle's urgent ask," *Politico*, May 4, 2023. https://bit.ly/3pnJFeh

196 Blow, Charles M., "L.G.B.T.Q. Americans Could Become a 'New Class of Political Refugees>" *New York Times*, June 14, 2023. https://bit.ly/3NPMSNg

197 Press release, "Equality Florida Issues Advisory Warning For Travel," Equality Florida, April 11, 2023. https://bit.ly/3qV6kPo

Drag Race season fourteen contestant.[198] That means thousands of people showing up, spending money. We can add that RuPaul's World Of Wonder productions, right there on Hollywood Boulevard, boasts "endless spin-off shows, massive audiences online and huge ratings on TV."[199] As the company says of itself, "We believe that today's Underground is tomorrow's mainstream."[200] Such movement, from the edge to the middle, is, of course, a classic formula for success in show business. And show business, being a business, is investor friendly.

There are other, related, elements that make up a business climate, including perceived friendliness to what Richard Florida—his name notwithstanding, a Blue—has dubbed the "creative class." For sure, "creative class" was a deliberately flattering term, and yet it captured something important about corporations and economies—the aura, or *qi*, that looms large in the success of many industries and cities. Indeed, it's fair to say that many firms see cultural issues as more important than taxes or red tape. Yes, culture counts. As they say about business, "Culture eats strategy for breakfast."[201] In 2023, Elton John decried "a growing swell of anger and homophobia that's around America." As a consequence, the seventy-six-year-old rocker declared, he would not be doing what many aging pop stars have done: set up a "residency" in Las Vegas.[202] That same year, more than 250 Hollywood celebrities and influencers, including Ariana Grande and Amy Schumer, wrote an open letter to Big Tech executives, declaring, "True allies do not profit from anti-LGBTQ hate." The letter continued, "There has been a massive systemic failure to prohibit hate, harassment,

[198] Hansen, Candace, "DragCon returns to L.A. in celebration as queens fight to keep their culture," *Los Angeles Times*, May 12, 2023. https://bit.ly/445tuRV

[199] Strudwick, Patrick, "RuPaul's Drag Race co-creator on a mission to take the show to Uganda, Russia and Iran," iNews, April 10, 2023. https://bit.ly/3pn9YBg

[200] https://www.worldofwonder.com accessed May 29, 2023.

[201] Guley, Gokhan and Reznik, Tracy, "Culture Eats Strategy for Breakfast and Transformation for Lunch," *The Jabian Journal*, Fall 2019. https://journal.jabian.com/culture-eats-strategy-for-breakfast-and-transformation-for-lunch/

[202] Salam, Maya, "Elton John Warns of 'Growing Swell of Anger and Homophobia' in U.S." *New York Times*, June 20, 2023. https://bit.ly/3JJ2uj4

and malicious anti-LGBTQ disinformation on your platforms and it must be addressed."[203] One needn't agree with these show people to nonetheless see, they do have power to shape at least some corporate practices, and corporate practices matter to money.

We can point to more avant-garde experimentation with an economic implication—medical and surgical transgenderism. In 2022, California made itself a "sanctuary state" for transgender youth seeking "gender-affirming healthcare."[204] The following year, Illinois governor J.B. Pritzker seemed to up the ante when he tweeted, "We've taken steps so that Illinois is a beacon of hope for the LGBTQ+ community nationwide. Here are just some of them: Expanded Medicaid to cover gender-affirming surgery; Brought LGBTQ+ curriculum into schools; Ensured single occupancy restrooms are gender-neutral."[205] *The Boston Globe* reported that not only are Blue and Red are moving in opposite directions on transgender policy, but furthermore, this splay in policies is resulting in a population shift. For instance, a family with a transgender child that picked up and moved from Texas to Massachusetts is one of "a small but notable exodus dividing the country into slightly deeper shades of red and blue." One Massachusetts transgender clinic told the newspaper that it was engaged in "a massive hiring push" to meet demand for its services.[206] For her part, the Bay State's governor, Maura Healey, herself a lesbian, declared to *Politico*, "There are people all across this country looking to us who need a safe haven," adding, "We are open for business in Massachusetts." The publication went on to explain that, while Healey had been focused on pro-business tax cuts for

---

[203] Complex, Valerie, "Letter Organized By GLAAD And HRC Calls On Social Media CEOs To Take Action On Disinformation About Transgender Healthcare And Malicious Anti-LGBTQ Narratives," *Deadline*, June 27, 2023. https://bit.ly/3JJ1z26

[204] McClurg, Lesley, "California Becomes First Sanctuary State for Transgender Youth Seeking Medical Care," KQED, October 18, 2022. https://bit.ly/3r0421A

[205] Pritzker, J.B. (@GovPritzker), X, April 14, 2023. https://bit.ly/3XoFOu7

[206] Johnston, Katie, "As bans on transgender care for minors grow, a migration of sorts is underway," *The Boston Globe*, July 14, 2023. https://bit.ly/3XT25QR

her state, "She's now adding abortion and LGBTQ rights to her pitch as red states impose more restrictions on both."[207]

We can see, here, a vision of social liberation, and, at the same time, a vision of a kind of economic development. And if the business model isn't quite Nevada-like, there's still big money involved. Anti-trans activist Abigail Shrier argues that Planned Parenthood, a multi-billion-dollar enterprise, is now a "factory" for transgenderism. Shrier quotes a former employee saying, "Trans identifying kids are cash cows, and they are kept on the hook for the foreseeable future in terms of follow-up appointments, bloodwork, meetings, etc., whereas abortions are (hopefully) a one-and-done situation."[208] Such treatment can cost in the tens, even hundreds, of thousands of dollars—and that's money in someone's pocket. For instance, Lupron, made by Abbvie, is used as a hormone suppressant sells for thousands of dollars a shot.[209] Some will be horrified at this sort of monetization, while others will be intrigued. By now we should be getting used to the idea that Red sees things one way, while Blue sees them differently. If we want to, we can even point to micro-examples of dubious Directionality. For instance, in San Diego, the "Boo Bash: Queerfest Family-Family Drag Show" was sponsored by Align Surgical Associates, a gender reassignment center.[210] On a larger scale, we can point to the extended billionaire family of Illinois' Governor Pritzker, which seems to be directing a movement toward transgenderism.[211] Is this philanthropy? Or ultra-cynical, ultra-ideological, directional investment? Perhaps both? Will it succeed? If the states are laboratories of democracy, it seems a cinch

[207] Garrity, Kelly, and Kashinsky, Lisa, "Healey's pride: Mass. LGBTQ protections," *Politico*, June 12, 2023. https://bit.ly/3NJUoaU

[208] Shrier, Abigail, "Inside Planned Parenthood's Gender Factory," Substack, February 8, 2021. https://bit.ly/3XpBnz4

[209] Allen, Arthur, "It cost $38,398 for a single shot of a very old cancer drug," NPR, October 26, 2022. https://bit.ly/3NqS1tI

[210] "Parents to protest Encinitas Union School District for distributing 'Queerfest' dragshow flyer," KUSI TV, October 10, 2022. https://bit.ly/3Jvfngk

[211] Bilek, Jennifer, "The Billionaire Family Pushing Synthetic Sex Identities (SSI)," *Tablet*, June 14, 2022. https://bit.ly/3JxrTvS

that at least one state, and maybe more, will be to transgenderism what Nevada is to gambling.

Of course, abortion is more widely accepted. Probably half of US states could be rated as "pro-choice." In 2023, New Jersey's Democratic governor, Phil Murphy, suggested that he and his state would defy the US Supreme Court if it ruled against mifepristone, the so-called abortion pill.[212] So under some possible stricter national abortion regime—including, perhaps one day, a restrictive Republican president—could the Garden State be an abortion Nevada? It could, although quite likely, many other blue states will join, too.

There's more. We've already considered the impact of the Black Swan of knowledge work. Now we can add that there's another sort of Black Swan lurking nearby. It's not technologically transformative, but it could be socially transformative—and in a rich area, where there's plenty of money to be found in social transformation. In 2023, the *New York Times* reported, "In recent years, Somerville, a four-square-mile city with 80,000 residents just outside Boston, has quietly turned into something of a haven for those who practice consensual non-monogamy, an umbrella term for relationship styles that involve more than two people."[213] Also known as polyamory. Assuming that the Commonwealth of Massachusetts doesn't mind, a new kind of Nevada-ish lifestyle enterprise zone could be in the making. We could go on in this vein, citing other social and cultural issues carrying an economic and investment impact.

THE LEFT DISCOVERS STATES' RIGHTS

The right has long favored decentralization, in keeping with its general distaste for a strong federal government. For its part, the left today might not

[212] Hanchett, Ian, "NJ Gov. Murphy: We'll Defy SCOTUS 'To Save Lives' If They Rule Against Abortion Pill," *Breitbart*, May 17, 2023. https://bit.ly/3XqzG4o

[213] Safronova, Valeriya, "Interested in Polyamory? Check Out These Places," *New York Times*, May 16, 2023. https://bit.ly/3PxM94l

want the federal government to be smaller, but the left does seem to want the central government to be weaker. Fifteen years ago, in *The Big Sort*, author Bishop called it: "One of the ironies of political segregation is that it's turned Democrats into the party of states' rights." He added, "State sovereignty, once the discredited viewpoint of segregationists, is now becoming the battle cry of mainstream liberals."[214] For instance, there's the state of California, which never much cottoned to Donald Trump. But California did more than just vote against Trump by near 2 to 1 margins in both 2016 and 2020. The Golden State's then attorney general, Xavier Becerra, filed no less than 110 lawsuits against the Trump administration, on matters ranging from climate change to immigration to consumer rights.[215] However, federal officials, at least on the Democratic side, were not troubled by Becerra's legal assault on the federal edifice. In 2021, President Joe Biden appointed him to be his Secretary of Health and Human Services.

So if we think about the issues mentioned above—deregulated drugs, school choice, transgenderism, abortion, non-monogamy—all can put states in opposition, at least potentially, to federal authority. And yet the fact that the states are winning speaks to the waning of federal authority. Whether the state is blue or red, it wants to go its own way. And whether the federal government's political leadership is red or blue, it seems either unable, or unwilling, to assert its authority. We've come a long way since President Eisenhower sent the 101st Airborne to Little Rock, and Arkansas, respectful of the commander in chief's power and prestige (Ike having been the military commander of many Razorbacks during World War Two), knuckled under.[216] Nobody these days, it seems, really thinks that the feds know best, and no more than half the country thinks much of the president—whoever it is. For their part, federal officials are now chary

---

[214] Bishop, *The Big Sort*, 247, 239.

[215] Lyons, Byrhonda, "California's bill for fighting Trump in court? $41 million so far," Cal Matters, January 22, 2021. https://bit.ly/3NOZNyI

[216] Clark, Alexis, "Why Eisenhower Sent the 101st Airborne to Little Rock After Brown v. Board," History, updated September 13, 2023. https://bit.ly/3TlM4Tx

of trying to push the states around.[217] So in the meantime, the states are free to push each other around.

FLORIDA V. CALIFORNIA

In 2020, Florida governor Ron DeSantis, a Red Jeffersonian, distinguished himself by opposing COVID mask mandates. His critics called him "DeathSantis," and yet DeSantis' popularity soared. His supporters say the ultimate COVID mortality data vindicated him. In any case, the voters vindicated him. Having been elected by a mere 32,000 vote margin in 2018, he was re-elected by a 1.5 million vote margin in 2022. DeSantis has liked to say that "the free state of Florida" is where "woke goes to die."[218]

Yet there's a counterview, epitomized by California. In 2023, its Blue Hamiltonian governor, Gavin Newsom—having just been reelected by a two million vote margin—formed "Campaign for Democracy," endowing it, just to start, with $10 million. Its purpose, in Newsom's words, "ringing this bell of alarm around issues of rights regressions"[219] in red states. Addressing a certain state in the Southeast, Newsom declared, "I urge all of you living in Florida to join the fight." He added, "Or join us in California, where we still believe in freedom: Freedom of speech, freedom to choose, freedom from hate, and the freedom to love." Amidst images of the gay rainbow flag, as well as the American flag, Newsom closed with, "Don't

---

[217] Part of federal diffidence might be traced to the changing nature of American political leadership. The last US president to have served in the active-duty armed forces in wartime was George H. W. Bush, who left office in 1993. The Congress and other top offices were similarly once heavy with military and wartime veterans, but no longer. That's a big difference from the days when presidents such as Eisenhower, U.S. Grant, or Andrew Jackson could confidently give orders, having done so before in uniform.

[218] Nusbaum, Lydia, "DeSantis Appoints People to Overhaul 'Equity' Ideology at New College of Florida," *Florida's Voice*, January 6, 2023. https://bit.ly/3NOA35F

[219] Reston, Maeve, ""Newsom forms new group to fight 'rising authoritarianism' in red states," *Washington Post*, March 30, 2023. https://www.washingtonpost.com/politics/2023/03/30/gavin-newsom-political-group/

let them take your freedom."[220] It's interesting to compare the January 2023 inaugural addresses of DeSantis and Newsom. The Floridian used the word "free" or "freedom" 15 times,[221] while the Californian used those words 22 times.[222]

Who has the better vision of freedom? That's for the American people to decide. Still, one data point is those who are voting with their feet, participating in their own Big Sort. California, having gained population steadily for the first 170 years of its existence, lost a congressional district after the 2020 Census. Indeed, from 2020 to 2022, it lost another half-million residents.[223] Some will say immediately, of course, that the quality of life matters more than the quantity of the population—and then argue that by their measures, the quality of life in California is better than Florida's. To be sure, California's success in rolling back smog and other kinds of pollution is a point of pride for many in the state, even if they brag less about crime and homelessness. Yet, as with Massachusetts, it's unlikely that many VIP Californians truly mind if the state's population shrinks. They might, in fact, see shrinkage as a step on the path to ecotopia—at least for their part of the seacoast. Indeed, one could even speculate that the people leaving California are mostly Republicans, and so their exodus doesn't bother Democrats much. Whether it's Malibu or Nantucket, the rule of the rulers seems to be—the fewer the better. Exclusivity is perhaps the ultimate luxury.

Although, of course, it's not just people in play, but also their money. In 2021, California lost residents who accounted for $29.1 billion in adjusted

---

[220] Dovere, Edward-Isaac, and Contorno, Steve, "Gavin Newsom goes on the air against Ron DeSantis as political rivalry grows," CNN, July 3, 2022. https://bit.ly/3Nt0o87

[221] "Governor DeSantis Delivers Inaugural Address, Sets Priorities for Second Term," Flgov.com, January 3, 2022. https://bit.ly/3JAcfQB

[222] "Governor Newsom Inaugurated to Second Term in Celebration of California's Values, Diverse Communities," Gov.ca.gov, January 6, 2023. https://bit.ly/3Xpjssl

[223] Schlepp, Travis, "New census estimates show which California counties are losing residents," KTLA, March 31, 2023. https://bit.ly/3Nv3Dvw

gross income (more than triple the figure from 2019), while Florida *gained* $39.2 billion (more than double the figure from 2019).[224]

Still, Newsom and his state have plenty of fat cats left. Of the 100 wealthiest people in America, California is home to twenty-six, boasting, overall, 189 billionaires.[225] To be sure, that's hardly the only metric of economic success, and yet as Newsom said in his 2023 inaugural, California is "now the fourth largest economy in the world." That's up three notches just since 2015.[226] Newsom continued, "The most venture capital and startups in America. Leading the world in the transition to a low-carbon, green growth future." How is this happening? Newsom's explanation— California has a "conveyor belt for talent."[227] That does seem to be true; California leads in brains. In 2023, after less than two years in Texas, Tesla moved its engineering headquarters (but not its corporate headquarters, nor its manufacturing operations) back to Silicon Valley.[228]

Indeed, if we match brains with funds, we see that the value of deals in the Bay Area matches the value of deals in the rest of the country put together.[229] Yet California must carry forty million people, and tech, rich as it is, does not provide enough wealth to lift all forty million boats. In 2022, the state's GDP grew by just 0.4 percent, compared to the national average

[224] Editorial, "The Blue State Exodus Accelerates," *The Wall Street Journal*, April 28, 2023. https://bit.ly/42VIrEV

[225] Karlamangla, Soumya, "Why So Many Billionaires Live in California," *New York Times*, March 8, 2022. https://bit.ly/46miMYP. The article quoted Richard Walker, an emeritus professor at U.C. Berkeley. "California has been the main engine for American growth for the last 50 years," attributing it to the state's "open, experimental culture."

[226] Newsom inaugural, https://bit.ly/3Xpjssl

[227] "Governor Newsom Welcomes New Tesla Global Engineering and AI HQ in California," Gov.ca.gov, February 22, 2023. https://www.gov.ca.gov/2023/02/22/governor-newsom-welcomes-new-tesla-global-engineering-and-ai-hq-in-california/

[228] Mihalcik, Carrie, "Tesla Returns to California for New Engineering Headquarters," CNET, February 22, 2023. https://bit.ly/435pKP0

[229] Pitchbook, National Venture Capital Association, 2023, p. 20. https://bit.ly/44zSrW1

of 2.1 percent, and Florida's growth of 4.0 percent.[230] So is California stagnating? Or is it just waiting for the Next Big Thing?

BLADE RUNNER IRL

Back in 1982, one of California's signature industries, Hollywood, brought forth the movie *Blade Runner*. It envisioned the Los Angeles of 2019 as a densely weird and dangerous place—high-tech, high pavilions, shadowy killers, all covered in grime. In addition to being at least a somewhat reasonable prophecy of urban life, as every film buff knows, *Blade Runner's* style—Raymond Chandler-ish tough guy-meets-brooding Big Tech—has made it one of the most influential sci-fi movies of all time. So perhaps it's not surprising that geek life as imitated this art. IRL (in real life), cities across the country—most spectacularly San Francisco—honor the film with their urban decay.

Digital tech originated, of course, in the bland-and-safe suburbia of the Santa Clara Valley. And yet by 2000s, restless techies were leaving Silicon Valley, migrating to the denser, funkier groove of the city forty miles north. That shift has survived the chaos that has overtaken the city's downtown in the last decade. It's worth noting that even amidst rampant crime and overall exodus of "normie" businesses, San Francisco was home to OpenAI, the company that, in late 2022, unleashed ChatGPT.

We might be tempted to say that AI is a piece of Blue Hamiltonianism—after all, OpenAI's main man, Sam Altman, is a big Democratic donor, and the entire company, is, well, tangled up in blue. Yet there's a distinctly libertarian, Jeffersonian, strain within AI. The actual coding of it seems to thrive on a twenty-first century updating of that twentieth phenomenon, also much associated with San Francisco, the hippie. Six decades ago, hippies and other counter-culturalists were given to saying, "Do not fold, spindle or mutilate"—that being their protest against the conformist corporatism of IBM and the analog punch cards it used for its monster mainframes. In

---

[230] Editorial, *The Washington Examiner*, May 7, 2023. https://bit.ly/3piv9oe

early 2023, Microsoft CEO Satya Nadella, lumped together the early AIs of Big Tech and jibed, "Whether it's Cortana or Alexa or Google Assistant or Siri, all these just don't work … They were all dumb as a rock."[231] Writing of the tech giants, Bloomberg News marveled at "how slow and cautious they have been to create services with the technology until a tiny firm … OpenAI, prodded them to act."[232] Recalling that genius companies were typically founded in someone's garage or dorm room, maybe we should know that the whole idea of a big office complex is wrongheaded for the best tech. In the hacker ethos, in the AI subculture, perhaps there's something de-synergizing about big organizations.

Ominously for Big Tech structure, Bloomberg even made the comparison between Alphabet and its AI problems and another high-flying company from the 1960s, Xerox. That company had developed, and then sat on, key innovations in computing, such as the mouse. Into the resulting innovation vacuum stepped smaller, (much smaller), nimbler (much nimbler) companies, most notably, Apple. Today, Xerox is still around, but it's a distant afterthought. So now in our time, Alphabet let its lead on AI slip away. Its pioneers left the company for their own AI startups, currently worth $4 billion.[233] To be sure, that's a pittance next to Alphabet, and yet it was little upstart critters that ended up eating the dinosaurs' eggs. So could Alphabet somehow be the next Xerox? The next T-Rex? That's hard, maybe even impossible, to believe, but for a reputable journalistic outlet to even breathe that comparison could get short-sellers thinking.

If the best AI makers are not working for Big Tech, where are they working? They're still in San Francisco, but elsewhere in the city. In fact, employment in "information" rose 31 percent from 2019-2023, even as

---

[231] Lee, Dave, "Amazon's big dreams for Alexa fall short," *Financial Times*, March 3, 2023. https://tinyurl.com/2bynhpwk

[232] Olson, Parmy, "Tech's AI Armies Are Huge, Yet Struggling to Innovate," Bloomberg News, March 27, 2023. https://bit.ly/3NrjTxG

[233] Olson, Parmy, "Meet the $4 Billion AI Superstars That Google Lost," Bloomberg News, July 13, 2023. https://bit.ly/3NLtsrs. See also: Fox, Justin, "Google's AI Blunders Rival Xerox's PC Mistakes," Bloomberg News. July 13, 2023. https://bit.ly/3RjTG7u

employment in other sectors, such as hospitality and construction, plum-meted.[234] San Francisco mayor London Breed says, "There's a reason why people continue to do business here. … It's because of the talent."[235] In particular, one residential neighborhood, Hayes Valley, is the hot hub. A few miles from downtown, it's an epicenter of hippieish "hacker houses," boasting so many AI startups that it's now known as Cerebral Valley.[236] We could say that the AI-ers have arbitraged themselves from yuppieish office towers to a noir netherworld—and maybe that's what they want. Nobody enjoys being mugged, but scoring exotic drugs might be the bump the hacker needs to rev up for the next all-nighter. In 2023, the *San Francisco Chronicle* reported that, since 2015, drug arrests in the city had fallen sharply. The article further detailed that San Francisco's status as a "sanc-tuary city" further emboldens drug dealers, and one is also left to wonder what other sort of trafficking could be occurring under the same sanctuary banner.[237] In this dark realm, nobody's asking questions about what hap-pens at the rave. Perhaps, in the spectrum imagination, squalor makes for a coolly authentic ambience; for sure, the frisson of danger encourages bros to stay inside and code.

Meanwhile, even as the city's urban core melted, other places in San Francisco flourished. The Presidio, a military base-turned-national park, a few miles from downtown, boasts federal protection, so criminals aren't allowed to roam free. So it's safer for Tesla-driving millennials, working in venture capital, to hang there. Revealingly, rents are higher in humble Presidio spaces than in the once-glittering, now guttering, downtown.

---

[234] Rezal, Adriana, "Charts show how San Francisco's job market is unusually strong despite 'doom loop' concerns," *San Francisco Chronicle,* June 8, 2023. https://bit.ly/44jwlGv

[235] Winkler, Matthew, "California Poised to Overtake Germany as World's No. 4 Economy," Bloomberg News, October 24, 2022. https://bit.ly/3CTr5xy

[236] Lindqwister, Liz, "What Is 'Cerebral Valley'? San Francisco's Nerdiest New Neighborhood," *The San Francisco Standard,* January 13, 2023. https://bit.ly/3PvH78q

[237] Cassidy, Megan, and Lurie, Gabrielle, "This is the hometown of San Francisco's drug dealers, *San Francisco Chronicle,* updated July 21, 2023. https://bit.ly/3rqEICg

[238] And yet Presidio, like Cerebral Valley, is still the city, and so it offers the hipster clustering that techsters and dealmakers crave. So we can see, there's at least something of a tech boom loop inside the urban doom loop. Indeed, so long as tech talent thinks blue, blue cities will hang in there.

If we're getting the idea that different people like different things— very different things—well, that's the point. Blue, including its tech niche, has its ways, and it's not certain that the twain shall meet with Red. Yet one can wonder, is there some other milieu of tech economic development that does not involve night and fog? Some sort of productive tech cluster friendlier to red sensibilities, including its political folkways? Finding the right answer will mean a lot to Red. And here we can take note of an interesting tech flowering from within the heart of Jeffersonia, emerging, ironically enough, from Red's cultural conservatism. Louisiana was the first state to impose an eighteen-years-old age requirement for online porn consumption. As a *New York Times* headline put it, the Louisiana bill has the potential to "remake the internet," with dozens of states following.[239] We can observe immediately, any time something finds itself in a "remake"— especially if it's as huge as the internet—profit opportunities abound. Most notably, the Louisiana law was good news for Envoc, a Baton Rouge-based software company that had previously contracted with the state to create a digital wallet for ID purposes. Now LA Wallet is used to verify age, too. This could be big for the Pelican State tech scene. Oh, and Envoc operates from two locations in Louisiana—an ordinary strip mall in Baton Rouge and an equally nondescript storefront in Hammond. So maybe tech can, in fact, flourish without the cyberpunk freak.

---

[238] Hu, Krystal, "San Francisco's new venture capital hotspot: The Presidio," Reuters, July 8, 2023. https://bit.ly/3XG6hDs

[239] "If the rules were not overturned, these experts argue, they could radically alter the internet—by changing the online world into a patchwork of walled-off fiefdoms or causing popular platforms to narrow their offerings to avoid triggering the rules." Singer, Natasha, "States' Push to Protect Kids Online Could Remake the Internet," *New York Times*, April 30, 2023. https://nyti.ms/3XuAtkJ

INVESTMENT TAKEAWAYS

- State-based arbitrage means that a portfolio can be diversified without leaving the US The more complexity—the more crenelations and involutions—the greater the potential for niche markets. So if one is so inclined, get a sex-change operation in blue Illinois, a green-energy deal in blue California, and thence to red Texas for lower taxes and to red Idaho to buy a bunch of guns. Make money in Blue, move to Red to keep it. Many options for arbs.

- Will the Big Sort keep sorting? Will it drain, say, Florida of a certain kind cultural fizz and help, say, California? Is a gay bar a better investment in West Hollywood than West Palm Beach? Is it possible that we could see a return to the old pattern in which a young gay or queer person sees their home state as oppressive and flees to a friendlier clime, bringing along earning power? That's certainly happened in the past. One can cite, for instance, such famous figures as Truman Capote (born in Louisiana), Andy Warhol (born in Pittsburgh), Halston (born in Iowa) and Tom Ford (born in Texas). All ended up in New York City in the twentieth century, bringing their talent with them. Creativity is, for sure, an economic driver, right alongside capital and patents. And of course, cultural conservatism is an economic driver, too, especially if one factors in children. Utah has a relatively low per capita income—much lower than New York—but that's in part because Utah, among the fifty states, boasts the highest percentage of its population under age eighteen, whereas New York ranks forty-first.[240] Energetic youth of all kinds is economic development, and investment potential.

- It's hard to know if this Sorting trend will last, but it does seem that we're seeing a strange kind of unity—a hardening of the attitude of

---

[240] "Per Capita Personal Income by State, Annual," FRED, St Louis Fed. https://bit.ly/3JzoblI. See also: "The U.S. Adult and Under-Age-18 Populations: 2020 Census," US Census Bureau, August 12, 2021. https://bit.ly/3NvNjL0

the states, whether blue or red. All of them wish to retain their sovereignty on key issues—and want the feds to butt out. So weaker federal power could be a long-term trend. As we know, the clearer the trend, the better the friend.

- Technology is all about rigorous structure, and yet technologists seem to require looseness. When the mix is done right, there is, yes, *a wholly unaccustomed energy.*

- The convention business is in a bit of flux. Some reports suggest that convention business in Florida has been affected. According to the *South Florida Sun Sentinel,* "Broward County has lost more than a half-dozen conventions as their organizers cite the divisive political climate as their reason to stay out of Florida."[241] On the other hand, conventioneers aren't going to San Francisco or Los Angeles as much. So where are they going? Given that convention conveners typically strive to be all things to all conventioneers, it's easy to imagine someone, somewhere, figuring out the most neutral space in the most neutral place—and making a mint.

- A note on the money value of culture: In addition to its aesthetic rewards, art offers great opportunities for arbitrage, as well as tax evasion and money laundering. So if you're rich and feel that you're paying too much in taxes, you might consider art as not just a tax shelter, but a money shelter. As a US Senate report from 2020 had it, "The art industry is considered the largest, legal unregulated industry in the United States. Unlike financial institutions, the art industry is not subject to Bank Secrecy Act's requirements, which mandate detailed procedures to prevent money laundering and to verify a customer's identity."[242] According to UBS, the world art market totals some $64 billion, with the US accounting for

---

[241] Huriash, Lisa, "'Unfriendly political environment': Broward convention cancellations blame Florida as reason for exodus," *South Florida Sun-Sentinel,* July 7, 2023.

[242] "The Art Industry and U.S. Policies That Undermine Sanctions," Permanent Subcommittee on Investigations, US Senate, 2020. https://bit.ly/44igxE0

about half that total.[243] But of course, with this many blanks and blind spots in the fiscal portrait, nobody really knows how much money is involved. For example, nobody knows who has paid how much for Hunter Biden's artwork. It's an unknown unknown. Occasionally, we get glimpses of the Biden family's moneymaking operation, and when we do, the sums are considerable.[244]

- In the meantime, there's the rest of the art world, from here to Beijing. With Luxembourg in between. In that country of convenience, art works are shuffled between rooms in a barbed-wire-walled and fortified warehouses, called free ports, so that oligarchs and drug kingpins can launder their money while posing as "collectors."[245] One investigative deep dive from 2023 found that just one of these free ports guards art worth $100 billion—although, of course, nobody really knows for sure.[246] The Switzerland-based UBS adds hintingly to prospective clients, "Approximately 25% of wealthy investors consider themselves to be collectors... their collections represent 10% or more of their total wealth on average."[247] So maybe art isn't just for art's sake—it's *art for arb's sake*. Art, of course, being worth whatever the buyer/seller/arbitrageur can agree upon, with the money concealed from everyone else (in this sense, fine art is a bit like crypto). Now we see better why so many artists do well, and how art galleries can have so many customers who don't care about art.

---

[243] "The Art Basel and UBS Survey of Global Collecting in 2023," UBS. https://bit.ly/3XsuAod

[244] Rogers, Katie, "Hunter Biden's Daughter and a Tale of Two Families," *New York Times*, July 1, 2023. https://bit.ly/43bU7Dk

[245] Letzing, John, and Colchester, Max, "Oligarchs and Orchestras: Inside Luxembourg's Secretive Low-Tax 'Fortress of Art' Warehouse," *The Wall Street Journal*, September 23, 2015. https://bit.ly/3Dd5twm

[246] Corbett Rachel, "The Inheritance Case That Could Unravel an Art Dynasty" *The New York Times Magazine*, August 23, 2023. https://bit.ly/3t2PLCK

[247] "The value of collecting," UBS, accessed July 1, 2023. https://bit.ly/3OfeFpc

- There's an interesting bit of political economy on the topic of tax enforcement. On the one hand, Democrats decry tax evasion. On the other hand, tax evasion makes it easier to be rich Democrat. And a party needs funders. So there's a good reason why those loopholes never get closed, even when Democrats are in charge.

- By one reckoning, the Big Sort is just another word for "creative destruction." Are old workways being creatively destroyed? If, for example, the "old" vision of Big Tech is being eaten by a newer AI vision of Little Tech, is something being "arbed" into creation in its place? If AI talent doesn't want to be downtown in an "old-fashioned" office tower, then maybe we're starting to see the future. Perhaps we will look back and see that office buildings were an artifact of paper, as well as people. That is, paper memos and documents that needed to be created, distributed, centralized and archived. But when the paper was replaced by pixels, the utility of centralization became a *dis*utility. And now, AI is scything through people (metaphorically). And yet, people aren't disappearing— they are, physically, somewhere. And there's an arb for that. The fact that the modest Presidio rents for more than audacious office buildings is a klaxon horn for trend-spotting Directional Investors. More will be said about the Direction of real estate in Chapter Ten.

- As seen in the case of the Louisiana age-restriction law, there's opportunity in diversity, of a kind. In business, it's known as "market segmentation," and, coupled with the forced innovation of the law, it could be setting in motion a red tech ecosystem.

CHAPTER SEVEN

E PLURIBUS DUO

I n the last chapter, we considered diversity, and in this chapter, we'll consider where it ends up—*polarization*. This is another trend to spot.

DIVERSITY BEGETS DUALITY

The US is dispersing from the central median of an idealized 1950s-type national unity.[248] To put that more precisely, the country is both diversifying and dividing. A headline in *The Economist* was clear enough. It stated, "American policy is splitting, state by state, into two blocs."[249] In 2023, the Associated Press took note of the continuing impact of Donald Trump, observing that he and his "ism" have "effectively split the United States

---

[248] In the words of one political scientist, "The mid-twentieth century was a period marked by unique levels of bipartisanship in U.S. lawmaking. Although often attributed to an overarching postwar 'consensus,' such cross-party collaboration is more accurately seen as a byproduct of the huge ideological range contained within the ranks of each of the two overlapping major parties." He continued, "From the 1980s on, party adherents sorted out along ideological lines, catalyzing a partisan resurgence that has continued, unabated, into the troubled present." This partisan resurgence is, of course, Republican Red v. Democratic Blue. Rosenfeld, Sam, "What History Teaches About Partisanship and Polarization," Scholars.org, July 23, 2018. https://bit.ly/3r3C9pq

[249] "American policy is splitting, state by state, into two blocs," *The Economist*, September 3, 2022. https://bit.ly/47W77Qw

in two, making almost every facet of modern life from sporting events to beer choice a referendum on whether people side with Trump and his movement."[250] One poll found that Trump voters, and Republicans overall, believed that racism against Whites was a greater problem than racism against Blacks. And Democrats, not surprisingly, took the opposite view.[251] We read all the time that the Republican Party has become more "right wing," and yet it's less often said that the Democratic Party has become more "left wing." In the words of the *Washington Post*'s Perry Bacon, Jr., "The average Democratic senator or governor is to the left of the person who previously held their job"—and the same is true for Joe Biden compared to Barack Obama.[252] Donald Trump, himself never a stranger to divisiveness, volunteered in 2023 that Biden "treats half the Country as Enemies of the State."[253]

This is the Big Sort, sorting more. And yet because our politics is based on the two-party system, and because the human mind cleaves toward the clarity of binary, the diversity among the states we noted in the previous chapter is clustering, heading to division. We can note that the words "diversity" and "division" have the same Latin root. And another word from the same root is "divorce." In late 2021, Rep. Marjorie Taylor Greene, a high-profile Republican from Georgia, made headlines when she tweeted about "national divorce."[254] We can pause right there and observe that the word "divorce" implies two sides to the split. Yet interestingly, Greene didn't seem to be talking about actual secession. A tweet in 2023 said, more fully, "We need a national divorce. We need to separate by

[250] Riccardi, Nicholas, and Kirk, Danica, "How Trump and Johnson, divisive populists with many similarities, ended up on different paths," Associated Press, June 16, 2023. https://bit.ly/3NOtu2X

[251] Francis, Marquise, and Romano, Andrew, "Poll: Trump voters say racism against white Americans is a bigger problem than racism against Black Americans," Yahoo News, August 2, 2023. https://bit.ly/3QrTXW3

[252] Bacon, Jr., Perry, "Biden's Democratic Party is to the left of Obama's. Thank a progressive," *Washington Post*," July 13, 2023. https://bit.ly/3ObDH9N

[253] Trump, Donald (@realDonaldTrump), TruthSocial, September 20, 2023. https://bit.ly/3uLiIn4

[254] Greene, Marjorie Taylor (@mtgreenee), X, October 11, 2021. bit.ly/3lXX9M7

red states and blue states and shrink the federal government."[255] So right there, we see that the "divorce" seems to be less than a divorce, and more like a separation, with the marriage intact.

To be sure, there's no need to overanalyze the tweets of a single member of Congress. Yet a much different political figure has drawn the same conclusion. Michael Podhorzer, former political director of the AFL-CIO, says, "We are more like a federated republic of two nations: Blue Nation and Red Nation. This is not a metaphor; it is a geographic and historical reality." Podhorzer counts twenty-five states as red, seventeen states as blue, and eight as purple. Red states account for 45 percent of the voting population, compared to 39 percent for Blue. (But as for economic output, Blue Hamiltonia leads, 46 to 40 percent.)[256]

It's certainly possible that some important figure will issue an outright call for 1861-type secession. And yet here's the thing. In this Trumpy era—and with the prospect of more polarizing figures, right and left, on the horizon—we seem to have all the preconditions for a civil war except one: *The willingness to actually fight.* We might ask, does anyone in Massachusetts really want to fight to keep, say, South Carolina in the union? Would Harvard students drop out to enlist and go to war? How many new Robert Gould Shaws are ready to lead charges on the Carolina coast?[257] In our time, the feeling is much more, go away! By this reckoning, the states can declare their states' rights and drift apart, while still staying in a much looser union.

After all, the states are different, in politics, culture, everything. In that sense, diversity is another way of saying "reality." And so of course they are Big Sorting. And yet having Sorted, they find it advantageous to cluster into two opposing blocs, Blue and Red. The political science term for

---

[255] Ibid. February 20, 2023. https://bit.ly/3pkRqBN

[256] Brownstein, Ronald, "America is Growing Apart, Possibly for Good," *The Atlantic*, June 24, 2022. https://bit.ly/3XuSJe6. Podhorzer also opined, "A national divorce may not be possible. But we're already sleeping in separate bedrooms and seeing other people." Walter, Amy, "America on Trial Separation," *The Cook Political Report*, March 30, 2023. https://bit.ly/432AMoj

[257] Robert Gould Shaw (1837-1863) was the Harvard man, killed in action at Fort Wagner, celebrated in the 1989 movie "Glory."

this phenomenon is bimodal, as in two modes, the two ends of a barbell. There's a solid logic for red states and blue states to make themselves into blocs—self-defense. In 2016, North Carolina enacted its so-called "bathroom bill," a first-in-the-nation law requiring people to use the bathroom according to their sex at birth. In the annals of trans politics, that was long ago and far away. And in that long-ago era, the establishment, including corporate America, regarded the bill as a frightful attack on transgender rights. And so boycotts, and threats of boycotts, came raining down on the Tar Heel State, including from—but hardly limited to—the NCAA, the NBA, Bank of America, Wells Fargo, and the by now very corporate Bruce Springsteen.[258] This corporate counter-attack was instrumental in the election defeat, later that same year, of the Republican governor who signed the bill, Pat McCrory.[259] The lesson for Red was clear—for the sake of their own defense, they had to stick together. As Ben Franklin quipped, admittedly in a different context, "We must, indeed, all hang together, or assuredly we shall all hang separately." Thus an overall Red consciousness has emerged, especially on "culture war" issues. There's strength in numbers. That's the value of a convoy. Since 2016, Red has much grown bolder on backlash/anti-woke issues, and yet Blue now suffers from "boycott fatigue."[260] So now, stalemate. Pro-transgender is policy in half the country, and anti-transgender is policy in the other half.

---

[258] Kreps, Daniel, "Bruce Springsteen Cancels North Carolina Gig to Protest 'Bathroom Bill,'" *Rolling Stone*, April 8, 2016. https://bit.ly/3DBRhNV

[259] Schneider, Elena, "The Bathroom Bill That Ate North Carolina," *Politico*, March 23, 2017. https://bit.ly/3OlSgq6

[260] To cite one of many instances of this "boycott fatigue," in 2023, a *Washington Post* sportswriter called for a boycott of baseball spring training in Governor Ron DeSantis' Florida. The result was a yawn. See: Blackistone, Kevin B., "Baseball can no longer ignore Ron DeSantis's culture wars," *Washington Post*, March 5, 2023. https://bit.ly/3QnCePk

DEEP ROOTS OF DIVISION

It should be no surprise that things split. No unity lasts forever. In fact, the roots of duality run deep. The Italian political scientist Gaetano Mosca (1858-1941) was interested in people, and yet prefaced his points about rivalry among bipeds by observing the rivalrous behavior of quadrupeds. "If a certain number of stags are shut up in a park they will inevitably divide into two herds which will always be in conflict with each other." Mosca then continued,

> "An instinct of very much the same sort seems to make its influence felt among men. Human beings have a natural inclination toward struggle, but it is only sporadically that the struggle assumes an individual character, that one man is at war with another. Even when he fights, man remains preeminently a social animal. Ordinarily, therefore, we see men forming into groups."[261]

Dualism is a profound feature of existence—of physics (positive and negative charges, centripetal and centrifugal forces), of biology (male and female, predator and prey), and of human nature (good and evil, right and left, and yes, too, Directional and Anti-Directional). So, understandably, almost all wars are two-way. Us against Them is about as much complexity as the human mind can handle on a mass scale. Henry Adams, the American man of letters, wrote in 1907, "Politics, as a practice, whatever its professions, had always been the systematic organization of hatreds."[262] Fortunately, we have a Constitution to manage hatreds and cool them down. Madison, Jefferson, and the other framers were fully aware of the passions that led to strife, civil war, and downfall. So their idea was that the states would be separate, and so the union would be compartmentalized, surviving and thriving because of its very looseness. Yet over the last century or so, that looseness has been challenged by the centralizing power

---

[261] Mosca, Gaetano, *The Ruling Class,* (New York: McGraw Hill, 1939), 163.
[262] Adams, Henry, *The Education of Henry Adams,* 1907. https://bit.ly/3NqeV4b

of the federal government and perhaps, too, the power of corporations—including media companies—who consider a national market to be most useful for them. Yes, centralization had a good run, but it's built a backlash. The primal forces of duality, and division, are reasserting themselves.

TOO BIG TO SUCCEED

It's worth keeping in mind that the population of the US, about 340 million, is well more than double what it was during World War II, and half again larger than it was in just four decades ago. So perhaps today the US is simply too large to administer through a federal government attempting to operate on the increasingly unpopular principle of one-size-fits-all. In previous chapters, we considered the states as laboratories of prosperity, and in this chapter we'll examine the laboratories as they have dualized, split into two big blocs. Call it *e pluribus duo*.

At the same time, for perspective, we can also look to business history to see how companies have dealt with the issues of bigness. As we already know, the interests of corporate managers do not always align with corporate shareholders. Then we'll illustrate the same point about political managers and the citizenry. In the middle of the last century, it was faddish for companies to "conglomerate." That is, to buy up unrelated companies and seek to run them all, different as they were. The "pro" argument was that companies needed to grow, but couldn't necessarily grow in their original line of business, in part because of antitrust concerns. So they would buy up other companies and grow outside their core competency. If diversifying an investment portfolio is a good idea, they reasoned, then so is diversifying corporate holdings. The "con" argument was that companies didn't know what they were doing, that it was all just disguised empire building. The matter came to the attention of Wall Street. Magellan Fund investor-pundit Peter Lynch worried that it was increasing *non*-core *in*competency and so he tagged it *diworseification*, a play on "diversification." Writing in 1989, Lynch recalled, "The 1960s was the greatest decade for diworseification … It's hard to find a respectable company that didn't diworseify in the 1960s, when the best and the brightest believed they could manage one business as well as the next." Lynch cited a long list of diworseifiers from that era, including Allied Chemical, Gillette, and Mobil. But then, nudged along by Lynch-type market players, companies realized that such empire conglomeration was a mistake. "Every second decade, corporations seem to alternate between rampant diworseification (when billions are spent on exciting acquisitions) and rampant restructuring (when those no-longer-exciting acquisitions are sold off for less than the original purchase price)," Lynch wrote. Restructuring "is a company's way of ridding itself of certain unprofitable subsidiaries it should never have acquired in the first place." He added slyly, "The same thing happens to people and their sailboats."[263] Thus costly conglomerization was followed by costly de-conglomerization.

To be sure, we can think of companies that have grown by carefully considered acquisition, including Google's purchase of DoubleClick, Microsoft's purchase of LinkedIn, and Facebook's purchase of Instagram. And yet the roll call of companies that have diworseified since Lynch's time is long and dolorous, starting with, of course, the epochally catastrophic AOL-Time Warner merger. Which brings us to a 2009 book, *The Curse of the Mogul: What's Wrong with the World's Leading Media Companies*, a classic study of empire-building at the expense of shareholder-valuing. "The curse of the mogul," the authors write, "is that while moguls' careers invariably begin with a great insight that creates value for shareholders, they somehow lose the thread of what the actual source of that initial value creation was."[264] Alas for the fate of emperors and their empires—the sclerotic pathologies of organizations build up to toxic levels. That's when we know, a change is gonna come.

---

[263] Lynch, *One Up.* 114, 143-144.
[264] Knee, Jonathan, et al., *The Curse of the Mogul: What's Wrong With The World's Leading Media Companies*, (New York: Portfolio, 2009), 1, 267.

THE SCHISM

A May 2023 headline in *The Atlantic* got attention—"How the Right and the Left Switched Sides on Big Business." The article took note of the fight between the State of Florida and Disney (more on that in Chapter Nine), as well as other instances where populist Republicans were upsetting the reigning Reagan pro-business orthodoxy, even as Democrats were embracing "neoliberalism." As the author put it, "When corporations advance voting rights or acceptance of gays and lesbians, or oppose racism or laws that restrict the ability of trans people to use the bathroom where they feel most comfortable, many progressives are happy to see corporate power exerted as a counter to majorities in state legislatures or even views held by a majority of voters in red states."[265] Indeed, as we consider such hot buttons as immigration, LGBTQ, gun control, and abortion, it's not at all clear that business—especially big business—is "conservative." Nor is it clear what social policies should be deemed as "pro-business." As free-market icon Ludwig von Mises wrote back in 1944, "Capitalism is progressive."[266] Another free-market hero, Friedrich Hayek, published a piece in 1960 entitled "Why I am Not a Conservative."[267]

So we come back to ESG (Environmental, Social, and Governance), the concept-turned-acronym-turned-controversy roiling the business world. Some say ESG is a needed corrective, even penance, for past sins. Others say that it's just a cynical diversionary tactic. Still others say that it's deeper than that, that it's a current of thinking akin to a religion, connected, as it is, to the belief systems of anti-racism, environmentalism, and transgenderism. But is ESG good for investors? Mogul and media personality Mark Cuban says yes. "There is a reason almost all the top ten market cap companies in the U.S. can be considered 'woke,'" he says. "It's

---

[265] Friedersdorf, Conor, "How the Right and the Left Switched Sides on Big Business," *The Atlantic*, May 19, 2023. https://bit.ly/46mfKDX

[266] von Mises, Ludwig, *Bureaucracy* (New Haven: Yale University Press, 1944), 124.

[267] Hayek, Friedrich, excerpt from *The Constitution of Liberty*, (Chicago: University of Chicago Press, 1960). https://bit.ly/3Nzx6EA

good business."[268] Not everyone agrees, of course, but Cuban has a point.
The big companies, starting with one of the most valuable ones, Apple,
are woke, or, as they would prefer to say, *inclusive… socially conscious*. Some
might wonder if rich blue companies are successful because they are woke,
including the variables that wokeness is what customers, stakeholders, and
regulators expect. Others might say they are successful despite being woke.
This argument will not be settled. Yet it's clear that in the last few decades,
wokeness and profitability have gone hand in hand, at least for some industries. So that's a trend. But of course, trends can change.

For instance, BlackRock. Journalist John Masko writes of the
Manhattan-based investment giant that's been at the center of so much
ESG agita, "BlackRock's leaders had an epiphany—one that would repeat
itself in the C-suites of several of its competitors in the early 2010s. What
if big investment houses could rebrand themselves as so unimpeachably
virtuous and civic-minded that their virtue outshone even their regulators
themselves? Such a strategy would be game-changing. Not only would it
afford investment houses a mile-wide road to limitless growth; it could
even, if played judiciously, accord the companies themselves quasi-govern-
mental power."[269] We can add that around the same time, the non-corpo-
rate left had its own version of the same epiphany. If corporate America was
willing to play ball, then the progressive agenda—minus the soak-the-rich
part, of course—could be enacted by stealthy corporate policy, as opposed
to noisy legislation.

For a long time, BlackRock was uncontroversial, as it grew and grew.
But then, around the time that it neared $10 trillion in assets under

[268] Zito, Salena, "Target and Bud Light are hurting, but Mark Cuban says wokeness is
good business," *Pittsburgh Post-Gazette*, June 11, 2023. https://bit.ly/3COVaP0

[269] Masko, John, "BlackRock's tyrannical ESG agenda," *UnHerd*, March 2, 2023.
https://bit.ly/44aCLb4. Another business figure who caught on the they'll-like-
me-if-I'm-left wing idea was the notorious convict Sam Bankman-Fried, who gave
somewhere between $40 and $100 million to Democrats, adding that the goal
was "giving to a lot of woke shit for transactional purposes. Pearson, Jordan, "Sam
Bankman-Fried Funded 'Woke Shit for Transactional Purposes,' Prosecutors
Allege," *Vice*, February 23, 2023 https://bit.ly/46CuJbB

management, the wokeness issue erupted. Maybe BlackRock had become "Too Big To Be Humble." For instance, in 2017, CEO Larry Fink shared with the world how his company intended to use its financial muscle, stating, "At BlackRock we are forcing behaviors."[270] And in a 2020 letter to clients, Fink mentioned "climate" nine times, writing, "Climate change is driving a profound reassessment of risk and we anticipate a significant reallocation of capital."[271] That same year, BlackRock released its annual "Investment and Stewardship Report," patting itself on the back for what it had done and would do.

> *"In 2020, we identified 244 companies that were making insufficient progress integrating climate risk into their business models or disclosures. Of these companies, we took voting action against 53, or 22%. We have put the remaining 191 companies 'on watch.' Those that do not make significant progress risk voting action against management in 2021."*[272]

Yet by the middle of the decade, these tactics were drawing significant pushback. In 2023, Oklahoma's Republican governor, Kevin Stitt, invoked his state's Energy Discrimination Elimination Act to sanction thirteen financial institutions, including BlackRock. Said the Sooner State leader, "Oklahoma will not do business with financial firms who boycott oil and gas companies and prioritize ESG over their fiduciary duty to Oklahomans' retirement funds."[273] That same year, thirteen red state attorneys general wrote a letter to Fortune 100 companies urging them to reevaluate their diversity programs. The letter ended on a tough note: "We urge you to immediately cease any unlawful race-based quotas or preferences your

[270] Spady, Aubrie, "BlackRock CEO slammed for 'force behaviors' comment after 2017 interview re-emerges about DEI initiatives," Fox Business, June 5, 2023. https://bit.ly/3NuRI13

[271] Fink, Larry, "Sustainability as BlackRock's New Standard for Investing," BlackRock, 2020. https://bit.ly/44ejfdE

[272] "Investment Stewardship Annual Report," BlackRock, September 2020, https://bit.ly/440zATJ

[273] Stitt, Kevin (@GovStitt), X, May 3, 2023. https://bit.ly/42XUdyA

company has adopted for its employment and contracting practices. If you choose not to do so, know that you will be held accountable—sooner rather than later—for your decision to continue treating people differently because of the color of their skin."[274]

Still, there's the question—does ESG help or hurt investments? Steven M. Rothstein, speaking for Ceres, a left-leaning investment organization, declares that anti-ESG states were taking on an "economic burden" if they act "to limit climate and other ESG considerations."[275] Yet West Virginia State Treasurer Riley Moore takes the opposite view. "Our latest performance clearly shows that when you focus on generating the best financial returns instead of social change, you will produce the best outcomes for your clients and investors." Moore adds that his funds are "outperforming the largest Wall Street firms," showing that "worship of ESG is a farce that's robbing returns and prosperity from their clients."[276] Interestingly enough, the Red response to Big Blue has been various forms of anti-Big-ness, including boycotts and also, from Congress, threats of antitrust action.[277]

Okay, so maybe the answer on the value of ESG for a firm is a decisive…it depends. Depends, that is, on who's working to make sure the investment works. In fact, on a limited scale, it is possible to plan for an investment to work. That is, if the plan is to rob Peter to pay Paul, then Paul can be said to have "invested" well. State planning doesn't work for a whole economy, and over-bureaucratization decreases efficiency, but so long as the government has wealth-transfer power, that power can work to enrich a sector. If Blue wants a blue investment to succeed, quite possibly it will,

---

[274] Open letter, July 13, 2023. https://bit.ly/47FSAIX

[275] "New Research Shows Legislation to Boycott ESG May Cost State Taxpayers up to $700 Million in Excess Payments," Ceres, January 12, 2023. https://bit.ly/43WIjGz

[276] Bliss, Jacob, "West Virginia Treasurer Riley Moore Says State Outperformed BlackRock, Other Blacklisted ESG Firms," *Breitbart*, February 23, 2023. https://bit.ly/3Pt3ITh

[277] "Judiciary Republicans: Woke Companies Pursuing ESG Policies May Violate Antitrust Law," House Judiciary Committee, December 6, 2022. https://bit.ly/44gEADl

because Blue will have put in place subsidies, tax breaks, and even consumer preferences. To be sure, such planning can be expensive, and quite likely, on net counterproductive. Yet if the costs are borne by the larger system—a city, a state, a country, perhaps even the world—while the benefits are concentrated on the favored company or industry, investors do fine. And this is a book about investments. So if the political matrix decrees that an investment will be good, it's quite likely it will make money—although, of course, if the politics change, the return could change.

In the meantime, ESG has put the Democratic Party on the side of big business and the free market, at least as it's defined by big corporate protagonists. "Democrats embrace free markets against GOP's anti-ESG blitz," read the headline in D.C. insider-y *Punchbowl News*. For their part, Republicans deny they're anti-capitalist. They are, they say, anti-woke capitalist, wokeness being, in their view, a perversion of the market. In the words of Rep. Andy Barr, Republican of Kentucky, "If ESG is capitalism, why do we need the government to interfere in the free market?...That's what the SEC is doing."[278] At the same time, blue states such as Illinois actively defend ESG. In the words of Michael Frerichs, the Democratic treasurer of Illinois, "ESG is data. ESG is simply additional information that investment professionals use to assess risk and return prospects. It is about value, not values."[279] Some corporate allies go further, at least rhetorically. One such is Salesforce CEO Marc Benioff, who suggested in 2022 that his company would not do business in states that restrict abortion, saying, "If you're not for equality and dignity, then this is something that I cannot work with, and then we're going to have to exit your city or your

---

[278] A publication for DC insiders continued: "Progressives—led by Reps. Maxine Waters (D-Calif.) and Sean Casten (D-Ill.)—are also spending a lot of time talking about the importance of free markets and free enterprise. They're sounding a lot like the Republicans of yesteryear in the process." Peterson, Brendan, "The Top," *Punchbowl News*, July 13, 2023. https://bit.ly/3JXQIBw

[279] "Statement Before the House Committee on Oversight and Accountability For the Hearing Entitled "ESG Part I: An Examination of Environmental, Social, and Governance Practices with Attorneys General" Michael Frerichs, Illinois State Treasurer, May 10, 2023. https://bit.ly/3qSTAZB

state." As of this writing, Salesforce has not actually exited from any pro-life states, although it has reportedly helped individual female employees relocate to pro-choice places.[280] So it could be argued that ESG and the other acronyms—DEI (Diversity, Equity and Inclusion) and CSR (Corporate Social Responsibility)—are just corporate virtue-signals. Indeed, it's interesting that ESG can be gamed by clever companies, such that tobacco companies score high.[281] The fact that tobacco rated higher than his own Tesla inspired Elon Musk to tweet, "ESG is the devil."[282] Yet whatever the source, the social and cultural wellsprings of ESG are deep.

But deep, too, are the wellsprings of opposition to ESG. Plenty of people "cling," as Barack Obama said awkwardly in 2008, to God, and guns, and all that.

So what will happen next with ESG ? The answer will come from whoever's in charge—although in an ironic way. That is, the prevailing current actually goes against whoever's in charge. In fact, we can say that the woke wave that BlackRock was riding actually crested on January 20, 2021. Why this precision? Because that was the day Joe Biden was inaugurated as president. As a general rule, ideology moves opposite to power. That is, whoever's in charge—Democrat or Republican—tends to build a backlash. Action creates reaction. To put that another way, political belief is countercyclical to authority. So Donald Trump had the effect of moving the country to the left, energizing Blue. (Even as he moved his MAGA following to the oppositional right, in keeping with the trend toward polarization and *e pluribus duo*.) Then Biden, governing on the left, had the effect of moving the country to the right.

Seeing events from this meta-perspective helps us put individual incidents in context. For example, the celebrated Capitol Hill exchange

---

[280] Letkeman, Ethan, "Salesforce CEO Marc Benioff Threatens to 'Exit' Republican-Led States If They Pass Pro-Life Legislation," *Breitbart News*, September 24, 2022. https://bit.ly/3NuUSSn. Benioff and Salesforce do not appear to have followed up on this threat—"boycott fatigue."

[281] Sibarium, Aaron, "How Tobacco Companies Are Crushing ESG Ratings," *Washington Free Beacon*, June 13, 2023. https://bit.ly/3NqR1FY

[282] Musk, Elon (@elonmusk), X, June 13, 2023. https://bit.ly/3phBHU6

between Rep. Elise Stefanik (R-NY) and three Ivy League presidents is often regarded as a watershed moment in the backlash against wokeness. For sure, it was seismic.[283] Yet the anti-woke trend line was already clear. Five months before, *The Wall Street Journal* had reported that job searches for chief diversity officers were down 75 percent from the previous year, to the lowest level in three decades.[284]

Companies will benefit from understanding this action-reaction cycle—and will get hurt if they don't. In the words of business adviser Andrew Essex, "There can be a myopia of the corporate boardroom—there's so much enthusiasm that they can piggyback into cultural relevance, that they forget the idea might alienate their core audience."[285]

One myopic company that alienated its audience was Anheuser-Busch, caught up in the Bud Light *brew*-haha. The AB brand, looking for a rebrand, hired transgender influencer Dylan Mulvaney—and blew up. Bud Light's customer base has always been on the right, but it was only under Biden that it got hopped up. So Manhattan-based marketers were pushing Bud Light to the left even as drinkers were edging right. Soon, "de-influencer" Kid Rock using Bud Light cans for target practice. AB had made an Edsel/New Coke level miscalculation. Sales fell by a quarter and the stock of parent InBev, downgraded.[286] "In Bud Light's effort to be inclusive," one wit put it, "they excluded almost everybody else, including their traditional audience."[287] The point here is not that it's automatically a mistake for a company to engage a transgender endorser, or to make any other move

---

[283] Green, Justin, "Elise Stefanik's star rises after college president takedown," *Axios*, December 10, 2023. https://bit.ly/3TlltGa

[284] Chen, Te-Ping, and Weber, Lauren, "The Rise and Fall of the Chief Diversity Officer," *The Wall Street Journal*, July 21, 2023. https://bit.ly/3DpCntM

[285] Weigel, David, "Pride Month is a war. Brands are the battlefield," *Semafor*, May 30, 2023. https://bit.ly/3CPPhRu

[286] Rigolizzo, John, "Major Bank Downgrades Anheuser-Busch's Stock Status As Sales Continue To Crater," *Daily Wire*, May 10, 2023. https://bit.ly/3VYcQAD

[287] Byrne, Kerry, "Bud Light suffers bloodbath as longtime and loyal consumers revolt against transgender campaign," Fox Business, April 11, 2023. https://bit.ly/3NuJCW8

that could be defined as woke. The point is, it's a *choice*. A choice best made with cognizance of which way the wind is blowing.

Yet at the same time, not everything shifts. For instance, one poll from mid-2023 found that 57 percent of Americans were conservative on trans issues, while 43 percent were liberal.[288] The side with 43 percent won't win an election, but it can still sell plenty of product. Transgenderism, for at least a part of the country, is here to stay. Similarly, even if DEI is in retreat, it still has many strongholds, including in corporate America. So for all the pendulum-swinging, there's also some permanent dividing.

WIDENING THE SCHISM

Some companies have long embraced a profile as distinctly blue or red, realizing—or not caring—that such profiling could limit the size of their market, even as it potentially intensifies their market share. For instance, Patagonia and Ben & Jerry's are branded on the left, while Chick-fil-A and Black Rifle Coffee are branded on the right. The supportive term for this corporate positioning is *purpose-driven marketing*, the idea being that the product, and the company, should stand for something good. Of course, the predominant assumption, put forth from big-city creatives, has been that the good purpose must be blue. The acme of this thinking was Nike's Colin Kaepernick campaign, launched in 2018, when being pro-Kaepernick could be styled as being anti-Trump. By the 2020s, the Biden years, Kaepernick had faded.

Understandably, most companies, mindful of being caught in a zeitgeistial downdraft, are purposeful only in wishing to dodge self-identification. They might seek to be purple, as in, friendly to both parties. The effort might be called "purplewashing," as a play on "greenwashing"—the ploy of company is making itself appear to be green, in the way that British

---

[288] Meckler, Laura, and Clement, Scott, "Most Americans support anti-trans policies favored by GOP, poll shows," *Washington Post*, May 5, 2023. https://bit.ly/3XqtQju. A Pew poll found 60 percent on the conservative side.

Petroleum changed its name to BP, which it then said stood for Beyond Petroleum.[289]

Can purplewashing work? We'll see. This is not only a polarized environment, it's also an information-rich environment. The internet notices, never forgets. Activists on one side or the other will scrutinize not only the company and its internal policies, but its employees, their social media, their campaign donations, their group affiliations, and so on. And a slew of new outfits have arisen to not only observe the schism, but to widen it. The left pioneered such corporate watchdogging. For instance, the Washington, DC-based Human Rights Campaign has its Corporate Equality Index, which it describes as "the national benchmarking tool measuring policies, practices and benefits pertinent to lesbian, gay, bisexual, transgender and queer (LGBTQ+) employees."[290] But the right is catching up, in this ratings game. For instance, the PublicSq shopping platform, launched in 2022, pledges to connect "freedom-loving Americans to the businesses that share their values." Among its investors: Donald Trump, Jr.[291]

All this info-granularity becomes fodder for campaigns, boycotts, and even, sadly, harassment. In the words of industry observer Allen Adamson, "Previously you could send a homogeneous message to the country, but there's so much divisiveness and polarization on so many issues that that's become almost impossible."[292] So purpling is harder, because people, including customers, will sniff out the choices a company has made. Conservative activist Charlie Kirk says, "I'm going through my refrigerator

[289] Cutter, Chip, and Weber, Lauren, "Companies That Embraced Social Issues Have Second Thoughts," *The Wall Street Journal*, June 6, 2023. https://bit.ly/42ZjRTq

[290] Corporate Equality Index, Human Rights Campaign, accessed May 28, 2023. https://bit.ly/3PqA6G6

[291] Cai, Sophia, "Trumpworld gets behind a MAGA-friendly shopping site," *Axios*, November 30, 2023. https://bit.ly/4a59lyQ

[292] Deighton, Katie, and Coffee, Patrick, "Combative Consumers Change the Marketing Strategy for Target and Bud Light," *The Wall Street Journal*, May 27, 2023. https://bit.ly/3Py66rY

and I'm starting to ask the question: 'Was this ketchup bottle woke? Is this mustard?' I mean, literally."[293]

We can see the dilemma that companies are facing. Decades ago, Peter Lynch wrote of "diworseification," by which he meant, companies being too clever by half in their expansion/conglomeration plans. So now we can add a twist on Lynch. Call it *revealed diworseification*. That is, the company realizes—too late—that it has an obnoxious (as judged by red or blue) subsidiary or activity. That could be the fate of Elon Musk. Tesla is clearly a blue company, and yet Twitter, now X, is red. So which is Musk? As of this writing, Musk himself is much more identified with red. Will this hurt Tesla? And SpaceX? One imagines short-sellers will be circling around one or more of Musk's assets. Of course, they always have been.[294]

Nothing will be easy for high-profile companies. Vivek Ramaswamy, the capitalist-turned-presidential candidate, socked it to the marquee ESG punching bag: "BlackRock will not be able to modulate its political stances because blue states won't let them back off the firm-wide commitments they've made." And so, he concluded, "market bifurcation becomes inevitable."[295] That is, blue bifurcated from red. *E pluribus duo.* Still, BlackRock seems eager to at least try to be "PurpleRock." After taking a beating, the company has been backing away from its forward stances. It shook up its comms team, even as Fink sighed about ESG, "it's been weaponized by the far left and weaponized by the far right ... we lose the conversation."[296] Part of the art of conversation, of course, is changing the subject, or at least the nomenclature. And so if ESG gets too loaded, well, there are plenty of let-

[293] Media Matters (@mmfa), X, June 13, 2023. https://bit.ly/3phBjF8

[294] On October 4, 2018, Musk tweeted, in his own droll way, "Just want to that the Shortseller Enrichment Commission is doing incredible work." Musk, Elon (@elonmusk), X, October 4, 2018. https://bit.ly/3Q7Qv2H

[295] Ramaswamy, Vivek, (@VivekRamaswamy), X, September 22, 2022. https://bit.ly/3XveDxB

[296] Ungarino, Rebecca, "BlackRock communications leaders exit as Larry Fink's messaging falls under a microscope," *Business Insider*, July 18, 2023. https://bit.ly/3DpBmln. See also: Poor, Jeff, "BlackRock CEO Fink: We Don't Say 'ESG' Anymore," *Breitbart*, July 5, 2023. https://bit.ly/3NXw1Id

ters in the alphabet, many more acronymic arrangements. So the future could be a contest between bashers of the underlying policy and changers of the overlying phrase. Yet it seems likely that the market—including, as it does, non-financial players empowered with more information than ever—will eventually force a clear-cut delineation.

Deepening the divide, *The Wall Street Journal* reports that companies are being whipsawed by pro-ESG Blue and anti-ESG Red. "We're caught right in the middle between these very different agendas," said David Sampson, head of the American Property Casualty Insurance Association. "What we're seeing is the weaponization of the business of insurance…to [try to] achieve certain public policy objectives." The point being, it's hard, and maybe impossible, to please both sides. Interestingly, Amy Barnes, head of climate strategy at the insurance broker Marsh & McLennan, told the *Journal* that companies were still committed to combating climate change. "None of the insurers are going back on the way they prioritize decarbonization."[297] We'll have to see about that, of course. But if, in fact, Blue is still committed to green, that's a clear signal to Red that it will need its own insurance operation. Most likely, the future holds a lot of red-blue bifurcation.

THE SCHISMATIC SOLUTION

As we know, there are dozens of left-leaning CSR funds. And now, opposing such liberalism, we're seeing emerging counterweights on the right, including Strive, founded by Ramaswamy, which declares, "We live by a strict commitment to shareholder primacy—an unwavering mandate that the purpose of a for-profit corporation is to maximize long-run value to investors."[298] Strive is reviving the argument of Nobel Laureate Milton Friedman, who argued for an exclusive focus on shareholder value. Back

---

[297] Eaglesham, Jean, "Insurers Are in the Hot Seat on Climate Change," *The Wall Street Journal*, July 13, 2023. https://bit.ly/3rs7wKs

[298] Home page, Strive, accessed June 12, 2023. https://strive.com

in 1970 Friedman wrote, "The doctrine of 'social responsibility' involves the acceptance of the socialist view that political mechanisms, not market mechanisms, are the appropriate way to determine the allocation of scarce resources to alternative uses."[299]

In the meantime, politics and policy are dividing all the more sharply and *duo*-ly. In 2023, twenty-five governors, all Republicans, wrote to the Biden administration, protesting transgenderism in girls' sports.[300] We might immediately note that twenty-five governors did *not* write in protest. Similarly, from 2021 to 2023, state membership in the National School Boards Association was cut in exactly half, as twenty-five red states exited the group, accusing it of going woke.[301] Other old-line groups, such as the National Governors Association (NGA), founded in 1908, are under similar stress. *Politico* reported that at the group's summer 2023 conference, just three of the nation's twenty-six Republican governors attended. GOPers find more time for the Republican Governors Association (and there's also a Democratic Governors Association, as well as regional associations). Said the chair of NGA, "A bipartisan organization in a partisan world is always going to struggle."[302]

Meanwhile, state legislatures were becoming more top-heavy, red and blue. The chambers in twenty-nine states were more than two-thirds controlled by one party or the other—it's "an era of supermajorities."[303] In such circumstances, when one party is enough for victory, there's no need for bipartisan compromise, and the blue-red divide widens.

[299] Friedman, Milton, "A Friedman doctrine—The Social Responsibility of Business Is to Increase Its Profits," *New York Times*, September 13, 1970. https://bit.ly/46qqZeo

[300] Hamilton, Katherine, "25 GOP Governors Say Proposed Biden Admin Rule Would Prevent States from Protecting Women's and Girls' Sports," *Breitbart*, May 12, 2023. https://bit.ly/43ZgblQ

[301] Pondiscio, Robert, "Who's Afraid of Moms for Liberty?" *The Free Press*, July 13, 2023. https://bit.ly/3NJNUsM

[302] Martin, Jonathan, "No-Show Republicans Shun NGA," *Politico*, July 16, 2023. https://bit.ly/3XVid4f

[303] Crampton, Liz, "Democratic governors lose their grip as Republicans nab supermajorities," *Politico*, April 19, 2023. https://bit.ly/3r4r7Aj

Adding to the dichotomous spirit, Biden administration Transportation Secretary Pete Buttigieg says, "Every transportation decision in the 21st century is a climate decision."[304] So nothing is neutral; everything is pushed to one side or the other. And in the transportation space, here's an investment implication. Gallup finds that 76 percent of Democrats said that they would consider buying an electric vehicle, while 71 percent of Republicans said they would not.[305] So EV sales will be better in Maryland than Montana. Where will this end up? History provides, if not the answer, then at least some helpful hints.

THE DIOCLETIAN DIFFERENTIATION

In the third century CE, the Emperor Diocletian, confronting the decline of the Roman Empire, chose to divide it, Eastern and Western, with the Eastern half ultimately headquartered in Constantinople (today's Istanbul). He would have known the phrase *e pluribus duo*. In the words of historian Edward Gibbon, Diocletian "was convinced that the abilities of a single man were inadequate to the public defence." In Gibbon's view, this division—the modern term might be "deconglomeration"—was a success. The historian compared the resulting duo to "a chorus of music, whose harmony was regulated and maintained by the skillful hand of the first artist."[306] Now it can be objected that Diocletian was not a nice guy—he was, for instance, a notable persecutor of Christians.

Still, in geopolitical terms, Diocletian's "spinoff" was vindicated. The Western Empire proved weak. Rome was sacked in 410, 455, and then, finally, in 476, extinguishing all its glory. Indeed, the city's population

[304] "Sec. Buttigieg: 'Every Transportation Decision in the 21st Century Is a Climate Decision Whether We Recognize It or Not,'" Grabien, January 23, 2023. https://bit.ly/46pPOra

[305] Brenan, Megan, "Most Americans Are Not Completely Sold on Electric Vehicles," Gallup, April 12, 2023. https://bit.ly/3NQtmAd

[306] Gibbon, Edward, *History of the Decline and Fall of the Roman Empire*, Chapter XIII, Part I. https://bit.ly/46nol9m

fell from as much as a million to as little as 30,000. And that must have caused a massive loss in property values. Yet the Eastern Empire proved resilient. The East lasted another eleven centuries, long enough to see the full flowering of Byzantine prosperity and culture. Indeed, the Diocletian Differentiation led to the emergence of two very different cultures, Catholic and Orthodox. And then, of course, in the sixteenth century, Catholicism was split by the Reformation, which unleashed wholly unaccustomed economic energy in Protestant Europe.[307]

One element of the Reformation, we might add, was the disposition of property in new ways, as the new Protestant regimes seized the land that the Catholic Church had accumulated over the previous thousand years. For instance, in England, King Henry VIII seized the property of the Church. It's estimated that that the "dissolution of the monasteries" transferred one-fourth of the cultivated land in the county to the Crown and its allies.[308] Which is to say, for all the theological imperatives of the Reformation, there was a financial angle. One could even say, an *investment* angle.

Following our rule that patterns of human behavior never disappear—and always reappear—we can point to a possible parallel in our own time. Today, the US government owns 640 million acres of land, or about 28 percent of the national total. And that's curious, because the only mention of federal land ownership in the Constitution is in Article One, Section Eight, which refers to "Places purchased by the Consent of the Legislature of the State in which the same shall be, for the erection of Forts, Magazines, Arsenals, Dock-yards, and other needful Buildings." So maybe Uncle Sam has gotten a little land-grabby. And since another theme of this book is that the Constitution still matters, it's possible to think of at least some of those federal lands as potential private assets. And to further see the

---

[307] Weber, Max, *The Protestant Ethic and the Spirit of Capitalism*, 1904-5. https://bit.ly/3JtgixN. The Scientific Revolution—from Bacon to Newton to Kepler—of the seventeenth century began in Northern Europe. Also beginning in Northern Europe: the Industrial Revolution.

[308] Johnson, Ben, "Dissolution of the Monasteries," Historic UK. https://bit.ly/3O8ACaE

Constitution as the basis of the argument that the feds shouldn't be controlling it. Without a doubt, federal lands, if unlocked, would be worth many trillions. In other words, they are a windfall waiting to happen. To be sure, federal ownership of land isn't much of a concern in Blue, where the feds own, for example, just .8 percent of the land in New York State. Well, actually, it is a concern, insofar as many people in Manhattan and Brooklyn insist on federal ownership of land west of the Mississippi—land they might quite possibly never even see in person. But nonetheless, for the sake of the environment, they want Uncle Green to own it. In effect, green plutocrats and activists are the absentee landlords. In Idaho, for instance, the federal government owns 62 percent of the land, and in Alaska, 61 percent.[309] In those Western states, federal ownership is a *big* deal. As a general rule in the West, Republicans favor at least some rollback of federal land power, while Democrats oppose it, or even support the expansion of federal land ownership. And yet the parties have Big Sorted themselves such that Republicans have overwhelming dominance in Red, while Democrats have overwhelming dominance in Blue. So current federal land ownership is an assertion of blue power in places where Blue is actually sort of the enemy. So how long will this sort of colonialist mismatch last? How long before a Henry VIII of red America seeks to dissolve legacy blue power? For sure, any such effort would be intensely controversial. But as we look around the national landscape, do we see political figures shying away from controversy? In an *e pluribus duo* America, political actors are often looking for opportunities to widen the divide.

Sure enough Sen. Cynthia Lummis, Republican of Wyoming, has proposed to build affordable housing on federal land.[310] The red-blue battle is joined on a new political field, which happens to be the home turf of of Red. Cowboy Staters will presumably never mess with Yellowstone National Park, but who can know the fate of the remainder of the 46.7 percent of Wyoming the feds currently own. In that same spirit, Native Alaskans have

---

[309] "Federal Land by State," Wise Voter. https://bit.ly/43zU84x

[310] Wolfson, Leo, "Lummis Wants To Use Federal Land For Affordable Housing," *Cowboy State Daily*, November 4, 2023. https://tinyurl.com/4jv4drrw

mobilized against Biden administration decrees about oil drilling. "We will not succumb to eco-colonialism and become conservation refugees on our own land," said Charles Lampe, president of the Kaktovik Iñupiat Corporation.[311]

Yet Blue might see the silver lining in this sort of separation, because it would allow Blue to protect other of its assets that Red is coveting. For instance, there's currently a small "r" reformation-like movement among Republicans to tax university endowments, the most sapphire-hued gems of blue finance—which Red regards as fat piggybanks, funding woke sacrilege.[312] GOPers note that in fiscal year 2021, the five richest universities, all blue, boasted assets of more than $210 billion.[313] In fact, as far back as 2017, Republicans coupled a substantial tax cut with a tax increase on higher education—a new excise tax on large university endowments. Leading Republicans—including Sen. Tom Cotton of Arkansas, born in Red, educated in Blue and now back in Red plotting against Blue—would like to soak these ivory tower riches.[314] So in the *duo*-ification of the nation, Red might grab the federal lands on its turf, but Blue would protect its academic crown jewels.

INVESTMENT TAKEAWAYS

- If the US does see a Diocletian Differentiation, the business and marketing implications will be enormous. There will be a blue style and a red style, and it will be a hard challenge to any national

[311] Catenacci, Thomas, "Alaskan Native Americans unleash on Biden admin's climate agenda," Fox News, December 1, 2023. https://bit.ly/484hKRf
[312] Shaw, Tim, "Republican Bill Would Raise Tax on University Endowments," Reuters, September 23, 2022. https://bit.ly/42VlOAd
[313] "U.S. and Canadian Institutions Listed by Fiscal Year (FY) 2021 Endowment Market Value," National Association of College and University Business Officers. https://bit.ly/3NOPsBG
[314] "Cotton Introduces Bill to Tax Private University Mega-Endowments, Support Workforce Training Programs," Tom Cotton, Senator for Arkansas, May 11, 2021. https://bit.ly/3PROnO7

brand to appeal to both. The obstacles won't just be cultural, they'll be political, as Blue chips away at Red, and vice versa. Yet of course, every trend plants the seeds of a counter-trend. So as soon as there's duo, there'll be an effort at knitting back the *unum*. That will have its own investment implications. It's always a challenge to know which trend to befriend.

- The Bud Light story is a B-school case study for the ages. In the meantime, other consumer-facing companies, such as Disney, Kohl's, and Target, have been similarly caught in the downdraft of the shifting trans zeitgeist. For instance, fifteen Democratic state attorneys general wrote to Target expressing dismay at its purported lack of support for LGBTQ.[315] That letter might have come as a surprise to Target HQ, as well as to the general public. So as if there weren't already enough mines in the minefield, companies must be mindful of state AGs. And if Democrats do it on one side, Republicans will do it on the other.

- Some economists will say that bifurcation is inefficient, arguing that economies of scale are lost with too many jurisdictions and borders. They won't be wrong, although one new reality is that computerization allows for more "batch processing," as opposed to "continuous flow" mass production; this was a trend noted back in 1980 by that noted trend-noter, Alvin Toffler.[316] So while it might be more convenient for Corporate America to have one big market, if the US goes bimodal, red-blue, capitalism will adjust. Companies have loved to celebrate diversity. They'll find a way to celebrate division. In the meantime, arbitrageurs will enjoy.

---

[315] Letter to Target CEO Brian Cornell from fifteen state attorneys general, dated June 16, 2023. https://bit.ly/3Xt0HUJ. The letter reads, in part, "We write to express our resolute and unequivocal support for the LGBTQIA+ community as well as our concern regarding recent events in Target stores involving intimidation and destruction of certain Pride-related merchandise and Target's resulting decision to remove some Pride merchandise from its stores."

[316] Toffler, Alvin, *Third Wave*, 92.

- Outright spinoffs, however, might be a different story. Even if management wishes to hold on to the empire, shareholders might be quite happy owning a new share of red, and a new share of blue, as opposed to a troubled older share of a legacy blue seeking to be purple.

- Equilibration—if a blue company has a big market share in a red state, it will be vulnerable to a marketing/boycotting campaign by a red competitor. And while it might seem hard to believe that a red company could rise to take on, say, Disney, it's hard to believe that Disney has found itself in as much difficulty as it has. In any case, now Red is ready to rumble. Conservative critic John Nolte writes, "Something's gonna give...and it ain't gonna be human nature."[317] Such a crunch spells investment possibility—either going short on the established player, or going long on a rivals. One such rival is DailyWire+, whose offerings include *Lady Ballers*, which one critic described as a"right-wing movie that farcically depicts cis-gendered men claiming to be women in order to dominate women's sports.[318] Another is Angel Studios, which released *Sound of Freedom*, a conservative film about child trafficking that proved to be a huge hit. Interestingly enough, Disney had once owned that film, but passed on releasing it.

- During those same years, several high-profile Disney films bombed amidst rampant accusations of wokeness, causing the company's stock to slump. Has Disney lost its touch, at least with Red? Disney worries that it might have. In a 2023 filing with the SEC, the company acknowledged, "We face risks relating to misalignment with public and consumer tastes and preferences for entertainment, travel and consumer products, which impact demand for our entertainment offerings and products and the

---

[317] Nolte, John, "Woke-Poisoned Hollywood Has Doomed the Once-Unbeatable Movie Industry," *Breitbart*, March 24, 2023. https://bit.ly/3pl1xXh

[318] Marx, Nick, "'Conservatives' 'anti-woke' alternative to Disney has finally arrived," *The Conversation*, December 2023, https://bit.ly/3t903RQ

profitability of any of our businesses."[319] In business as in politics, ideas have consequences.

[319] The Walt Disney Company, Form 10-K, September 30, 2023. https://bit.ly/41aZC5P

CHAPTER EIGHT

SCHISMOPROSPEROUS: DUALITY CREATES PROFITABILITY

SCHISMOPROSPERITY

A theme so far has been that the national divide has actually been healthy for the country, given that the alternative is open strife. And happily, our constitutional system enables the fifty states to express their differences in peaceful competition, even if, as we have observed, they are choosing to form themselves into dueling blocs, red against blue. Now we can add a further point, of particular importance to investments. The divide will create *energy*.

We've already noted Herbert Croly's idea that the interplay of Hamiltonianism and Jeffersonianism would release "wholly unaccustomed energy." Now we can add a further kind of energy from splitsville. In 1935 the British anthropologist Gregory Bateson coined the word "schismogenesis," which he defined as "symmetrical differentiation" among peoples, leading to reciprocal rivalries, culminating in widely diverging modes of thinking and behaving.[320] We can see this dynamic in ordinary human relationships. In a breakup, the level of anger often escalates. As they say, it's easier to leave mad than it is just to leave. Yet even if schismogenesis means that the two antagonists don't like each other, it doesn't mean that they won't learn from each other, and gain energy from each other. In addition, the rival sides often develop stronger in-group loyalty, a sense of pride and purpose, even of localized patriotism, pitted against the other side.

As we saw in the previous chapter, the Diocletian Differentiation led to the emergence of two very different cultures in Europe, each challenging, informing, and stimulating the other. After the Reformation of the sixteenth century, came another differentiation in the seventeenth century, the Counter-Reformation. That led to a whole cultural efflorescence of its own, including, for example, the baroque. To be sure, these cultural advances coincided with huge wars and destruction, but they also led to economic creation. Indeed, the astonishing rise of Europe during this era—it's estimated that, wars and all, the West's per capita GDP rose nearly seven-fold from 1500 to 1850—supports one of Daniel Bell's arguments: the "disjunction of realms" unleashes a "furious energy."[321]

And so today, we can think about the schismogenesis of American culture over LGBTQ. On the conservative side of the divide, the Republican Party is rethinking its stance on education policy and cultural issues and the energy level on the right is picking up. At the same time, on the left side, LGBTQ and its allies are doubling down. New York City's Stonewall has become not only a blue cultural lodestone, but also a tourist-rich attraction.[322] And in 2023, San Francisco displayed an acre-sized pink trian-

[320] Bateson, Gregory, "Culture Contact and Schismogenesis," *Man*, Vol. 35 (December, 1935), 178-183. https://www.jstor.org/journal/man. Writing with World War II in prospect, Bateson observed that "the nations of Europe are far advanced in symmetrical schismogenesis and are ready to fly at each other's throats."
[321] Maddison Database, https://bit.ly/3Kkj34W. See also: Bell, Daniel, *Cultural Contradictions*, 82.
[322] Rajamani, Maya, "Stonewall's impact, 50 years after the riots: 'It's much more than a bar'," *AMNY*, June 24, 2019. https://bit.ly/3XJUcgs

gle—the largest in the city's history.[323] Meanwhile, Montgomery County,
Maryland, just outside of Washington, DC, moved its public schools to
the left. It eliminated students' "opt-out" provision for LGBTQ material.[324]
That same year, California's attorney general announced a ban on state-
funded travel to offending red states.[325] Generating still more energy for
Team Blue, the Democratic governor of Massachusetts, Maura Healey,
has been delighted to use Florida, in the words of *The Boston Globe*, as a
"foil."[326] And yet even as the blue governor was attacking Red, Blue was
enticing Red. Healey hoisted the pride flag over her state's Capital, hosted
a drag show on the statehouse steps—and posted billboards in Florida urging LGBTQ Floridians to move to Massachusetts.

And it's not just big cities and states that are seeing schismogenic
energy. For instance, Ottawa County, Michigan, is going right, and left,
at the same time. First, right-wing activists mobilized and pushed aside
more moderate Republicans to take over the county government, cancel-
ing funding for diversity programs and all that. Whereupon folks in Grand
Haven, population, 11,000, decided to hold an LGBTQ parade. Organizers
were expecting hundreds, but drew thousands.[327] We can see, there's not
much that can't be polarized and energized by schismogenesis. Whatever
happens in these duels, it's safe to say that billions, if not trillions, are leaving one pocket, and going to another pocket—so arbitrage will abound.

[323] Daley, Haven, "San Francisco displays the largest ever pink triangle for Pride
month in a stand against pushback, AP, June 22, 2023. https://bit.ly/3JAInUa
[324] Asbury, Nicole, "How the fight against LGBTQ+ books in Montgomery County
became a national issue," *Washington Post*, July 5, 2023. https://bit.ly/3OztgMz
[325] Schrupp, Kenneth, "California bans state-funded travel to Missouri, Nebraska and
Wyoming," *The Center Square California*, July 17, 2023. https://bit.ly/3rBWAKw
[326] Van Buskirk, Chris, "Massachusetts declared a 'safe haven' as Pride flag is raised
at State House," *Boston Herald*, June 7, 2023. https://bit.ly/3XOOEBy. See also:
Stout, Matt, "In promoting Massachusetts, Healey has found a foil: Florida and
its conservative governor, Ron DeSantis," *Boston Globe*, July 16, 2023. https://bit.
ly/44uiduv
[327] Cappelletti, Joey, "Midwest small town's Pride festival attracts thousands who
reject far-right local politics," Associated Press, June 14, 2023. https://bit.
ly/3PxRVmC

So maybe that's not only our destiny, but our best possibility—to live in a country where rival ideas contend with each other, even as they're linked with each other, in a kind of homeostasis, orbiting each other like binary stars. To further illustrate the power of schismogenesis, we can point to different moments in business history where splits were profitable.

STANDARD OIL, SCHISMO ENRICHED

In 1911, Department of Justice antitrust action broke the Standard Oil monopoly into thirty-four corporate pieces. That breakup didn't make John D. Rockefeller happy, but the result was surprisingly good for him. Compared to the original intact company, the total value of the pieces at least doubled.[328] This might seem paradoxical, but as with Diocletian and the Romans, sometimes an empire can be too big to be managed effectively. Yet for reasons of ego and stasis, the entity stays together, even if it could be more profitably run in separate units. Breakup, however unwanted, can lead to positive results. This is not an argument for more aggressive antitrust enforcement today, it's simply an observation as to what we already knew—sometimes adversity creates opportunity. Another antitrust case in point was the 1984 breakup of the Bell System. It seems to have opened up space permitting the full flowering of telephony, which in turn supported the growth of the internet.

GENERAL MOTORS, SCHISMO SLOANED

A century ago, General Motors was a hot company. And it got hotter when it was internally divided in an intelligent way. The best teller of this tale is

---

[328] Desjardins, Jeff, "Chart: The Evolution of Standard Oil," Visual Capitalist, November 24, 2017. https://bit.ly/3CMioVN. According to Peter Drucker, the Rockefeller fortune increased ten-fold. See also: "Sage Advice: The foremost business thinker of our age tells what is wrong (and right) with the New Economy," Ghandchi.com, August 22, 2000. https://bit.ly/3CP5mqU

Alfred P. Sloan, president and/or chairman of the board of GM from 1923 to 1956. In his memoir, Sloan recalled the earliest days of the company, started by William Durant in 1908. Durant was a genius as a starter, but not as a manager. Not an unfamiliar pattern—a brilliant empire builder is not the same person as the effective corporate consolidator. Sloan writes, "By various means, mostly exchanges of stock, Mr. Durant between 1908 and 1910 brought into General Motors about twenty-five companies. Eleven were automobile companies, two were electrical lamp companies, and the remainder were auto-parts and accessory manufacturers." Was that genius at work, or diworseification—or maybe a little of both? In any case, it now fell to Sloan to make sense of it all. Amidst the welter, the new chief saw promising patterns—"variety in cars for a variety of tastes and economic levels in the market." At the time, that was Buick, Oldsmobile, Oakland, Cadillac, and, a little while later, Chevrolet. So we can see, here, some Diocletian Differentiation—only five-way, not two-way. Those car brands, Sloan added, "were to have a permanent place—first as companies, later as divisions—in the evolution of the corporation." He continues, "By placing each division on its own profit-making basis, I gave the general office a common measure of efficiency with which to judge the contribution of each division to the whole." It was, Sloan concluded, "a happy medium in industrial organization between the extremes of pure centralization and pure decentralization."[329]

We can pause to observe that while some companies, such as GM, thrived when they decentralized, others have thrived when they centralized, or engaged in any other form of reorganization. As we have seen, it's the change in the state that releases energy. In organizational science, there's term for this—the Hawthorne Effect. It argues there's a positive value in shaking things up. Everyone intuits the Hawthorne Effect. That's one reason why people feel better when they change their hairstyle, or redecorate their home, or get outside for some air. The best cure for humdrum is to

---

[329] Sloan, Alfred P., *My Years With General Motors* (New York: Doubleday, 1990), 5-6, 16. 25, 46-7, 52, 55.

do something fresh—that's the deep wisdom, derived from both physics and the psyche. Is the Effect a short-run thing? Sure it is. Which is why people keep changing, or redecorating, or getting. Not a day goes by that some big company, somewhere, isn't reorganizing, consolidating, acquiring, selling, streamlining—pick a gerund, that's what companies are doing. Such personal and institutional restlessness keeps things moving. All those short runs add up to a long run. We can now look at other "schismos" that generate wealth.

SCHISMO IMAGINATION

No less than Albert Einstein said, "Imagination is more important than knowledge. Knowledge is limited. Imagination encircles the world."[330] Who can argue with him? Scientific knowledge is vital, and historical perspective can help, but ideas and imagination are perhaps even more important. In the contemporary economy, the key factors of production are IQ, adrenaline, and caffeine. So no wonder wealth creation is highly mobile—as mobile as people and their laptops. That's why Indiana, a relatively low-tech state, is seeking to beef itself up with incentives to blue techies to become Hoosiers.[331]

Now that the Red-Blue rivalry is instantiated in our culture, we're seeing new schismogenic energy. For instance, Blue chooses to flaunt its wealth. Here's a typical headline from just after the 2016 presidential election. "Another Clinton-Trump divide: High-output America vs low-output America." Data-crunchers found that the 472 counties carried by the Democratic nominee, Hillary Clinton, accounted for 64 percent of US economic output, while the 2584 counties the Republican carried accounted

---

[330] Viereck, George Sylvester, "What Life Means to Einstein," *Saturday Evening Post*, October 26, 1929. https://bit.ly/3XoPuor

[331] Steussy, Lauren, "One family ditched California for an Indiana town that offered them $5,000 cash, an unlimited golf membership, and coffee with the mayor," *Business Insider*, June 13, 2023. https://bit.ly/3r2zuw6

for just 36 percent.[332] In addition to partisan rivalry, we can detect more than a little snobbery, but that's schismogenesis in action. California's Gavin Newsom combined dismissiveness and haughtiness when he tweeted, "7 of the top 10 dependent states are red states. We're subsidizing red states. Progressive economic policies work."[333] So Blue is now bragging on its knowledge-economy prowess. And that will inevitably bring push-back from Red. Still, Blue does, indeed, have things to brag about.

"If you can imagine it, you can probably make it through biology. That's the promise of biomanufacturing."[334] So said Kate Sixt, principal director for biotechnology in the Office of the Under Secretary of Defense for Research and Engineering. Sixt is taking us into territory that's both unfamiliar and familiar. The technology is new to us, and to everyone, and yet the backdrop is Hamiltonian. So this Pentagon official, serving under a Democratic president, is talking about not only defense, but also the components of economic growth—making plastics, chemicals, food, and fuels through biological processes. It seems almost magical. Indeed, one is reminded of the wisdom of sci-fi legend Arthur C. Clarke, who famously postulated, "Any sufficiently advanced technology is indistinguishable from magic." Technology that's magical, we pause to say, is also profitable. We might note that Dr. Sixt has a rhapsody-in-blue resume. She earned her undergraduate degree in New York State, then a PhD at Johns Hopkins, then did a postdoc at the National Cancer Institute. Now, in addition to her work at the Pentagon, she has taught at Georgetown University, just across the Potomac.[335] Blue through and through.

To be sure, there's no guarantee that any of the defense industrial policy that Sixt is supervising will actually work. And yet the Pentagon's track

---

[332] Muro, Mark, and Liu, Sifan, "Another Clinton-Trump divide: High-output America vs low-output America," Brookings Institution, November 29, 2016. https://bit.ly/42ZJTWL

[333] Newsom, Gavin (@GavinNewsom), X, June 17, 2023. https://bit.ly/3r3OeLi

[334] Griffin, Riley, "Biden Plans to Spur Biological Production of Fuels, Chemicals, Plastics," Bloomberg News, March 22, 2023. https://bit.ly/3XoOYXx

[335] Dr. Kate Sixt, US Department of Defense, accessed March 31, 2023. https://bit.ly/44bNWAs

record of Clarke-type magic—from radar to the A-bomb to GPS—offers hope. Yes, there've been plenty of Pentagon boondoggles, but history shows that if you get a few big things right, you've more than covered the dogs. Indeed, Blue Hamiltonianism is bringing its own policy ideas to the table. In 2022, Brian Deese, chair of the National Economic Council at the Biden White House, outlined "Modern American Industrial Strategy." Defying Red, he declared, "If you do public investment in a thoughtful way, what you'll actually do is crowd in private investment."[336] This point about "crowding in" is a direct challenge to the conservative argument that taxes, regulation, and deficits have the effect of "crowding out" investment. Deese's counter-argument is that a good enough idea—or a good enough deal—will attract the needed capital. By this reckoning, the extra taxes, regulations, and wokeness that Blue imposes will seem small next to the potential capital gain. That's certainly been the story of, say, California and Massachusetts. To be sure, the economic stories of those states hardly settles the argument, as Red can point to the success stories of Florida and Texas. So what we're seeing is a rivalry, a clash of intellectual paradigms, the Hamiltonian Framework v. Jeffersonian Liberty. Schismogenesis advances schismoprosperity.

SCHISMO BIG TECH

Few industries are more avowedly blue than Big Tech. We can start with one of the biggest of the blues—Apple. Probably no company in history has gone further on the "coolness factor." Indeed, Apple is so cool that most red staters seem happy to have an iPhone, never mind the company's on-its-sleeve progressivism.

Still, the red-blue divide is so deep that we could potentially even see an *e pluribus duo*-ing of Apple's mighty market. In 2022, reports emerged that

---

[336] Mattingly, Phil, "Biden and his team feeling vindicated by a 2022 turnaround built on the same decades-old principles," CNN, December 28, 2022. https://bit.ly/444KcAT

Apple might ban the Twitter app from its phones. Whereupon Twitter's owner, Elon Musk, said, "If there is no other choice, I will make an alternative phone."[337] Now that would have been exciting, not just for Musk, but for wherever the new phone would have been designed and built. As it happened, Apple stood down, and so the specific tiff was mooted. Yet other technologies could be sharpened by competition with a schismo ideological subtext. In 2023, Musk tweeted that he had helped in the creation of OpenAI as a counterweight to Google.[338] Then, not satisfied with what OpenAI had become, he told Tucker Carlson his competitors were "training the AI to lie."[339] A few months later, he announced he built his own AI, giving it the Heinleinian name of "Grok."[340]

It's no secret that most AIs are woke. If that continues, it would be, indeed, an epic defeat for red states— leftism algorithmed onto red screens as the Truth. So it behooves Red, with or without Musk, to have its own indigenous AI, lest it be reduced to hewers of wood and drawers of water for Blue.(More on AI in Chapter Fourteen.)

SCHISMOCULTURE

Jayme Chandler Franklin, a former Trump White House staffer, is the founder of *The Conservateur,* an online publication that aims to be a *Vogue* for conservative women. *Politico* reported, "Franklin's theory of the case is that American culture is hopelessly split, with mainstream organizations—from sports leagues to fashion magazines—incapable of being welcoming places for her kind of conservatives." The site continues, "She sees the rise of a 'dual economy,' where different sectors of society turn to

[337] Serrano, Jody, "Elon Says He'll Make His Own Phone If Apple and Google Deplatform Twitter," *Gizmodo,* November 25, 2022. https://bit.ly/430HZoA
[338] Musk, Elon (@elonmusk), X, February 17, 2023. https://bit.ly/3CPQcSe
[339] Jin, Hyunjoo, and Dang, Sheila, "Elon Musk says he will launch rival to Microsoft-backed ChatGPT," *Reuters,* April 18, 2023. https://bit.ly/3NukSNw
[340] DeVynck, Gerrit, "Musk's new AI company, xAI, will aim to solve scientific mysteries," *Washington Post,* July 14, 2023. https://bit.ly/46QyOue

different companies for all manner of entertainment and lifestyle services, as a massive opportunity." Franklin herself says, "It's an incredible niche that I want to capitalize on. If the left wants to take all the companies and stuff to the left, there's room for us."[341]

INVESTMENT TAKEAWAYS

- Schismogenesis will make for difficult politics, but it also opens up opportunity-filled economics. As we have seen, involuntary breakups, such as that of Standard Oil, can unleash value. And yet even as we see what happens with the Biden administration's turn toward tougher antitrust enforcement—which is, we can add, a kind of Directed Investment in antitrust lawyers, pro and con— we will have to ponder, in a trend-is-your-friend way, the implications of the schism. With apologies to the Bob Dylan song, Blue Go Your Way, And Red Go Mine.

- Yet the magnetic power of Blue moneymaking is not to be gainsayed. In 2012, *The New Yorker*'s Ken Auletta profiled Stanford University, dubbing it "Get Rich U." Auletta cited all the Big Tech types who were teaching part-time at Stanford, observing that their students were often the next crop of Big Tech-ers.[342] In other words, a circular economy of prosperity. That's exactly the formula for creating the next Google, even if, along the way, it might also create the next Sam Bankman-Fried, who grew up on the Stanford campus. Is Stanford woke? Sure. However, as Bankman-Fried proved, wokeness can be just a facade for capitalist avarice, outright crime. In the face of such sophisticated predation from Blue, Red will need its own defensive tech capacity. And that

[341] Schaffer, Michael, "A MAGA Answer to Vogue Offers Advice on Owning the Libs – and Season's Best Fashions," *Politico*, September 2, 2022. https://bit.ly/3JuquWY

[342] Auletta, Ken, "Get Rich U," *The New Yorker*, April 23, 2012 https://tinyurl.com/23yxbhfs.

takes brains, and educated brains at that. It's bad strategy for Red to see so many of its smartest students going to Blue for higher education. And it's also bad for Red if the smartest people from around the world receive their further instruction in California or Massachusetts, as opposed to Florida or Texas. History is clear. Smart techies get their best ideas in college or grad school, often in conjunction with fellow students, and perhaps with a professor. So they all stick around and start up near alma mater. That's not only how Blue stays rich, it's also how Blue gains power, as with ascendant AI. So what to do? As a matter of good civics, as well as good economic development, some enterprising red state ought to announce that it is offering a free ride to any student who gets an 800 on his or her math SAT. Call it 800 U. It would be costly up front, but the cost could be reduced by situating the 800 U "campus" in an empty office building...and in this work-from-era, there're going to be plenty of them. Since the goal is to attract nerds, there'd be no need for the usual higher-ed frippery, including athletic facilities. Frisbee in the abandoned parking lot will be fine for the circulation, at least until the alumni contributions start rolling in. In any case, 800 U would be for nerds, not jocks. Various "magnet" ideas have been tried, including the North Carolina School of Science and Mathematics, and yet they are always watered down, as the education "blob" pseudopods its way in to regain control of the institution. Yet with 800 U, the rigor would be right there in the name. And while the newbie school would no doubt suffer catcalls from the anti-academically inclined, that hostility would create useful schismogenic energy, encouraging the school and its students to redouble their defiant nerd-dom. The result? In a few years, a new tech cluster could arise in, maybe, Tulsa or Twin Falls. Many investment opportunities would open up from such an brainiac flowering, but here's the easiest—buy real estate near 800 U.

CHAPTER NINE

FROM TREND-SPOTTING
TO TREND-SHAPING

The previous chapters have mostly been concerned with *spotting* directions, about making friends with existing trends. Now we can think about *shaping* directions, about making friends with new trends, trends we help start. Yes, that requires more effort, but there's more reward.

FIELD OF CAPITALISM

In the 1989 movie, *Field of Dreams,* a voice tells Kevin Costner, "If you build it, he will come." So Costner got active, shaping a baseball diamond out of a cornfield. Soon his investment was rewarded by visits from ghostly ball players, legends of yore. So there's much to be said for designing to win. Indeed, if we stay with baseball, we can recall the cleverness, a century ago, of the New York Yankees. Knowing that its star slugger, Babe Ruth, was a left-handed hitter, the team designed the new Yankee Stadium, opening in 1923, with its right field fence a mere 296 feet from home plate. That short distance, of course, was set to maximize the home runs of left-handed hitters. By comparison, the distance to the left field line was 395 feet, and the maximum depth of center field was 460 feet. No wonder the Sultan of Swat felt so at home there in the Bronx, banging homers over that close-in "right porch," while right-handed sluggers, not so much. Only in 1958, long after Ruth's retirement, did Major League Baseball designate that the distance to the fence had to be at least 325 feet.[343]

So now, in that same design-to-win spirit, we can strategize about designing the investment field. We've called it, in previous chapters, the Hamiltonian Framework. But now, in honor of *Field of Dreams*, we can say, "If you build a safe place for investment, capital will come."

It's a proven technique. To illustrate, we can look back to 1965, when Walt Disney announced that he and his company, riding on the success of Disneyland, would build a second theme park, this one in Orlando, Florida. The locals were thrilled. "Disneyland Produces Fantastic Prosperity" bannered the Orlando newspaper's front page.[344] Walt Disney died the following year, and so his brother Roy took over, telling the Jeffersonians of Florida that the company needed Hamiltonianism. "We must have a solid legal foundation before we proceed with Disney World," Roy said. "This foundation can be assured by the legislative proposals we are presenting at the next session of the Florida legislature. If these requests are granted, I believe that we can make the new theme park a reality by 1971."[345] In other words, a solid Framework would yield solid results. Florida obligingly established the Reedy Creek Improvement District (RCID), a thirty-eight-square mile entity controlled by the Walt Disney Company. The deal was totally Hamiltonian. Give Disney control over roads, building permits, zoning, and the like, then let the company go. It was, in effect, an enterprise zone—its own little Nevada—and Disney would, in turn, build not only a theme park, Disney World, but also EPCOT, the Experimental Prototype Community Of Tomorrow, which promised dramatic innovations in mass transit, construction, and overall urban design. As it happened, Disney's

---

[343] Landers, Chris, "Yankee Stadium's short porch in right field is responsible for some of baseball's biggest moments," MLB.com, January 29, 2019. https://bit.ly/3XrdbMG

[344] "Orlando Sentinel front page breaks the news of new Disney project in Florida," Newspapers.com, October 24, 1965. https://bit.ly/3prHiqI

[345] Korkis, Jim, "Walt Disney's EPCOT '66 Film Debut," *Mouse Planet*, July 11, 2018. https://bit.ly/44kuQbb

end of the deal was not completely kept. Disney World opened in 1971, but the company was less interested in EPCOT. Soon enough, the brave new city aspects were forgotten and EPCOT submerged into Disney World. Yet still, RCID, the ultimate in "walled garden," fulfilled its purpose and rewarded its creator, decade after decade, governor after governor. A 2021 estimate showed that the overall economic impact of Disney in Florida was $75.2 billion annually, including $5.8 billion in additional state tax revenue and nearly half million jobs.[346]

To be sure, the idea of a special district for special tasks is hardly unique or new. There are more than 2,900 such districts in Florida, and more than 50,000 across the country.[347] We could also note a cognate structure that emerged only in the 1970s: the business improvement district (BID).[348] And while none of these other districts have been as ambitious as RCID, they have all at least attempted to fulfill a Hamiltonian purpose—focusing effort on a bottom line. But alas, all things must pass. As we have seen with the Frameworks protecting the rails and highways, protective legal structures have a way of eroding over time. In 2022, Disney came embroiled in Florida school legislation, which critics dubbed "don't say gay." The fight erupted into the national consciousness, as did Florida Governor Ron DeSantis. Disney's CEO was pushed out for not being sufficiently opposed to DeSantis. He was replaced by Bob Iger, who came out of retirement to once again lead his old company. That took the spat up a notch. DeSantis called Disney "woke," accusing it of "sexualizing children." Iger rejected the accusations and labeled DeSantis "anti-business and anti-Florida."[349]

[346] Call, James, "The Mouse that need not roar: How Disney World at 50 shapes Florida, wields influence," *Tallahassee Democrat*, October 14, 2021. https://bit.ly/3r8Ejnx

[347] Maciag, Michael, "Number of Local Governments by State," *Governing*, September 14, 2012. https://bit.ly/44gfBQA

[348] Kudla, Daniel, "Fifty years of Business Improvement Districts: A reappraisal of the dominant perspectives and debates," *Sage Journals*, February 1, 2022. https://bit.ly/3r2qx65

[349] Lakhani, Nina, "Disney chief Bob Iger calls Ron DeSantis 'anti-business and anti-Florida'" *The Guardian*. April 4, 2023. https://bit.ly/46Amq1s

Whereupon Florida retaliated. RCID was liquidated. The area is now the Central Florida Tourism Oversight District (CFTOD). An exasperated Iger asked, "Does the state want us to invest more, employ more people and pay more taxes or not?"[350] Disney cancelled a plan to move employees from California to Orlando, citing Florida's supposed intolerance. DeSantis partisans clapped back that the project was canceled in keeping with Disney's poor corporate performance, that Iger was trying to shift the onus for his own failures onto DeSantis. It remains to be seen whether CFTOD will be much different, in terms of its actual operations and effect, than the old RCID.

In the meantime, that ace Blue Hamiltonian, Gavin Newsom, weighed in on Disney's cancellation of its Florida expansion. "Authoritarian policies have consequences," the governor of California said. Referring to Disney's decision to keep jobs in Burbank, Newsom added, "This announcement is a victory for California, and the tens of thousands of Disney employees who know they can live in a state where they are respected and safe. Disney has invested billions of dollars in California, and we look forward to their increased investment and growth in our state."[351] Another Blue Hamiltonian, Michigan governor Gretchen Whitmer, piled on. The one thing for a state not to do, she jibed, is "wage war with Mickey Mouse." Putting the Wolverine State "on the right side of history," Whitmer continued, "is going to be good for business."[352]

In the end, who will win? Florida? California? Some third state? It's a never-ending story of cat and, er, Mouse. The only thing we know for sure is that businesses craves the stability (and profitability) of a Framework, and if they have it, they will move toward it, and if they don't, they will look elsewhere.

---

[350] Palmeri, Christopher, "Disney CEO on Florida Fight: 'Does the State Want Us to Invest?'" Bloomberg News, May 10, 2023. https://bit.ly/3XoCfE9

[351] "Disney bailing on Florida project is 'victory' for California, Newsom says," KTVU, May 19, 2023. https://bit.ly/431OO9I

[352] Martin, Jonathan, "Bypassing Biden: Democrats Think of What Could Have Been," Politico, July 6, 2023 https://bit.ly/3NDWTMc

HOW DARPA DOES IT

The Pentagon's Defense Advanced Research Projects Agency (DARPA) is all about stability. The most Framework-y of federal agencies, it offers private contractors the Hamiltonian assurance that the agency will see the project "end to end." Since the assurance is coming from the deep-pocketed Pentagon, it's impactful. To mix a metaphor, contractors know they're in good hands. With this careful comprehensiveness, DARPA has brought forth wonders, including the internet, GPS, stealth technology, and voice command. To be sure, DARPA has had plenty of strikeouts, and yet the home runs still win the game. Frameworks work.

So it's not surprising that other outfits have attempted to follow the model. In 2021, *The Economist* surveyed the vast ranks of DARPA wannabes—including America's ARPA-E (energy), IARPA (intelligence) and ARPA-H (health), Germany's Federal Agency for Disruptive Innovation, plus their Cybersecurity Innovation Agency, Japan's Moonshot R&D, and Britain's Advanced Research and Invention Agency. But the magazine hammered the key distinction, writing, "Whereas most focus on basic research, DARPA builds things."[353] That is, it brings the product to "market"—the market, of course, being the military. Still, we can all see the results, both in military success and then in future civilian spinoffs. Can any other agency, anywhere, equal DARPA's success? Can other sectors and economies flourish using DARPA techniques? It can be argued that what makes DARPA so effective is its tie to the military. That is, plenty gets done that wouldn't otherwise get done, in the name of national security. Yet with creative thinking, just about everything can regarded as "national security," or at least as a top national priority. In the meantime, billions in capital languish in the bardo between idea and action—and trillions await creation.

---

[353] "A growing number of governments hope to clone America's DARPA," *The Economist*, June 3, 2021. https://bit.ly/3NOtY9i

ACCENTUATING THE NEGATIVE: FIELD OF NO DREAMS

If special districts and DARPA are ways to get things done, here's a way to get things undone—bring in the Naderite NIMBY Naysayers. Ralph Nader emerged as a significant figure in 1965, with his muckraking attack on the auto industry, *Unsafe At Any Speed*. For better and for worse, Nader became a significant figure, such that "Naderite," and "Naderism," became memes. For better, Nader inspired a new emphasis on safety. For worse, Nader helped create legal regulatory systems that helped trial lawyers more than citizens. Naderism soon joined with another idea, NIMBYism, that being the reflex—perhaps even the ideology—of Not In My Back Yard. And NIMBY-ism links to other "isms," including environmentalism and legal hucksterism.

The legislative encapsulation of the Naderite spirit is the National Environmental Policy Act (NEPA) of 1970. NEPA put in motion legal procedures—most notably, the environmental impact statement (EIS)—which have probably helped the environment in places but have definitely, always, engorged consultants, lawyers and form filler-outers. Unsurprisingly, in the decade of the 1970s, American industrial production stagnated, while lawsuits, as well as other kinds of post-industrial production, expanded.[354] One study found that NEPA documents have mushroomed from a handful of pages in the early '70s to an average of 1626 pages today, even as the litigious process stretches for years.[355] Illustrative of this de-industrialization is Bethlehem Steel, which traced its roots to 1857. For the next century, it provided, the the most literal sense, the sinews of industry; in 1957, it was rated the eleventh-largest company of the Fortune 500.[356] The it fell on hard times, dissolved in 2003. By contrast, Apple, founded in 1976, in now valued at $3 trillion.

---

[354] The website WTF Happened in 1971? Offers charts making this and related points. https://wtfhappenedin1971.com/

[355] Mackenzie, Aidan, and Ruiz, Santi, "No, NEPA really is a problem for clean energy," *Noahpinion*, July 19, 2023. https://bit.ly/43MZPfz

[356] "Fortune 500," 1957 CNN Money https://bit.ly/44e7gg4. Accessed, April 10, 2023.

This shifted environment—from analog to digital, one might say—became all the more clear in 2009, when President Barack Obama persuaded Congress to pass his stimulus package, promising New Deal-ish "shovel ready" projects that would get Americans working and rebuild the nation's infrastructure. Yet the following year, surveying the failure his near trillion-dollar package to stimulate much more than paper-shuffling, Obama sighed, "There's no such thing as shovel-ready projects."[357] And it wasn't just the Obama administration that was flummoxed. Other examples of cost overrunning delays include Boston's ultimately completed Big Dig to California's still (and possibly forever) uncompleted high-speed rail.[358] In 2020, the Heritage Foundation's Diane Katz scorned EIS as "an anachronism that unduly politicizes environmental protection and encourages judicial activism."[359]

To illustrate the continuing naysaying syndrome, on November 13, 2022, the *Washington Post* reported on the new plan of the Federal Railroad Administration, a unit of the Department of Transportation, to remodel Union Station, the Amtrak rail and mass-transit hub serving Washington, DC. The cost would be $10 billion, the *Post* said, and, oh, by the way, the projected finish date is 2040. And of course, that target-date could slip. "Much of the timetable is unclear," the *Post* warned its readers. "The federal environmental review of the project, which began in 2015, is at least three years behind schedule."[360] Such slowness seems strange, given that President Biden declares himself to be the special friend of rail. After all,

[357] Roig-Franzia, Manuel, "Obama Brings 'Shovel-Ready' Talk Into Mainstream," *Washington Post*, January 8, 2009. https://bit.ly/3PrLvp7. See also: Condon, Stephanie, "Obama: 'No Such Thing as Shovel-Ready Projects,'" CBS News, October 13, 2010. https://bit.ly/3NsdTon

[358] "Big Dig Billions Over Budget," *Taxpayers for Common Sense*, April 12, 2000. https://bit.ly/3r8f6tK. See also: Obando, Sebastian, "California's high-speed rail cost rises to $105B, more than double original price," *Construction Dive*, February 15, 2022. https://bit.ly/3Pw5zGI

[359] Katz, Diane, "Curbing Abuses of a Politicized NEPA," Heritage Foundation, August 25, 2020. https://bit.ly/3JzUWyZ

[360] Lazo, Luz, "Union Station in line for $10 billion facelift, but questions remain," *Washington Post*, November 13, 2022. https://bit.ly/3Jz5wWT

as a US senator from Delaware, self-declared "Amtrak Joe" commuted on Amtrak for thirty-six years.[361]

Moreover, rail and mass transit are central to Democratic goals on climate change. That is, if Americans are going to be persuaded to give up their automobiles (which, for reasons of traffic and aesthetics are deemed undesirable, even if they are electric), they will need nice transit alternatives. In a 2019 video, Rep. Alexandria Ocasio-Cortez (D-NY) depicted herself riding happily on Amtrak as she touted the Green New Deal.[362] And the 2020 Democratic platform declared, "We will launch our country's second great railroad revolution by investing in high-speed rail and passenger and freight rail systems, and commit to public transportation as a public good."[363] Yet even with all that enthusiasm for rail and mass transit, Democrats still couldn't see how to complete the Union Station project in less than two decades. With a few exceptions—which we will get to—Democrats have been unwilling, even uninterested, in establishing the sort of Framework that could speed up, even make possible, the projects they say they want.

Once upon a time, things were different. There was, for sure, a Framework around big construction projects. A Democratic president, Franklin D. Roosevelt, oversaw the building of the Pentagon—6.5 million square feet of office space—in just sixteen months. He also oversaw the construction of two oil pipelines, from Texas to the East Coast, each in about a year.[364] And the construction of the Alaska Highway, connecting the lower forty-eight to the future forty-ninth state, carved out of the rug-

[361] Shalvey, Kevin, "Amtrak Joe: A brief look at President Biden's long history of supporting America's railroad," *Business Insider*, April 10, 2021. https://bit.ly/44iBcrI. See also: Yen, Hope, and Woodward, Calvin, "AP Fact Check: Biden tale of Amtrak conductor doesn't add up," Associated Press, October 26, 2021. https://bit.ly/44eaMag

[362] "A Message From the Future With Alexandria Ocasio-Cortez," *Intercept*, 2019. https://bit.ly/3NRBmAZ

[363] "2020 Democratic Platform," The American Presidency Project, University of California Santa Barbara, August 17, 2020. https://bit.ly/3JVdYQL

[364] Palmer, Jerrell Dean and Johnson, John G., "Big Inch and Little Big Inch," Texas State Historical Association, updated June 30, 2023. https://bit.ly/44EHemw

ged Pacific coast, that 1382-mile artery was also built in just seven months. To be sure, those feats of rapid construction were during the emergency of World War II. And yet today's Democrats routinely describe climate change as an emergency. Biden himself says, "Climate change is literally an existential threat to our nation and to the world."[365] Okay, if the matter is that urgent, then one might expect…urgency.

Ironically, some from the post-industrial digital world are now clamoring for a return to the physical. They want to see things built. In 2020, Silicon Valley mogul Marc Andreessen wrote,

> *"Our nation and our civilization were built on production, on building. Our forefathers and foremothers built roads and trains, farms and factories, then the computer, the microchip, the smartphone, and uncounted thousands of other things that we now take for granted, that are all around us, that define our lives and provide for our well-being. There is only one way to honor their legacy and to create the future we want for our own children and grandchildren, and that's to build."*[366]

So will progressive attitudes toward NEPA and associated legalisms change? There's evidence that's happening. Ezra Klein, columnist for the *New York Times*, calls for "liberalism that builds." Shrewdly, Klein has defined the issue in a way friendly to the left—"state capacity." That is, the capacity of the state to build a Framework to build things.[367] Bloomberg's Matthew Yglesias observes, "governments at various levels have opted for over the past half century, regularly prioritizing community input and litigation avoidance over the goal of getting something done quickly." And so, he concluded, "delay is a policy choice." Some elected Democrats are

---

[365] "Remarks by President Biden on Actions to Tackle the Climate Crisis," The White House, July 20, 2022. https://bit.ly/3Pwxzu4

[366] Andreessen, Marc, "It's Time to Build," a16z, April 18, 2020, https://bit.ly/3JA2BNF

[367] Klein, Ezra, "What America Needs Is a Liberalism That Builds," *New York Times*, May 29, 2022. https://bit.ly/3r4Jghv

getting the message about getting things done. The rapid restoration of a fallen bridge on I-95 in Philadelphia—rebuilt in less than two weeks in the Summer of 2023—demonstrates that speediness can also be policy choice. To put that another way, a bad choice that's been made can be unmade. In the mission-critical words of Pennsylvania's Democratic governor, Josh Shapiro, "I hereby suspend the provisions of any other regulatory statue proscribing the procedures for conduct of Commonwealth business, or the orders, rules or regulations of any Commonwealth agency, if strict compliance with the provisions of any statute, order, rules or regulations would in any way prevent, hinder, or delay necessary action in coping with this emergency event."[368] That wasn't so hard. If pols are motivated, a Hamiltonian Framework can be put in place in one quick hurry.[369] Yet we shouldn't gain the impression that NIMBY, NEPA and EIS are always bad for investment. For certain kinds of investment, they're a boost.

MALIBU'S NIMBY INVESTMENT STRATEGY

Its defeat at I-95 notwithstanding, NIMBYism is doing fine in plenty of places, especially when it's linked to induced scarcity, aka, property protectionism. For instance, there's Malibu, California, where a relative handful of existing property owners have cornered the market on oceanfront real estate. Back in 1892, Malibu land sold for $10 an acre. But the population of Los Angeles County was only around 100,000. Then came Hollywood, aerospace, and suburbia. By 1950, the county's population had surged to more than four million. Yet here's the thing—during that time, the population of Malibu didn't change much. It was still in the low thousands. All those miles of oceanfront, and so few people. How'd that happen? The answer, of course, was that Malibu directed—more like

---

[368] Mackenzie, Aidan, "Can I-95's Repairs Teach Us to Build Faster?" Institute for Progress, July 7, 2023. https://bit.ly/3PIKGIJ

[369] In 2023, bipartisan lawmakers put forth the Building Chips in America Act, which would suspend NEPA for computer-chip manufacturers. The argument was simple. We want computer chips to be made in America. And soon.

shunted—development away from its sandy and foamy stretch of paradise, making that which was already there worth all the more. Shrewdly, Malibu made itself into its own district, upping its just-for-us exclusivity. According to one chronicler, "The Colony soon had its own police force, courthouse, grocery, post office, and general store, giving the most famous one-mile stretch of beach in the country the outlines of a small town, albeit one whose gate was guarded at all times by armed patrolmen."[370] Want to keep developers, and everyone else, at bay? Have your own armed guard!

In 1962, the City of Los Angeles decided to build a nuclear power plant in Malibu, and a newly formed group, Malibu Citizens for Conservation, fought it off. Interestingly, one of the leaders of the group was a highly situational conservationist, the president of Richfield Oil, which is now, a few mergers later, part of BP.[371] In that same decade, the Colony fought off a housing plan that would have increased Malibu's population to 400,000.[372] To gain still more autonomy, Malibu made itself a city in 1991. And in 2014, a well funded coalition—including Steven Spielberg, Tom Hanks, James Cameron, Barbra Streisand, and Rob Reiner—helped to vote down, by a wide margin, a referendum allowing chain stores. Asked if he was a NIMBY, Reiner was frank: "This is 100 per cent Nimbyism. Everybody who lives here is concerned about their way of life. That's Nimbyism writ large, baby...Not in my back yard! You bet!"[373] Today, Malibu's population is barely more than 10,000, and yet its few-but-affluent residents ably defend their grip on twenty-one miles of coastline, while the other 20 million people in the greater metro area look on. So the "Malibu Protection Plan" is working. Aside from eyepopping prices for estates with

---

[370] Meares, Hadley, "How Malibu Grew," *LA Curbed*, November 21, 2018. https://bit.ly/440Zu9I

[371] Wellock, Thomas Raymond, *Critical Masses: Opposition to Nuclear Power in California, 1958-1978.* (Madison: University of Wisconsin Press, 1998), 62-64

[372] "Malibu Development Battles," *Los Angeles Times*, February 12, 2015. https://bit.ly/46lBrE7

[373] Allen, Nick, "Malibu at war over celebrity Nimbyism," *Telegraph*, October 28, 2014. https://bit.ly/3XGVOI9

breathtaking views, prices for just an acre of land that's zoned residential run in the millions.

We could read the same script, starring other luxury reserves, across the country. They all have the same plot—mandate scarcity. Investors dream of some sort of "moat" around their investment. In Malibu, they've dug a good one. For all the talk of "character," "traffic," and "more study needed," there's a voice that says, "If you don't build it, they *won't* come." Malibuers hear that, loud and clear—exclusivity makes property worth more. NIMBYism is a proven price raiser.

INVESTMENT TAKEAWAYS

- Beginning with the Trump administration, and carrying over into the Biden years, thinking among the elites, in both parties, shifted on domestic industry. Before 2017, the exodus of American factories was generally seen as somewhere between inevitable and desirable. Inevitable because that's how globalism was deemed to work, and desirable because manufacturing brings unwanted externalities—and besides, things were cheaper if they were made in China. During that time, as we have seen, Bethlehem Steel rusted, while Apple blossomed. The friendly trend was digital, or financial, not industrial. And investments reflected that. Then came Donald Trump, putting a sledgehammer to that consensus, and unfriending its trends. Trump demonstrated that there was, in fact, a substantial constituency for re-industrialization. Love him or hate him, Trump was a trend-shaper on trade. Since then, Democrats have become more hawkish on trade, especially with China. Moreover, Democrats such as Josh Shapiro have shown their willingness to challenge the NEPA/NIMBY regime for the sake of the economy and, well, normalcy. So this could be a new trend. The US will probably never again see huge factories with tens of thousands of workers in them, but we could see huge factories with thousands of robots. That prospect has vast investment implications…assuming, that is, the trend continues. We can say of any trend, there are no lost causes, and no won causes. As the Greeks said, the world is matter in motion, and it can flow one way, or it can flow the other way. It's just a question of the correlation of forces. Who's for it, who's against it, and then who wins—more on politics in Chapter Sixteen.

- In 2020, Elon Musk weighed in, opining, "In the United States especially, there's an over allocation of talent in finance and law. Basically too many smart people go into finance and law."[374] In 2023, he further elaborated, "Major misallocation of capital imo [in my opinion]….Not enough talent in manufacturing & heavy industries." Continuing, he added, "It's silly to have 10 talented entrepreneurs all chase same SaaS [software as a service] niche when they could be epically successful in heavy industry."[375] The owner of Twitter, now X, boasts more than 170 million followers on his site. Will his voice be heard nationwide? Or has he gotten himself so pegged as a tribune of Red that's he's a pariah to Blue? The answer to those questions could speak loudly to whether re-industrialization is regional, or national, or happens at all.

- One thing's for sure. Some parts of the US are no more interested in factories—or for that matter, much of any kind of economic development if it involves more people—today than they were in the pre-Trump era. In fact, following the rule of schismogenesis, their hostility to anything Trumpy might make them *more* NIMBY. In any case, NIMBYism is a proven investment strategy, and proven strategies never go out of style. Yet at the same time, there will also always be YIMBYs—Yes In My Back Yard. As we know, multiple paradigms can coexist. The trick is to know which is which—and in which Direction.

---

[374] Bursztynsky, Jessica, "Elon Musk: 'Too many smart people go into finance and law,'" CNBC, May 7, 2020. https://bit.ly/3Xre0oK
[375] Musk, Elon (@elonmusk), X, April 9, 2023. https://bit.ly/3CPOgJs

CHAPTER TEN

CUI BONO?
IDENTIFYING DIRECTIONAL
INVESTMENT

NAMING THE NAME

Some might say that what's described here, Directional Investing, is not new. And that's true, it's not. Indeed, it's fair to say that every dollar, and every bit of value, anywhere, has been a part of someone's plan. That is, it's already an investment.

However, the actual Directional nature of investment is little discussed. Why is this dollar here? And not there? How to optimize Direction going forward? One reason why such questions aren't much discussed is that those in the know aren't inclined to talk. After all, a good investment strategy is best kept to one's self. If everyone knows about it, it's not valuable. We can compare this point, about investment strategies, to trade secrets. Over the ages, plenty of people figured out better techniques of doing something—from stonecutting to winemaking to horse-breeding to financial engineering—and kept that better technique to themselves. Who knows what strong techniques are still held in secret—or which ones might have died out over the ages, because somebody forgot, and nobody wrote them down. In any case, the best strategies, like the best conspiracies, are those we've never heard of. And sometimes, too, an idea can seem so obvious that nobody bothers to record it—they just do it. As English majors joke, "I didn't realize that I'd been speaking in prose all my life." Prose, of course, being everyday speech.

Still, Confucius was right—it's useful to give things names, as the beginning of greater wisdom. The Master declared 2500 years ago that if were in charge of the kingdom, his most urgent task would be "to rectify names." He explained, "If names are not right then speech does not accord with things; if speech is not in accord with things, then affairs cannot be successful."[376] So with that Confucian injunction in mind, let's name some contemporary examples of Directionality, even if they might choose not to speak for themselves.

We've already considered Alexander Hamilton, that great Directional Investor, and we've even allowed that Thomas Jefferson, too, in his way, was Directional. In fact, buying Louisiana was perhaps the best investment ever. But some directed investments might be grimmer. For example, there's the idea that wars are started, or at least promoted, by arms manufacturers, aka "merchants of death," seeking to profit from weapons sales. One such character, from fiction, is Daddy Warbucks, from the comic strip Little Orphan Annie.[377] To cite a more recent war, we can pause over this 2023 headline, "Ukraine War is great for the portfolio, as defense stocks enjoy a banner year."[378] And for the ultimate in evilly amoral directionality, small "d," we can look to this headline: "Hamas may have profited from Oct. 7 assault with informed trading."[379] The allegation: short-selling the

---

[376] Confucius, *Analects*, 13.3.
[377] From 1934 to 1936, Sen. Gerald P. Nye of North Dakota led Congress to a directional accusation. "The long exhaustive investigation ... produced a sordid report of intrigues and bribery; of collusion and excessive profits; of war scares artificially fostered and [disarmament] conferences deliberately wrecked." See Detzer, Dorothy, *Appointment on the Hill* (New York: Henry Holt, 1948), 169-171.
[378] Clifton, Eli, "Ukraine War is great for the portfolio, as defense stocks enjoy a banner year," *Responsible Statecraft*, February 24, 2023. https://bit.ly/44lyjq8
[379] "Hamas may have profited from Oct. 7 assault with informed trading — study," *Times of Israel*, December 4, 2023. https://tinyurl.com/czm6r6tm

Israeli stock market. For sure, the military-industrial complex and high (or low) finance deserve scrutiny. But there could be more directionality in other places, too.

For instance, did Big Pharma plot to make the COVID virus worse in order to sell more medicines and vaccines?[380] In 2023, one Jordon Trishton Walker, apparently an executive at Pfizer, spoke to a hidden camera of "directed evolution."[381] That's sort of close to Directional Investment—unless, of course, it's an unethical conspiracy, in which case we denounce it. We can leave it to the satire site Babylon Bee to blare the unproven suspicion, "Pfizer Pleased To Announce Their New Vaccine 90% Effective Against New Virus They Created."[382]

Yet it is for sure true that Big Health is committed to new vaccines, to the point where the plan seems to be that everyone should get a shot every year.[383] Is that a good idea? A bad idea? It depends on who you ask. One who's skeptical is hedge funder Bill Ackman. He argues that vaccines are a loophole in the Food and Drug Administration's regulatory regime, and through that loophole, Big Pharma has stampeded cash-cows. That is, in contrast to other pharma drugs, the FDA rushes vaccines to approval, and then the federal government urges, perhaps even mandates, that everyone get vaccinated. Furthermore, the feds pay for vaccinations and then shield the drug companies from liability.[384] Whether or not the argument is fairly put, that's a formula for profitability.

[380] "Rubio Sends Letter to Pfizer CEO on Alleged Gain-of-Function Research," Sen. Marco Rubio, January 26, 2023. https://bit.ly/431sL2E
[381] "Pfizer Executive: 'Mutate' COVID via 'Directed Evolution' for Company to Continue Profiting Off of Vaccines," Project Veritas, January 25, 2023. https://bit.ly/3NQGR2S
[382] The Babylon Bee, (@Babylon Bee), X, January 29, 2023 https://bit.ly/44lyfqo
[383] Diamond, Dan, "White House launching $5 billion program to speed coronavirus vaccines," Washington Post, April 10, 2023. https://bit.ly/3D6ub1j
[384] Ackman, Bill (@BillAckman), X, July 5, 2023. https://bit.ly/43e4N4F

THE SECRET OF DIRECTIONAL INVESTING

FREQUENTLY ASKED QUESTIONS

So let's pause for some FAQs about Directional Investing:

Is it...*corrupt*? Here we can once again distinguish between trend-*spotting* and trend-*shaping*. Trend-spotting is just observation, of say, the red-blue split. Playing it as it lays. Nothing wrong with that. Trend-shaping, the way Alexander Hamilton did it, was above board. In President Washington's cabinet, he said America needed to industrialize, and the country, after a time, agreed. Was there corruption along the path to industrialization? Of course. But there's corruption along the way of everything—and yet if it's a good idea, it should continue, even as prosecutors perform cleanup. What distinguishes trend-shaping Directional Investing—capital "D," capital "I"—is that it aims honestly to gain public support for the plan. That's not goody-goody, that's practicality, striving toward long-term sustainability. Support for the railroads in the nineteenth century, or for automobile roads in the twentieth century, was real and genuine. To be sure, sly special interests abounded in both industries (as they do in all industries), and yet for the most part, the policy discussion was open and above-board. Everybody knew what was going on, and they had a chance to vote and otherwise make themselves heard. In those days, rails and roads were popular; that's why we got so much of both. And when rails and roads became *less* popular, we got *less* of both. We can see, there's always an interplay between Jeffersonian Liberty and the Hamiltonian Framework. People freely and Jeffersonian-ly decide to pursue a certain course of action, and then a Hamiltonian Framework comes into place to make it so. And then, perhaps, Jeffersonian populism takes some of it away. So now, in our time, political leaders and investors can think about the Frameworks they might wish to pitch. And then the public process of consideration—politics and markets, both—will begin.

Hmm. Big shots in on it together? So maybe Directional Investing is... *corporatist*? Even...*fascist*? Nope and nope. Directional Investment is open about its goals and thrives on time-tested constitutional mechanisms. To be sure, there's a presumption of expertise here—and that expertise is often clustered at the top. But history proves that voters don't mind being led by smart people, so long as they're not snobby. Elected officials who seek a mandate, all the while respecting the values and interests of their constituents, will find that they have a lot of leeway to get things done.

So is Directional Investing some sort of... *runaway privatization scheme*? Yes, it's partial privatization, in the sense that it sees private enterprise as the prime motor of progress, but it's the opposite of runaway. It's actually constrained, in ways that Polanyi, Hamilton, and Walt Disney would recognize. As with the railroads in the 19th century, or Florida's Reedy Creek Improvement District, it's the free market in a defined Framework, for a designated purpose.

So is Directional Investment... *insider trading*? Actually, if anything, it's outsider trading. Directional Investing, in its trend-spotting mode, is about watching the world go by—and making money as it goes. Directional Investing, in its trend-shaping mode, includes building public support for ambitious projects. And, in the course of generating wealth for the commonwealth, making money for one's self. This is not a book for crooked schemers, although it certainly takes note of crooked schemes—pointing out their limitations.

Okay, so is it... *cronyism*? Answer: Cronyism is a slur, aiming to slug the argument. But if we define cronies as friends, then we could say that Directional Investment is friendly. After all, not many collaborative deals get done with strangers. There's usually some degree of schmoozing, first. So perhaps developmentalism should really be called, "Rotarianism"—as in the Rotary Club, the civic and social group that was into networking before networking was cool. Friendly networks are simply how the world works, and today, of course, much of that friendliness has migrated online, most notably to LinkedIn.

CASE STUDIES IN CUI BONO

So let's consider some sightings of Directionality, answering the ancient question, cui bono—"who benefits?" Peter Thiel slyly suggests that the federal student loan program—which is now measured in the trillions—is actually a real estate hustle. He writes, "If you analyze the universities in economic terms, you might even conclude that the dorms and residences are the profit center driving an elaborate real-estate racket."[385] Thiel might have been thinking, perhaps, of the University of Kentucky. *The Wall Street Journal* describes how the school spent $3.66 billion on its Lexington campus. The improvements included "new homes for the law, business and visual-arts schools, state-of-the-art hospital facilities, a student center, a 900-spot parking garage, a theater for videogame competitions and dorms sporting full-size Tempur-Pedic mattresses, granite countertops and in-unit washer-dryers."[386]

Speaking of real estate, one has to wonder, is the value wipeout of America's downtowns in the early 2020s really just as simple as toxic politics? What caused the "politicide" of, first, lockdowns and, second, letting criminals and crazies run wild in the streets? To be sure, the trend toward working from home has also been an important factor, and yet the drop-off in the '20s has been so staggering that one wonders, is there some force, perhaps a financial force, directing the political craziness that led to the economic carnage? In 2023 New York-based real estate scholars Arpit Gupta and Stijn Van Nieuwerburgh reported that commercial real estate in their city had fallen as much as 45 percent.[387] Said one Wall Street

---

[385] Thiel, Peter, "The diversity myth," *The New Criterion,* June 2023. https://bit.ly/3PJp8Ma

[386] Korn, Melissa, et al. "Colleges Spend Like There's No Tomorrow. 'These Places Are Just Devouring Money,'" *The Wall Street Journal,* August 10, 2023. https://tinyurl.com/4kmjbhxk

[387] Gupta, Arpit, and Van Nieuwerburgh, Stijn, "The real estate industry is at risk. Here's how to soften the blow," *Washington Post,* May 22, 2023. https://bit.ly/46V3WJa

real-estate banker, "My clients are scared shitless."[388] Hudson Yards, a high-end development in Manhattan, was staring into the abyss of a 50 percent vacancy and a 50 percent fall in prices and rents.[389] *New York* magazine's cover punned "Worth Less" and "Worthless," referring to New *Glut* City.[390]

The same has held true on the other coast. In Los Angeles, property giant Brookfield shuddered when the value of its downtown office buildings had fallen by more than 80 percent.[391] "We're at the point here where the Z [zombie] Apocalypse has started," said one LA real estate hand.[392] Also in 2023, a twenty-two story San Francisco office building sold for a whopping 75 percent less than its pre-pandemic value, while other companies, across the country, are simply walking away from their property, giving the keys back to the bank.[393] Where will it end? According to one fintech chief, "The top 5 percent of office buildings will be resilient and still able to select tenants. For the bottom 95 percent, people are going to have to figure out how to reposition those buildings. They're going to have to figure out how to rezone, convert, or they're just going to have to be willing to sell at a pretty significant loss."[394]

There's something happening here. Even if, according to the '60s song lyric, what it is, ain't exactly clear. Yet still, as we sort through the forensics of these trillions in losses, we might perhaps see the outlines of a giant short. That is, the silhouette of someone, or something, selling what it does

[388] Cohan, William D. "Fade to Blackstone," *Puck*, May 17, 2023. https://bit.ly/44iie4K

[389] Clarke, Katherine, "The Luxury Tower Built for New York's Elite Still Sits Half Empty," *The Wall Street Journal*, July 13, 2023. https://bit.ly/43qbl06

[390] Rice, Andrew, "New Glut City," *New York*, July 17, 2023. https://bit.ly/3De3iJ8

[391] Hoffman, Liz, "Leaning towers: Office-building loans are looking shaky," *Semafor*, April 11, 2023. https://bit.ly/44y7Wgu

[392] Gittelsohn, John, "Downtown LA's Office Distress Shows Pain Coming for Cities," Bloomberg News, May 24, 2023. https://bit.ly/44cZDHp

[393] Ohanian, Lee, "San Francisco Falls Further into the Abyss as Office Values Plunge 75 Percent," Hoover Institution, May 16, 2023. https://bit.ly/3O1j7co. See also: Valinsky, Jordan, "San Francisco Hilton investor will stop making loan payments," CNN, June 6, 2023 https://bit.ly/3pxd9qf

[394] Hoffman, Liz, *Semafor Business*, July 11, 2023. https://bit.ly/44HjC0u

doesn't own, with the plan of buying it back later at a lower price. So who's famous for executing shorts? One famed short-player is George Soros. Back in 1992, he profited mightily from shorting the British pound.[395] Indeed, in the course of his long life, Soros has made tens of billions—and has given away $32 billion.[396] It's an interesting way to play, giving, with one hand and investing, with the other. It's sometimes called "philanthrocapitalism."

Yet with that word in mind, we can note Soros' involvement in financing the political campaigns of "restorative justice" prosecutors, whose tenure always seems to lead to higher crime rates.[397] In fact, across the US, Soros has given hundreds of millions, if not billions, to support progressive—many would say pro-criminal—policies.[398] Given Soros' track record as a master macro strategist, we might wonder, is it possible that there's investing going on here, alongside the giving? Could donating and moneymaking be tied together? Soros himself wrote in 2009, "In the course of my life, I have developed a conceptual framework which has helped me both to make money as a hedge fund manager and to spend money as a policy oriented philanthropist."[399] So the two go together as "philanthrocapitalism." That sounds kind of directional.

Without a doubt, it takes some special way of looking at the world to think that criminals need freedom, and that it's a good idea to use tax dollars to distribute free crack pipes and other drug paraphernalia.[400] Some

[395] Beattie, Andrew, "How Did George Soros Break the Bank of England?" *Investopedia*, updated July 10, 2023. https://bit.ly/44ayYuR

[396] "The Open Society Foundations and George Soros," Open Society Foundation, October 12, 2023. https://osf.to/3N7bb8k

[397] Hinton, Rachel, "Another billionaire weighs in on state's attorney's race: George Soros gives $2M to group backing Foxx," *Chicago Sun-Times*, February 20, 2020. https://bit.ly/3JRC5zK

[398] Soros, George, "Why I Support Reform Prosecutors," *The Wall Street Journal*, July 31, 2022. https://bit.ly/44cY0th

[399] Soros, George, "General Theory of Reflexivity," *The Financial Times*, October 26, 2009. https://bit.ly/3XQRBBn

[400] Morphet, Jack, and Fitz-Gibbon, Jorge, "NYC vending machines cater to drug users with free crack pipes, lip balm—and Narcan for ODs," *New York Post*, June 5, 2023. https://bit.ly/3JLjgOn

suggest that it's simply misanthropic malice. Elon Musk tweeted of Soros, "He wants to erode the very fabric of civilization. Soros hates humanity."[401] That's one answer. But perhaps we just haven't sussed out the directionality here. We've already noted, in Chapter Six, the arbitrage inherent in the fall of real estate prices in downtown San Francisco compared to the rise in prices elsewhere in the city. So has someone already done this arb? Including, possibly too, an arbitrage that goes short on retail stocks, hit hard by the crime wave, and long on e-commerce stocks, which have done better? In 2023, *The Wall Street Journal* reported on financial players betting against urban paper, not just municipal bonds, but also REITs (real estate investment trusts) and commercial mortgage-backed securities. Okay, that much makes sense, given what we've seen. And yet if something goes down, oftentimes, something else goes up. The *Journal* quoted one analyst saying, "The suburbs are going to be one of the big winners in this."[402] So maybe the force causing the fall is also reaping the rise.

We might further speculate: Maybe the crime wave is a way of washing out incumbent property owners. If urban valuations go low enough, could that be the moment financial players *spot* the bottom and start buying? Notably, the physical city of San Francisco—classy structures on steep hills, surrounded by water on three sides—would have a bright future under better management. Maybe the new owners will *shape* the glorious future history of San Francisco. After all, geeky investors know the city is home to Starfleet Command in *Star Trek*.

In fact, as soon as 2023, the techtropolis was making a comeback. Salesorce's Marc Benioff tweeted, "San Francisco is the #1 AI City! SF will soon be sold out again! Never seen commercial real estate leasing at this rate. # of companies looking for huge amounts of space is incredible.

[401] Musk, Elon (@elonmusk), X, May 15, 2023. https://bit.ly/3pATTrL
[402] Gillers, Heather, "Wall Street Sours on America's Downtowns," *The Wall Street Journal*, June 20, 2023. https://bit.ly/3CXYt6D

'AI companies seek up to 1 million square feet of office space in the city, according to JLL [Jones Lang Lasalle].'"[403]

One thing San Francisco has taught us: It's not hard to squelch squalor. In September 2023, authorities swept part of the city clean for Benioff's Dreamforce convention, and swept even more of it clean for the APEC meeting two months later.[404] Happily, the criminals who have been marauding the city are not the high-tech virtuosos of, say, *Neuromancer*. In fact they are so low-tech that even medium-tech puts a quick stop to them. Muggers, shoplifters, drug dealers, and carjackers don't stand a chance against beefed up security, including surveillance cameras, many of which, thanks to a tech donor, are already in place.[405] This security can be further strengthened by facial- and gait-recognition technology, as well as cellphone tracking (an obvious solution authorities have shied away from, fearful of backlash).

But what about all the office buildings? Even if law and order were restored, would people want to commute back to work on the thirty-fourth floor? Perhaps not. According to one report, the percentage of workers in the office full time actually fell during 2023, from 49 in the first quarter to 42 in the second quarter.[406] Perhaps the story of AI workers shunning buildings tells us something about the future, as well as, of course, that AI might wipe out much office work.

If so, that's sad news for office building owners. And yet we should all realize that commercial buildings don't stay the same for very long, anyway. Applying our Peter Lynch-type powers of observation, we have all seen

---

[403] Benioff, Marc (@Benioff), X, September 29, 2023, https://tinyurl.com/yc2h3c39

[404] Novet, Jordan, and Levy, Ari, "Salesforce CEO says Dreamforce is staying in San Francisco after reaching deal with mayor," CNBC, November 7, 2023, https://tinyurl.com/mr435y6r

[405] Lapowsky, Issie, "Ripple's chairman funded a 1,000-camera surveillance network. Now SFPD can watch it," *Protocol*, September 23, 2022. https://www.protocol.com/policy/sfpd-cameras

[406] Samuels, Alana, "Return-to-Office Full Time Is Losing. Hybrid Work Is On the Rise," *Time*, May 19, 2023. https://tinyurl.com/vdnzj8p7

that most buildings are remodeled, rewired, rehabbed, overhauled, gutted, or demolished every few decades. One study found, for example, that the average chain drugstore location lasts a mere twenty-four years.[407] There's always some defect, some new need, that requires "creative destruction." This has been just the normal churn of the march of time, as well as the march of progress. Indeed, as we think about office buildings, we can think about shopping centers. Long before COVID and crime, couch based e-commerce took its toll. Hundreds of malls had been decommissioned. In fact, the US has had five times as much brick-and-mortar retail—square feet measured against population—as Europe.[408] That's evidence of serious bubbling, and bubbles have a way of popping. So office buildings could be next. As we have seen, they're all due for a rendezvous with reconstruction of some kind—it just might be more drastic, that's all. But what about landmarks? What about, say, the Chrysler Building? Someone will eventually figure out something good to with must-keep edifices. Perhaps they'll become luxury hospitals—every patient gets his or her own floor!—or perhaps homeless shelters, or sanctuaries, or vertical farms, or, who knows, book depositories. As with all the many empty cathedrals of Europe, they might keep their fancy artwork and become new kinds of shrines, or perhaps hubs for living, lifestyling, and partying—including spooky tours, epic climbing, and even more epic rappelling. That doesn't guarantee that these edifices will have anything close to their old value, but then, we can't always get what we want.

INVESTMENT TAKEAWAYS

- Directional Investment with a capital "D" and a capital "I" displays, as Thomas Jefferson wrote in the Declaration of Independence, a

[407] Feldstein, Stuart A. "Age of U.S. Commercial Buildings," SMR Research, accessed July 13, 2023. https://bit.ly/3JZ2Hi9
[408] Bain, Marc, "America's vast swaths of retail space have become a burden in the age of e-commerce," *Quartz*, July 19, 2017. https://bit.ly/46yMYQx

"decent respect for the opinions of mankind." That is, whatever the relevant audience—in the case of the United States, the American people—Directional Investment strives to show that it's in the public interest. And strives, furthermore, to be duly rewarded for its actions on behalf of the public interest. That's how Americans roll. To be sure, there's an infinity of stealthy ploys that may be small "d" directional, but they aren't as good. Yes, they may be quick-score enriching, but they can't be as long-term rewarding, for the simple reason that they don't last as long. And at the risk of sounding sappy, we can say something that's true—most people, including investors, wish to be thought of as good, not bad.

- In this chapter, we've devoted much attention to cities, which are, of course, the greatest repositories of wealth. So it's worth noting that one of the hottest urban trends is the "electronic cottage" that Alvin Toffler wrote about four decades ago. It's the pre-modern idea of living and working in a cozy village, with, of course, a post-modern digital twist. From an investment point of view, whoever can make life easier for these e-villagers will be rewarded. For instance, one trend is the "15-Minute City," which holds that a city dweller ought to be able to get to anything necessary for work, life, or play, within fifteen minutes—ideally, by walking or bicy-cling. All this opens up opportunities for trend-shaping, as well as trend-spotting. For instance, who will provide the curbed bike lanes that makes bicycling safe? Who's going to ban cars in some places? And undertake all the other changes needed for maximum micro-mobility? The dollar opportunities are macro. To be sure, the "15-Minute City" is a mortal threat to the old idea of commut-ing to a distant downtown. To which "15-Minuteers," pioneering this new lifestyle, say, in effect, "That's okay, we want to evolve."[409]

---

[409] Rogger, Caitlin, "Downtown DC's recovery hinges on one word," *Greater Greater Washington*, May 18, 2023. https://bit.ly/43fSuo8

- We might ask the analytical question put forth by management guru Peter Drucker: "If we did not already do this, would we go into it now?"[410] This "Drucker Test" can be applied to office space: Will they ever again seem like a good idea? In that clarifying spirit, New York City real estate mogul Scott Rechler says he is engaging in "Project Kodak," after the fallen film and camera company. Buildings he rates as worth saving are labeled "digital," whereas duds are dubbed "film." That's a hard-nosed thought process that appears to condemn 70 percent of the office space in New York City.[411] Yes, human nature is cyclical, and that might argue for a swing back to office working. But technology is cumulative, and that suggests that intensely verticalized white-collar work will go the way of whale oil. People still wish to cluster, but they'll likely do it in some place other than a cube farm.

- Having said all this about office buildings, creative destruction brings new energy, and puts new life into old forms. As Daniel Bell wrote back in 1976, "the repudiation of institutions" opens up "an enlarged repertoire of mankind ... from which individuals can draw, in a renewable fashion, to remold an aesthetic experience."[412] Cities have been compared to furnaces, millions of people firing each other up, new ideas being forged. So it's likely that many cities can reposition themselves, post white-collar towers, gaining new culture and so retaining their economic vitality. This is already working in many places, where devastated downtowns coexist with energized residential areas. *The Wall Street Journal* caught the contrast, of high-vacancy downtown and the high-vitality nearby, saying "Anyone walking through New York's Jackson Heights or Silver Lake in Los Angeles looking for a deserted hellscape will

---

[410] Drucker, Peter, *The Effective Executive*, (New York: HarperCollins, 2006), 104
[411] Rice, Andrew, "New Glut City," *New York*, July 17, 2023. https://bit.ly/3De3iJ8
[412] Bell, Daniel, *Cultural Contradictions*, 13-18.

be disappointed."[413] It's the neighborhoods that now function as distributed economic engines—distributed, say, between the sofa, the backyard, and the nearest Starbucks—stabilizing urban economies.[414]

- Real estate experts Gupta and Van Nieuwerburgh advocate federal funding "to encourage the conversion of brown offices to green apartments."[415] They add hopefully, "Such programs would pay for themselves." It's fair to say that supporters of just about every government program say it will pay for itself. Sadly, that's not always the case. Still, in 2023, the Democratic leaders of both chambers of Congress, the House and Senate, were from New York City. With that much political power on the side of Gotham and other blue dots, there'll be action to save cities. Red might not go for it, but Blue will. In fact, investors may have already gotten the message that a salvific Framework is being put in place. In the five years, 2018 to mid-2023, the stock price of real estate colossus Vornado, headquartered and heavily invested in Manhattan, fell by more than 70 percent. Yet in the second half of 2023, Vornado rose sharply.

- For reasons seen, San Francisco probably has more economic resiliency than any city in America—and perhaps the world. Yet the sort of tech destined to make that city safer could be scaled widely. For instance, a license-plate-reading camera in Beverly Hills ID'd an alleged serial killer.[416] In fact, the scarier the status

---

[413] Putzier, Konrad, and King, Kate, "American Cities Are Starting to Thrive Again. Just Not Near Office Buildings." *The Wall Street Journal*, May 30, 2023. https://bit.ly/3r2VUxh

[414] Fahey, Ashley, "Emptying offices alone not expected to dry up city coffers, S&P Global finds," *Business Journals*, June 26, 2023. https://bit.ly/3pnTusz

[415] Gupta, Arpit, and Van Nieuwerburgh, Stijn, "The real estate industry is at risk. Here's how to soften the blow," *Washington Post*, May 22, 2023, https://bit.ly/46V3WJa

[416] Pulliam, Tim, "Beverly Hills license plate reader used in capture of murder suspect draws mixed reviews," ABC7, December 4, 2023. https://tinyurl.com/ms9m842f

quo, the better the market for new tech. Thousands of police and fire departments have partnered with Amazon Ring; as a further public-safety measure, some cities are even giving the tiny cameras to away to their residents.[417] So the crime plague could be reversed, quicker than a pixel. If so, exciting prospects for real estate.

- Not every city will stay strong, or even alive. With evolution comes devolution, and even, extinction. In the 1950s and '60s, "white flight" robbed the cities of much of their working and middle class—and some cities never recovered. Meanwhile, suburbs boomed, with lots of money being made in the construction of all those tract homes. Then, beginning in the 1980s, in some cities, gentrification set in, and crime fell, and so billions and trillions of wealth was either traded or created. But in the mid 2010s, crime started to rise again, and gentrification looked iffier.

- The Big Sort is being seen in the cities, as some conurbations have not seen much of the recent ebb. According to *The Financial Times*, "Many parts of the west and the south—such as Nashville, Dallas, Austin, Raleigh and Phoenix—are thriving, and indeed sucking people away from cities elsewhere. Americans are being attracted to them because they offer warmer weather, lower real estate prices, and low taxes."[418]

- As for surveillance tech, which will be essential in any crime turnaround, it's worth recalling that back in 1972, the science-fiction writer Larry Niven envisioned drones as a crime control device— he called them "copseyes."[419] A reminder—tech-minded sci-fi can be a great source of insight into future Directional opportunities.

---

[417] McCollum, Rod, "Do Video Doorbells Really Help to Deter Crime?" *Undark*, December 4, 2023. https://tinyurl.com/2nu3cmty

[418] Editorial, "The risk of an urban doom loop for America's old-line cities," *The Financial Times*, May 1, 2023. https://bit.ly/3JwQkto

[419] Niven, Larry, "Cloak of Anarchy," LarryNiven.net https://bit.ly/3Oek9St

CHAPTER ELEVEN

ENERGY EVERYWHERE ALL AT ONCE

In the previous chapter, we considered Directional Investment as an honest attempt to synthesize Jeffersonian Liberty with the Hamiltonian Framework. But what about *dishonest* attempts? What about honest attempts that nevertheless prove to be failures? How, exactly, do we judge? In the yeasty world of human paradigms, there are no "correct" answers. There's just what people choose, through the market and also through politics. As different as they are, those two forces can never be fully separated.

With that in mind, we can consider the fate of different energy sources, investments—and environmental outcomes—as described in a November 2023 news article in *The Wall Street Journal*: "Offshore wind projects are being scrapped, and renewable-energy companies' share prices are tanking. In the U.S., automakers are reining in electric-vehicle plansas demand falters. Meanwhile, the oil-and-gas industry is embarking on a round of megadeals enabled by soaring profits and is pushing more forcefully the idea that fossil fuels will be around for a long time yet." The *Journal* added, "Climate-warming carbon emissions are expected to climb to a record this year."[420] The following month came a report from *Politico* on the COP 28

---

[420] Dvorak, Phred, "The Path to Green Energy Is Getting Messier," The Wall Street Journal, November 13, 2023. https://tinyurl.com/yfbhtutt

climate conference in Dubai, headlined, "Open secret at climate talks: The top temperature goal is mostly gone"[421]

It's plain: The whole strategy of "decarbonization"—of the atmosphere and of the economy—that the greens have been pursuing for decades is sputtering. This approach, opposing carbon fuels while supporting renewables, is simply *ineffective*.

The result is a shifting in the conventional wisdom, which will, in turn help shape the paradigm of energy/environmental policymaking and moneymaking. We're *not* going green in the way that Al Gore or John Kerry (and many other investors) had hoped. Instead, we're going "all of the above." That is, three (and perhaps more) types of energy paradigms, will likely coexist—green, oil/natural gas (and perhaps cleaned-up coal), and nuclear. We might call it *e pluribus trio*. All three energy "silos" will be searching, of course, for Frameworks, but most likely, none will get the benefit of a worldwide Framework to the exclusion of the others. The energy paradigms will have to coexist. That might be bad news for producers of any one category of energy, but it's good news for energy consumers. And as we shall see, it's still possible to decarbonize the atmosphere.

In the meantime, we'll likely see energy abundance. That's good because civilization, as it advances, is voracious for energy. Back in 1943, anthropologist Leslie A. White explained, "Everything in the universe may be described in terms of energy." He added, "Other things being equal, the degree of cultural development varies directly as the amount of energy per capita per year harnessed and put to work."[422] To illustrate, in 1800, the world consumed an estimated 5.6 thousand terawatt hours (TWh). By 1900, energy consumption had more than doubled, to 12.1 thousand TWh. But by 2021, it exceeded 176 thousand TWh.[423]

---

[421] Harvey, Chelsea "Open secret at climate talks: The top temperature goal is mostly gone," *Politico*, December 3, 2023 https://bit.ly/4a4XS2d

[422] White, Leslie A., "Energy and the Evolution of Culture," *American Anthropologist*, July-September 1943. https://bit.ly/3JwXwWl

[423] Ritchie, Hannah, et al., "Global Energy Consumption," Our World in Data, July 10, 2020. https://bit.ly/3CN6XNH

This ever-increasing need for energy undercuts the stance of those Malthusians we might dub to be green traditionalists. That is, those romantics who yearn for a simpler, lower-tech life. Although, of course, "simpler" really means poorer. Society-wide, the traditionalist position is, simply not viable. Yes, of course, a few people might wish to live closer to nature and to nature's deities. They will be noisy, but not numerous.[424] But as a civilization, we're not going to cut back on energy. Even if more people install solar panels on their homes or ride bicycles, we'll always be consuming more energy through the use of old and new energy sucks—air conditioning, digital assistants, AI, and perhaps cryptocurrencies. So with this energy hunger in mind, let's look at the circumstances under which one kind, or another kind, of energy might be chosen.

THE TEN-STRIKE TEST

When it comes to choosing something, venture capitalist Peter Thiel makes the point that for a new thing to be adopted, it must be ten times better than the thing that went before it.[425] If we think about epic big-delta, big-alpha technologies—fire, the wheel, the plow, the printing press—they all fell into the 10x (or better) category. So it's easy to see why they were adopted. More recently, railroads, automobiles, and the internet were all obvious 10x winners. We can think of these technologies as having passed

---

[424] In 1997, this author argued that greens were ensorcelled by New Age romantic poetry. See: Pinkerton, James P., "Enviromanticism: The Poetry of Nature as Political Force," *Foreign Affairs*, May-June 1997. https://bit.ly/3JylcJU

[425] In 2014, Peter Thiel wrote, "As a good rule of thumb, proprietary technology must be at least 10 times better than its closest substitute in some important dimension to lead to a real monopolistic advantage. Anything less than an order of magnitude better will probably be perceived as a marginal improvement and will be hard to sell, especially in an already crowded market." *Zero to One: Notes on Startups, Or, How to Build the Future*, (New York, Crown Business) 2014, 41. We can observe, though, that Thiel is describing *proprietary* technology. We can broaden the point to *all* technology. The wheel, vastly superior as it was, immediately went into the public domain, and the returns have been accruing to all since.

the "Ten-Strike Test." By contrast, if a new technology is *not* ten times better, it won't be adopted, even if it is somewhat better. We can illustrate by
recalling the evolution of video playback technology. VHS was easily 10x
better than nothing, so it was adopted. Betamax was a little better than
the VHS, and it actually came first, but Sony had trouble distributing it,
and so it disappeared. Betamax wasn't 10x better, so it wasn't worth the
effort. Then DVD was 10x better than VHS, and so it was adopted. And
while Blu-Ray was better than DVD, it was not 10x better. So, like Betamax,
Blu-Ray fizzled. We can cite many other examples of better-but-not-that-
much better, from quadrophonic sound to eight-track cassettes to Steve
Jobs' NeXT computer (made in between his stints at Apple). All honorable
efforts, none successes.[426]

So now, with the Ten-Strike Test in mind, how do we rate green energy?
Let's start with an easy one—electric vehicles (EV). Are they 10x better
than vehicles relying on internal combustion engines (ICE)? Of course
not. They're good in many ways—they do look cool, tooling around suburbs—but they're not so good in cold weather, nor in hot weather, nor
for carrying heavy loads, nor if you're in a hurry and don't have time for
a lengthy recharge, nor if you're not near a charger that hasn't been van-
dalized.[427] Will EV improve? Sure. But it's doubtful EV will improve fast
enough to keep up with the political calendar that's been set for it. The
Biden administration wants America to be 50 percent new EV by 2030.[428]
We can take a step back to consider a key concern about Green—energy
density. Gasoline, for instance, is about ninety times denser, measured by

---

[426] Some "retro" systems will likely retain at least some market share as people realize
that advanced digital systems can not only be hacked, but also monitored and
censored—and perhaps closed down altogether. So the solution is to own a
stand-alone system for recordings, data, and the like.

[427] Kalmowitz, Andy, "It's Too Hot For Evs To Work Right," *Jalopnik*, July 21, 2023.
https://bit.ly/44A6Hhu

[428] "Biden-Harris Administration Announces New Private and Public Sector
Investments for Affordable Electric Vehicles," The White House, April 17, 2023.
https://bit.ly/3JWGnWz

megajoules per kilogram, than a lithium battery.[429] That's why you can fill your ICE tank with gas, quickly, go a long way—and pull a heavy load. Even when it's hot or cold outside. It doesn't take a scientist to see that there's more energy densely packed into a jerrycan of gasoline than a ray of sunlight or a waft of wind.

Of course, we mustn't underestimate the potential for breakthrough innovation. Lots of effort is being put into making batteries faster, cheaper, and better; we can add that schismogenesis is further spurring the effort. That is, green visionaries are inspired not only by clean energy, but also by their disdain for ICE. Yet batteries aren't the only energy source being innovated. Toyota, for instance, is advancing other energy paradigms, such as hybrids. In 2022, Akio Toyoda, president of the firm, expressed his skepticism about EV, saying, "People involved in the auto industry are largely a silent majority. That silent majority is wondering whether EVs are really OK to have as a single option. But they think it's the trend so they can't speak out loudly."[430] Greens ripped those words, and Mr. Toyoda has been quiet since. And yet Toyota is holding open the option of selling cars of all kinds—and they're always improving. By this reckoning, it's a decent bet that EV will never enjoy Ten-Strike status over ICE, including in its future variations, such as hydrogen fueled. Which suggests that EV might fail in their mission to displace the 250 million ICE vehicles in the US, and the billions more such vehicles around the world.

WIINIMBYS, LOCAL AND GLOBAL

We've already noted, in Chapter Nine, Democrats' shifting attitude toward the National Environmental Policy Act and its associated paper obstacles, including the environmental impact statement. Green capitalists are at the

---

[429] Energy Density in Some Combustibles," The Geography of Transport Systems. https://bit.ly/3PErrjc

[430] Davis, River, and McLain, Sean, "Toyota Chief Says 'Silent Majority' Has Doubts About Pursuing Only Evs," *The Wall Street Journal*, December 18, 2022. https://bit.ly/3XQ5vE6

forefront of rethinking NEPA and EIS, even if, of course, green traditionalists like the old ways. Hence the conflict—what "green caps" abhor, "green
trads" adore. In the Biden era, as the US government has allocated trillions
to green energy, the capitalists have had the upper hand, but the traditionalists have hardly gone away. In fact, green trads seem destined to be part
of a new coalition, joining with elements of the right, in overall opposition
to, at one time or another, *everything*. That is, we can pack in environmentalism, Luddism, and safetyism, and add anti-vaccine-ism, anti-globalism,
and anti-Great Reset-ism. The resulting brew of conspiratorialism can be
called WIINIMBY (Whatever It Is, Not In My Back Yard). We might recognize this feeling as an updating of the alienation that backlashed against
capitalism in centuries past. Which is to say, even people who are benefi-
ciaries of a system can end up as its opponents. Human nature is like that
sometimes. As wits say, friends come and go, but enemies accumulate.
That's how an old-line Green such as Robert F. Kennedy, Jr. found himself in league with such a complicated—and culturally potent—character
as Joe Rogan, who endorsed Bernie Sanders and has flirted with Donald
Trump. This is the so-called "horseshoe"—the bending of the left and right
wings so that they curve around and connect with each other. As with any
new political commingling, there's a new burst of energy, at least as strong
as the Hawthorne Effect.

In the meantime, green capitalists have work to do—including bulldoz-
ing. Specifically, they must roll over EIS to ease permitting for their projects. In the words of "green-preneur" John Delaney, a former Democratic
Member of Congress, "We cannot build the clean energy economy of the
future, which will involve the largest capital deployment in history, without permitting reforms that accelerate approvals/construction. Approval
delays are a major obstacle in fighting climate change."[431] We can see, Green
Inc. damns NEPA and EIS with the same vehemence that an American
manufacturing firm might have used a generation ago—before it gave up
and went to China.

---

[431] Delaney, John (@JohnDelaney), X, February 1, 2023. https://bit.ly/3r1HayI

Sympathetic journalists and pundits feel the green capitalists' pain. They are duly swinging around to support new construction. "Fighting climate change will require building a lot of new infrastructure," Robinson Meyer declares, "and NEPA could slow down that process...If America doesn't double its rate of new transmission construction, then 80% of the [Biden administration's plans for] carbon reductions will be squandered."[432] Speaking for the political class, California's Gavin Newsom, tribune of green capitalism, says of NEPA/EIS-minded foes, "These guys write reports and they protest. But we need to build. You can't be serious about climate and the environment without reforming permitting and procurement."[433]

Yet anyone in touch with the news knows that heavy green construction is running into the same WIINIMBY blockade as heavy construction of any other kind. One 2021 study found that 42 percent of the Department of Energy's active reviews under NEPA were for clean energy, compared to just 15 percent for carbon energy.[434] Here's *The Atlantic*'s Derek Thompson. "We *say* that we want to save the planet from climate change—but in practice, many Americans are basically dead set against the clean-energy revolution, with even liberal states shutting down zero-carbon nuclear plants and protesting solar-power projects."[435] Worried about such threats, the *Los Angeles Times*' Sammy Roth counsels his fellow greens that progress means "accepting that large-scale solar farms will destroy some wildlife habitat."[436] This is a genuine conflict of visions. Green capitalists want economic action, while green traditionalists do not.

[432] Meyer, Robinson,"The Real Climate Defeat in the Debt Ceiling Deal." *HeatMap*, May 31, 2023. https://bit.ly/3prsmcf
[433] Klein, Ezra, "'What the Hell Happened to the California of the '50s and '60s?'" *New York Times*, June 18, 2023. https://bit.ly/44honxz
[434] Mackenzie, Aidan, and Ruiz, Santi, "No, NEPA really is a problem for clean energy," *Noahpinion*, July 19, 2023. https://bit.ly/43MZPfz
[435] Thompson, Derek, "A Simple Plan to Solve All of America's Problems," *The Atlantic*, January 12, 2022. https://bit.ly/3Q61Dg6
[436] Roth, Sammy, "Would an occasional blackout help solve climate change?" *Los Angeles Times*, July 20, 2023. https://bit.ly/3Q8Uj3r

Indeed, the problem has been enlarged, because conservatives, too, are joining the naysaying. There have always been some agrarian "crunchy cons" who opposed "dark satanic mills," but they've been bolstered by folks who oppose green power projects, for all the usual reasons, and perhaps, too, for reasons of partisanship. That is, if the bicoastal elites are *fur* it, they're *agin* it.[437] In any case, right wing opposition is proving effective. Energy pundit Robert Bryce writes, "Since 2015, there have been at least 375 rejections of restrictions and those have occurred in states from Maine to Hawaii."[438] Bryce has assembled a database of such rejections, including one from Piatt County, Illinois, where local authorities vetoed a proposed 300 megawatt wind farm. In the words of board member Jerry Edwards, "I have heard from a lot of residents of Piatt County and for the vast majority, this is something they do not want."[439] Indeed, the legal tentacles of a well-funded conservative group, the Texas Public Policy Foundation, have reached all the way to Massachusetts, squeezing offshore wind farms. In its brief, TPPF cited "multiple federal statutes" that protect fishermen from the green energy machines.[440] We can see, the right, too, can practice NEPA/EIS lawfare.

But if Red is angry, schismogenesis says that Blue will be equally angry. So some blues are gearing up to put down the ornery red provincials. In the militant words of a Princeton professor, "We must also quell counterproductive nimby impulses and keep focused on the greater project

---

[437] We might also speculate that rising crime and social alienation have expanded the ethos of "Get off my lawn."

[438] Bryce, Robert, "Voters in Ohio and Michigan Join 375 Other Localities in Vetoing Large Wind Projects," *Heartland Daily News*, December 5, 2022. https://bit.ly/44e3MKC. Bryce adds, "Let me remind readers that you won't see these rejections being reported by *The New York Times* or National Public Radio. Those news outlets routinely ignore what is happening in rural America when it comes to land use conflicts."

[439] Barlow, Kevin, "County Board votes no on wind farm," *Piatt County Journal-Republican*, March 16, 2023. https://bit.ly/3JxuMwP See also: Bryce, Robert, "Renewable Rejection Database," accessed May 11, 2023. https://bit.ly/3Jz3Aho

[440] "TPPF: Vineyard Wind Project Violates Federal Law," Texas Public Policy Foundation, December 15, 2021. https://bit.ly/3K1ypvj

at hand."[441] Yet it's simply not clear that the green capitalists, and all their chattering class allies, will win. The WIINIMBY bloc is blocking, viz. this 2023 *The Boston Globe* headline, "As wind projects stall off Massachusetts coast, industry wonders: What's next?" According to one close-in observer, "Clearly, the near-term clean energy goals are going to be missed."[442]

In fact, the greater greener project is threatened, not just in the US, but around the world. A decade or two ago, it was assumed that expensive and obscure elements, such as cobalt and terbium, needed for batteries and other "green" production, would come from China, or maybe from somewhere in Africa. (The US was presumed to be off-limits because of environmental concerns.) But wherever the source, we're going to need a lot. According to a 2022 report from Just Security (a former perch of White House national security adviser Jake Sullivan), "By 2040, the clean energy sector will demand more than 60 percent of the world's cobalt and nickel, 40 percent of its copper, and 80 percent of its lithium. In a high-growth scenario, mineral demand will increase by 400 percent by 2040." The report concluded, "The world is going to need vast new quantities of critical minerals."[443]

To be sure, our friend innovation can help. In the past, we thought we were running out of things that we later discovered we had in abundance— or that we didn't need anymore, because something better came along. Still, optimism about innovation should not morph into magical thinking. In the words of hard-nosed energy expert Mark Mills, "Only in comic books does energy tech advance at the pace of information tech (a.k.a. Moore's Law). The analogy is worse than wrong, it's backwards: building an EV

[441] Jenkins, Jesse, "What 'Electrify Everything' Actually Looks Like" *Mother Jones*, May/June 2023. https://bit.ly/3NQMLRC

[442] That downbeat headline has since been changed. Newspapers have been known to bend to pressure from irate readers and advertisers. Chesto, Jon, "For the wind farm industry in Mass., it's back to square two," *The Boston Globe*, June 25, 2023. https://bit.ly/3NoHOhj

[443] Brew, Gregory and Bazilian, Morgan, "The Mining Gap: Critical Minerals and Geopolitical Competition," Just Security, November 7, 2022. https://bit.ly/43XYCmt

instead of a conventional car entails a 400 percent to 7,000 percent greater use of mined minerals to produce the same vehicle-mile. The technology around EVs will get better of course, but incrementally and not at anything resembling a Moore's Law rate."[444]

So even as our highest hopes for a deus ex machina are lowered, we must contemplate disruptions in the supply chain. Today, America must confront the geopolitical threat from China, including the prospect of a rare earth element embargo. And as for Africa, there's moral revulsion about labor exploitation, as well as environmental depredation. To top it off, we're now told that some vital "green" inputs, such as manganese, are poison.[445] So maybe green capitalism isn't so green, and maybe, all in, green energy can't be counted as green. If so, it's hard to see how its favorable framework in the West will survive.

THE FLY IN THE ARGUMENT

In fact, the United States is nowhere near united on green goals. At a 2022 hearing on Capitol Hill, Rep. Rashida Tlaib, Democrat of Michigan, demanded of JP Morgan Chase CEO Jamie Dimon, "Answer with a simple yes or no, does your bank have a policy against funding new oil and gas products?" Dimon answered, "Absolutely not and that would be the road to hell for America."[446] *The Economist*, mostly green-leaning, concedes with a sigh, "The...hard truth is that fossil fuels will not be abandoned over-night."[447] The even harder truth, of course, is that carbon fuels might not be abandoned at all. That's the conclusion one could draw from this 2023

---

[444] Mills, Mark, "The Year of Electric Vehicle Inevitability?" *RealClearMarkets*, December 15, 2022. https://bit.ly/44iNSPf

[445] Chason, Rachel, and Godfrey, Ilan, "In scramble for EV metals, health threat to workers often goes unaddressed, *Washington Post*, June 8, 2023. https://bit.ly/44nCUIp

[446] Propper, David, "Jamie Dimon says stopping oil and gas production would be 'road to hell' for US," *New York Post*, September 22, 2022. https://bit.ly/3JxaROs

[447] "The world is missing its lofty climate targets. Time for some realism." *The Economist*, November 3, 2022. https://bit.ly/3nWkP4n

headline: "Brazil Gears Up To Become Fourth Largest Oil Producer."[448] We can point out that this is not news from the right wing Brazil of former president Jair Bolsonaro. This is from the left wing Brazil of his replacement, Luiz Inácio Lula da Silva. If even Third World leftists are pro-oil, where does that leave Team Anti-Oil?

Indeed, to the extent that the rest of the world is opening its eyes to anything, it's seeing that it needs carbon fuel. In 2022, Nigeria's then vice president, Yemi Osinbajo, declared, "We need to have access to energy, access to electricity just to be able to survive and create industry for the millions of people." Therefore, he added, "We need to have investments in fossil fuels.... No country in the world has been able to industrialize using renewable energy."[449] We can note that the population of Nigeria is 223 million, crowded into territory not much bigger than Texas. And while its economy is growing, its population is growing faster, and so it suffers periodic "food emergencies."[450] Given that level of desperation—including the possibility of mass migration—is the West really going to insist that Nigeria be green, and stay poor? Would such insistence be heeded? Writing about the Global South, Joel Kotkin and Bheki Mahlobo declare, "Net Zero orthodoxy, with its embrace of degrowth and austerity, has little appeal."[451] Indeed, reading about such planetary pushback, one gets a whiff of the old spirit of anti-colonialism. Once again, White people are telling People of Color how to live—and the latter doesn't like it. So what will Big Green do? Most likely, rich liberal countries will either acquiesce to Nigeria staying with carbon fuels, or else subsidize green energy on a scale heretofore unimagined. Yet for context as to the larger dilemma, Nigeria

---

[448] Smith, Matthew, "Brazil Gears Up To Become Fourth Largest Oil Producer," *Oil Price,* June 12, 2023. https://bit.ly/3NoLAat

[449] Odutola, Abiola, "We need access to energy to survive, create industry—VP Osinbajo," *Nairametrics,* May 13, 2022. https://bit.ly/3PwFW8R

[450] Olaoluwa, Azeezat and Macaulay, Cecilia, "Nigeria's President Bola Tinubu declares state of emergency over food," BBC, July 14, 2023. https://bit.ly/46HpHMi

[451] Kotkin, Joel, and Mahlobo, Bheki, "Why Africa is turning its back on the eco-obsessed West," *Spi!ked,* June 4, 2023. https://bit.ly/43X18t5

accounts for only about a sixth of the population of sub-Saharan Africa. So whatever happens in Africa—and other poor parts of the world—will make for huge investment deltas.

These looming realities are being noticed. In the wake of the strains of the Ukraine war, QatarEnergy CEO Saad al-Kaabi declared, "The growing economic burden has fizzled the euphoria over the series of energy transition plans, causing severe erosion in public support for reducing carbon emissions." He continued, "Many countries, particularly in Europe, which had been strong advocates of green energy and carbon-free future have made a sudden and sharp U-turn. Today, coal burning is once again on the rise reaching its highest levels since 2014."[452] Perhaps the hardest truth comes from Saudi Aramco CEO Amin Nasser, who says the world is now "transitioning to coal."[453] And it's not just Arabs who are talking this way. The International Energy Agency offered this headline, "Global coal demand is seen to return to its all-time high in 2022."[454] Indeed, *Semafor* points out that of the 143 countries submitting climate strategy plans as part of the 2015 Paris Agreement, just five of the plans included "any commitment to phase down fossil fuel production."[455]

THE NEW IN NUCLEAR

Nuclear power is about as Hamiltonian as one can get. The idea of nuclear energy was born in places such as the University of Chicago and the University of California at Berkeley. The Manhattan Project, the building

[452] "Europe makes sharp U-turn from green energy - Qatar energy minister" Reuters, September 29, 2022. https://reut.rs/3T7mzoP

[453] Barbee, Darren, "Saudi Aramco CEO Warns Global Energy Supplies on Razor's Edge," *Hart Energy*, October 4, 2022. https://bit.ly/3NQO8Qg

[454] International Energy Agency, "Global coal demand is set to return to its all-time high in 2022," press release, July 28, 2022. https://bit.ly/3pmaOhB

[455] McDonnell, Tim, *Semafor Net Zero*, June 16, 2023. https://bit.ly/46zYAD0. McDonnell adds that of 2,554 climate-related projects financed—total cost $119 billi8on—by the World Bank between 2000 and 2022, many "actually contribute little or nothing to solving the problem."

of the A-bomb, was, on a relative basis, one of the largest government pro-grams ever. After World War II it was understood that anything to do with uranium was dangerous, and so Uncle Sam built a Framework around nuclear energy. For instance, the Price-Anderson Act of 1957 put a cap on the liability of nuclear operators; liability shields are often included in a Frameworks.[456] Yet as we know, the nuclear Framework fell apart in the '80s and '90s, in the wake of Three Mile Island and Chernobyl. Nuclear power in the US has been flat for a quarter-century, even as it has remained strong in some countries, notably, France. And while concerns about cli-mate change have bolstered the case for safe nuclear power, it's fair to say that there'll be little enthusiasm for—and much opposition to—a new nuclear plant anywhere in the US.

Still, goosed on by Hamiltonians, nuclear technology continues to evolve. In December 2022, *The Financial Times* took note of a hoped-for breakthrough, the first "energy positive" *fusion* reaction, achieved at the Lawrence Livermore National Laboratory, a unit of the US Department of Energy. As the *FT* put it, "Fusion reactions emit no carbon, produce no long-lived radioactive waste and a small cup of the hydrogen fuel could theoretically power a house for hundreds of years."[457] As one outside expert put it, "it's one of the biggest results of science in the past 20-30 years."[458] Biden administration Energy Secretary Jennifer Granholm declared, "This is game-changing, world-improving, livses-saving history unfolding in real time."[459] And yes, Livermore is in California, providing a lift to Blue Hamiltonia.

---

[456] "Price-Anderson Act: Nuclear Power Industry Liability Limits and Compensation to the Public After Radioactive Releases," Congressional Research Service, February 5, 2018. https://bit.ly/3JVuXC8

[457] Wilson, Tom, "Fusion energy breakthrough by US scientists boosts clean power hopes," *The Financial Times*, December 12, 2022. https://bit.ly/3NkaSGI

[458] Lefebvre, Ben, and Morehouse, Catherine, "'It's one of the biggest results of science in the past 20-30 years,'" *Politico*, December 12, 2022. https://bit.ly/432VdkV

[459] Granholm, Jennifer (@SecGranholm), X, December 13, 2022. https://bit.ly/3CP1qXa

Elsewhere in Blue, NuScale, based in Oregon, announced a $7.5 billion deal to build small modular reactors to the Philippines.[460] Interestingly, the company says its success "wouldn't have been possible without our partners...the U.S. Department of Energy."[461] Score another win for the Hamiltonians. We can see, for all the government's emphasis—some would say *over*-emphasis—on solar and wind, Uncle Sam has also been backing less fashionable technologies that might prove more saleable.

There are easily a dozen different ideas for nuclear power. Its energy density is so great, it's hard to resist. So as we wait to see what comes next, let's recall the wisdom of Leslie Groves, head of the Manhattan Project during World War II. He said, "When man is willing to make the effort, he is capable of accomplishing virtually anything."[462]

HAIL, CARBON!

There's an irony to carbon. In the right place, it's essential, in the wrong place, it's harmful, and in most places, it's merely valuable. Robert Hazen, executive director of the Deep Carbon Observatory, declares that carbon is a "symphony," singing to us in myriad ways. "We live on a carbon planet and we are carbon life," he writes. Expanding on his favorite element theme, Hazen adds, "Look around you. Carbon is everywhere: In the paper of every book, the ink on its pages, and the glue that binds it; in the soles and leather of your shoes... From your first baby clothes to your silk-lined coffin, carbon atoms surround you." Continuing in this lyrical vein, "Carbon is the giver of life: your skin and hair, blood and bone, muscle and sinews all depend on carbon. Bark, leaf, root and flower; fruit and nut; pollen and nectar; bee and butterfly... Carbon is the chemical essence of your

---

[460] "US firm plans to build small nuclear power plants in the Philippines," *Straits Times*, updated May 3, 2023. https://bit.ly/3XtL1AA

[461] Company History, NuScale https://www.nuscalepower.com/en/about/history

[462] Norris, Robert S. *Racing for the Bomb: General Leslie R. Groves, the Manhattan Project's Indispensable Man*, (Hanover, NH: Steerforth Press, 2002), 546

lover's eyes, hands, lips and brain. When you breathe, you exhale carbon; when you kiss, carbon atoms embrace."[463] Okay, so carbon is cool.

As a reminder of what can be done with carbon—with the help of a Hamiltonian Framework—we can think back to synthetic rubber in World War II. For a long time, the easiest way to get rubber was from nature—from a rubber tree. Yet after Japan bombed Pearl Harbor in 1941, plunging the US into World War II, it also seized the rubber plantations of the Dutch East Indies (today's Indonesia). So the US was cut off from its familiar source of rubber. In response, American industry built, from scratch, a synthetic rubber industry in a matter of mere months. After the fighting started, the Big Four rubber companies—Firestone, Goodrich, Goodyear, and United States Rubber—joined together and pooled their patents, figuring out how to use the hydrocarbons of crude oil as the feedstock. Rubber is ultimately, after all, just a polymer, five carbon atoms and eight hydrogen atoms. So with enough chemical noodling, rubber can be manufactured easier than it can be harvested. Such Applied Hamiltonianism was spectacularly successful. US production soared more than 400-fold, from 2,200 tons in 1942 to 920,000 tons in 1945.[464] Thus the lesson,: The exigency of the war forced the innovation that not only helped to win the war but also created a future industry.

So we're starting to see that carbon isn't so bad. And that's good, because we have plenty of it, including carbon-based fuel. According to the U.S. Energy Information Association, America possesses proved reserves of 41 billion barrels of oil.[465] We can add that "proved reserves" is an elastic concept, as it refers to the amount of a resource that is producible under existing economic conditions. Which is to say, costs, prices, and the regulatory environment can change the total of reserves dramatically, up or

---

[463] Hazen, Robert "Why Carbon?" *Scientific American*, October 22, 2019. https://bit.ly/3QndxTi

[464] "U.S. Synthetic Rubber Program," American Chemistry Society, accessed November 26, 2022. https://bit.ly/3NNMwqf

[465] "U.S. Crude Oil and Natural Gas Proved Reserves, Year-end 2021," U.S. Energy Information Administration, December 30, 2022. https://www.eia.gov/naturalgas/crudeoilreserves/

down. So another measure of supply is useful—oil *resources*. Just within the US, oil resources—the actual total of the stuff believed to be in the ground—are estimated to 198 billion bbl. And if we add in shale, the total of oil resources climbs to 2.8 trillion bbl.[466] So how much is that worth? In 2023, about $210 trillion. That's more than six times the US national debt. To put the sum another way, $617,000 per resident of the U.S. One has to believe that if the American people understood how much money is involved, they'll be willing to make some policy changes in order to make sure they got some.

Now of course, it can be immediately argued that not all that oil is actually recoverable, and/or that recovering it all would depress the price. Yet still, it's undeniable that there's a *lot* of wealth underground. Whether we ever use it is substantially a political choice. As we've seen, at first the Biden administration tried to restrict oil, as a way of helping green energy, and yet when that proved unpopular, the Bidenites relented, somewhat. All of which suggest that our civilizational energy hunger is going to win out over any stated desire to cut back.

We could do the same bullish survey for natural gas. Proved reserves in the US total 625 trillion cubic feet (Tcf) and resources are estimated to be 2.9 quadrillion Tcf.[467] And we can see the same humongous sums for coal. The US possesses 471 billion short tons of coal reserves.[468] Yes, coal is "dirty," heavy as it is with heavy metals. Yet the *techno miracle* of the Manhattan project and of synthetic rubber reminds us that if it fits within the laws of physics, we can figure it out. So we can see that concerns about an "energy crisis," or that we are hitting "peak oil," may be popular with Greens (both traditionalists and capitalists, for different, but over-

---

[466] "US Energy Facts," Institute for Energy Research, accessed December 2, 2023 https://bit.ly/3GorcTK

[467] "U.S. Crude Oil and Natural Gas Proved Reserves, Year-end 2021" U.S. Energy Information Administration, December 30, 2022. https://bit.ly/3uNOEHj see also, "Natural gas explained: How much natural gas is left," U.S. Department of Energy, accessed December 2, 2023. https://bit.ly/46qa4su

[468] "US Coal Reserves," U.S. Energy Information Administration, October 3, 2022. https://www.eia.gov/coal/reserves/

lapping, reasons), but the plain fact is that thanks to fracking and other technological advances, we keep finding more carbon fuel. Since 1980, world oil reserves have more than doubled.[469] And more coal and gas, too. And there's whole 'nother source of carbon energy, *methane hydrates*. This is natural gas frozen in ice crystals on the ocean floor. According to the Department of Energy, the total quantity is thought to be at least one quadrillion cubic feet.[470] So yes, there's a lot of carbon fuel. And that's good, because under practically any future scenario, we'll need it to make plastics—and of course, a by-product of plastic is…methane, aka, natural gas.[471] To be sure, we can't get at all the carbon fuel. Nobody's about to start drilling or mining in, say, Yosemite or the Vatican. But we've proven that we can drill horizontally, at great distance, such that a tourist gazing at El Capitan, or the Sistine Chapel, would never know there's an active rig, miles away.

THE PLANETARY PLETHORA

In 2023, we learned there's 70 billion tons of phosphate rock in Norway. That compares nicely to the previously known reserves, worldwide, of 71 billion tons. This phosphate can be used for fertilizer, and it can also be used for batteries, semiconductors, and computer chips.[472] Humans have been actively prospecting for thousands of years, and yet we're still finding vast new resources in Norway. There's a reason for this—valuable materials are all over. Why? The answer goes back to the origin of the Earth, formed 4.6 billion years ago by the coalescing of gases, dust particles,

---

[469] "Oil Reserves, 1980 to 2020," Our World in Data. https://bit.ly/3NCNpk9

[470] "Gas Hydrates," National Energy Technology Laboratory, https://bit.ly/3JzJWBA

[471] Royer, Sarah-Jeanne, et al. "Production of methane and ethylene from plastic in the environment," *PloS One*, 2018. https://www.ncbi.nlm.nih.gov/pmc/articles/PMC6070199/

[472] Simon, Frédéric, "'Great news': EU hails discovery of massive phosphate rock deposit in Norway," *Euractiv*, June 29, 2023. https://bit.ly/3NZzZAi

and asteroids surrounding the Sun. As Carl Sagan liked to say, it's all "star stuff," scrambled around by the forces of the universe. So that's why natural resources are scattered all over the Earth, and, too, all within Earth. That explains why everything is abundant. If we think about it, we realize that the earth is nothing *but* natural resources. Our planet weighs 6 sextillion tons (that's twenty-one zeros) so there's plenty of everything. For instance, this globe contains 122 billion tons of gold.[473] Of that weighty total, only about 208,000 tons have ever been mined.[474] Indeed, no mine of any kind has gone deeper than 2.5 miles, and it's 1800 miles to the earth's core. So in the most literal sense, we've only scratched the surface. Now we're seeing why we keep discovering more, whenever we go looking. And so long as resources are valuable, self-interest will keep people looking.

Still, one could ask, why should ordinary people—the folks needed to bolster a Framework—support all this production of energy and energy-related minerals? Here's a good answer—*money*. As a model of what's possible, we might look the sweet deal in the oil rich forth-ninth state. There, the Alaska Permanent Fund delivers a dividend to each resident. In 2022, the per person sum was $3,284.[475] That's a useful way to think about political problem-solving—put money in people's pockets. To be sure, not everyone will want free money if it means more carbon fuel production, but it's a proposition worth testing, state by state. Yet the biggest single issue with carbon, as we know, is that it gets into the atmosphere. So the solution is easy enough—*take it out.*

---

[473] "How Much Gold is Left on Earth?," West Coast Placer, accessed June 10, 2023. https://www.westcoastplacer.com/how-much-gold-is-left-on-earth/#

[474] "Above-ground stocks," Gold.org, accessed June 10, 2023. https://bit.ly/46WgAGJ

[475] "2022 Permanent Fund Dividend Hits a Record $3,284.00," State of Alaska, September 8, 2022. https://bit.ly/3R6J4aF

THE GRAND CARBON BARGAIN

Under its 2023 headline, "Climate Startup Removes Carbon From Open Air in Industry First," *The Wall Street Journal* reported on the first successful use of a direct air carbon capture facility, in Iceland. "This is an important inflection point," said one stakeholder. "It isn't just science fiction. It's reality."[476] That same year, Warren Buffett announced that Berkshire Hathaway had taken a huge position, more than $42 billion, in two oil companies, Occidental and Chevron. Why? As the *Journal* explained, Buffett "seems to firmly believe that even as a growing number of companies set ambitious goals to reduce their carbon emissions, the world will continue to need oil. Lots of oil." The *Journal* added, "Occidental has also, with Mr. Buffett's blessing, invested more than $1 billion in a carbon capture process."[477] Oxy has built STRATOS, a direct-air-capture facility near Midland, Texas. A second *Journal* article dubbed it "a budding technology with fuzzy economics." Yet that fuzz can be cleared up with government subsidies—45 percent of the cost of carbon is already being covered by tax credits enacted in 2022. STRATOS, which partnered with a Bill Gates startup, Carbon Engineering, in 2019, plans to have more than a hundred carbon capture plants up and running by 2035.[478] Said one industry insider, "It's been a sort of land rush. Emitters are recognizing the former trash they were emitting into the air is now a treasure. It was previously something they were ashamed of, a byproduct. Now it's a currency."[479] To be sure, this buildup could be affected by variance in national policy. And yet even Republicans who loathe green energy often have a soft spot for carbon capture, as it furthers the logic of continuing with carbon fuel.

---

[476] Ramkumar, Amrith, "Climate Startup Removes Carbon From Open Air in Industry First," *The Wall Street Journal*, January 12, 2023. https://bit.ly/3r4Fqox

[477] Otani, Akane, "Warren Buffett Has Been Betting Big on Oil. It's Time to Find Out Why," *The Wall Street Journal*, May 9, 2023. https://on.wsj.com/3JD7Gon

[478] Morenne, Benoît, "Occidental Makes a Billion-Dollar Climate Moonshot—So It Can Keep Pumping Oil," *The Wall Street Journal*, April 10, 2023. https://bit.ly/46qhOec

[479] LeFebvre, Ben, and Colman, Zac, "A crucial climate technology provokes fears in oil country," *Politico*, May 16, 2023. https://politi.co/46zgTYP

So what then becomes of the captured carbon? Many plans involve turning it into pellets, which can either be buried or used for some other industrial purpose, including enhanced oil recovery. But we can ask, does that sort of carbon plan meet the Ten-Strike Test? Quite possibly, no. And yet we're not through innovating. For instance, there's hope for energy circularity—with the help of a little hydrogen, buried carbon might be turned back into carbon fuel. Indeed, engineers have even figured out how to make gasoline out of atmospheric carbon.[480] Element No. 6 is, after all, a symphony of a resource.

Another way to capture carbon is in the ocean. According to one study, "The ocean is the largest carbon sink on the planet and contains almost 50 times more carbon dioxide than is currently in the atmosphere. The ocean's ability to remove and store CO_2 can be enhanced through a suite of approaches known collectively as ocean carbon dioxide removal." These approaches include an electrochemical "swing" in seawater toward producing CO_2, as well as fertilizing the ocean with nutrients "to increase photosynthesis and CO_2 uptake."[481] That last point reminds us, most of the ocean is "desert," with little life, so nothing much is happening, in terms of carbon capture or anything else. So there's plenty of opportunity for productive improvement—more life, more fish, more fun. Speaking of oceanic fun, what if we took the captured carbon, perhaps the pellets, and poured them all in one place in the Pacific? Would a new Hawaiian island be a good investment?

In fact, we're already sort of getting there on undersea construction.

In 2017, the University of Texas at Rio Grande Valley created a 1650-acre artificial reef off South Padre Island, specifically for the purpose of carbon capture. "Every nation that has a coastline may be able to build

[480] Riebeek, Holly, "The Carbon Cycle," NASA, June 16, 2011. https://bit.ly/3pw8qF0. See also: Myers, Andrew, "Stanford engineers create a catalyst that can turn carbon dioxide into gasoline 1,000 times more efficiently," Stanford, February 9, 2022. https://bit.ly/3CLsPsQ

[481] Chen, Sifang, "Depending on the Ocean," Carbon 180, accessed May 3, 2023. https://bit.ly/3XoMfNN

artificial reefs that could help in the climate battle," says Friends of RGV Reef head Gary Glick, "while at the same time restoring precious habitat and bringing back fish and other marine habitat around the world."[482] Talk about a win-win. Carbon is also—and this should come as no shock—the key material in carbon nanotubes, which are already the superstrong stuff of many industrial uses, and could be the structural material for future reefs or islands. (Indeed, with a solid foundation, carbon nanotubes could gird the world's tallest high-rise, becoming a vertical carbon sink.)

Okay, so how much would all this carbon capturing cost? The short answer, of course, is that nobody knows, because projections about the future, especially when technology is involved, are almost always wrong. Yet whatever the cost, it must be compared to two other kinds of costs. First, there's the anticipated estimate of achieving "net zero" CO_2 by 2050. This cost is variously estimated at, $125 trillion, $276 trillion, and $1.6 quadrillion.[483] Second, the anticipated cost of *not* succeeding in reducing CO_2, because the green forces chose a nonviable approach to net zero and were defeated by the opposition. So perhaps it's best for the greens to achieve their net zero victory any way they can, including by making peace with carbon fuels. Indeed, we can see, here, the makings of a "Grand Carbon Bargain." Under its terms, we keep doing what we're clearly going to keep doing, which is using carbon fuels. And at the same time, we capture the carbon. Doesn't seem so hard. And in fact, there are some pretty cool, and cooling, ways to do the capturing.

[482] "Carbon Capture Research Begins at Largest Artificial Reef in Texas," Friends of the RGV Reef, October 19, 2022. https://bit.ly/3PvutGw
[483] "What's the cost of net zero?" United Nations Framework on Climate Change, November 3, 2021. https://bit.ly/3OE0Y4o. See also: "COP27: Playing offense on the path to net zero," McKinsey & Company, November 11, 2022. https://bit.ly/3JwlOzU and Steve Milloy tweet citing Rep. Scott Perry (R-PA). Milloy, Steve (@JunkScience), X, July 13, 2023. https://bit.ly/3JTGXnO

TREES ARE AN ANSWER

Another kind of solidified carbon is wood. Back in 1990, President George H. W. Bush planted a tree in Indianapolis, declaring, "Trees, of course, can help ensure clean air. Consider: One recent study showed that trees, much more than water, consume the carbon dioxide that is building up in our atmosphere."[484] It's been a long and winding road since Bush's vision thing, and yet by the mid-2020s, Republicans were on board, pushing a plan to plant a trillion trees. That many carbon sinks wouldn't actually fit in the continental US, but one could look around the world for empty space, including, of course, the oceans, where landfill could create new ground, inviting substrate for our leafy friends.[485] Indeed, it could be that for all our new tech, we can't beat the good ol' tree. In the words of "tree-preneur" Yishan Wong, a former CEO of Reddit now running Terraformation, an organic carbon capture company, "If I were to say to you, 'Hey, I just invented this self-replicating carbon-extracting machine that only requires water and sunlight, and it can be operated by anyone,' you'd be like, 'That's awesome, that's what we need to address climate change.'…Well that's literally a tree."[486]

In fact, there's evidence that, across the world, thanks to carbon, the world is already getting greener. That is, green vegetation is enlarging. Makes sense—for green plants, carbon dioxide is food. One report concluded that global greening is likely already "helping to mitigate global warming more than climate models suggest."[487] So if vegetation and trees are a great carbon sink, one could imagine making them bigger, perhaps

---

[484] "Remarks at a Tree-Planting Ceremony in Indianapolis, Indiana," George H.W. Bush Presidential Library and Museum, April, 3, 1990. https://bit.ly/43x8Rgf

[485] Groves, Stephen, "House Republicans propose planting a trillion trees as they move away from climate change denial," AP, July 18, 2023. https://bit.ly/44AuPjV

[486] "How to address climate change? Plant a trillion trees" Withers advertisement, *The Financial Times,* accessed March 1, 2023. https://withers.ft.com/yishan-wong

[487] Knapton, Sarah, "Trees are growing larger than ever before to help ease global warming," *Telegraph,* October 8, 2022. https://bit.ly/4407kjV

modifying trees so they grow to *Avatar* size. That way, all the more carbon is captured, and there'd also be benefits to tourism and movie sets. Giants trees would be a worthwhile project for someone with a very green thumb, as well as, of course, mastery of genetic modification. To be sure, such tree engineering couldn't happen without controversy, and yet by now we've figured out that everything is controversial. Realizing the reality of tradeoffs, we must make choices, and once those choices are made, we can reify them into Frameworks. And then, solve the problem.

RENEWABLES

Even as we think about nuclear and carbon, there's no reason to stop thinking about green energy, for two reasons:

First, there's so darn much money in green energy. One study found that green investment totaled $1.1 trillion in 2022, for a total of almost $7 trillion invested since 2004."[488] Observing the ongoing gold rush, Biden climate envoy John Kerry said this is the way the fight against climate change had to be. "The lesson I've learned in the last year," he observed, "is money, money, money, money, money, money, money."[489] Indeed, the Blue Hamiltonians seem to have perfected the art of tapping this money. Will they ever change? Will the money flow ever change?

Second, there's so much energy in green, especially solar. After all, in a single hour, more energy from the Sun strikes the Earth than we earthlings consume in a year. According to MIT professor Washington Taylor, "A total of 173,000 terawatts (trillions of watts) of solar energy strikes the Earth continuously. That's more than 10,000 times the world's total energy use." The problem of course, is that the energy is diffuse—each square meter of solar paneling just doesn't capture that many photons. Taylor suggests

---

[488] "Global Low-Carbon Energy Technology Investment Surges Past $1 Trillion for the First Time," BloombergNEF, January 26, 2023. https://bit.ly/3PwwylK

[489] "Kerry on how to keep climate goals alive: money, money, money, money, money, money, money," *MarketWatch*, January 17, 2023. https://bit.ly/44nBP3j

putting the panels in deserts, calculating that covering just 10 percent of the world's deserts would provide electricity equal to the projected growth in worldwide energy demand over the next half-century.[490] Or we could put panels on the ocean. But we can immediately see, any such installation, including the transmission wires, would require a worldwide Hamiltonian Framework. And maybe we'll have that.

In the meantime, other kinds of green energy can be explored. Texas is not especially abundant in geothermal, and yet the federal government owns just 2 percent of the land in the state (compared to a national average of 28 percent), and so the Red Jeffersonians who run the Lone Star state have happily opened up the other 98 percent to development, including geothermal. According to *The Economist*, "Houston has become a capital for geothermal startups."[491] So we see a Nevada-like play—provide a protective Framework for something people want, and the money will come rolling in. Even if the territory is otherwise nothing special, a Framework can make it special.

Then there's hydrogen, the most abundant element in the universe, accounting for around 75 percent of all matter. The sun is hydrogen in a plasma state, so we know it's a great fuel. The problem is that hydrogen is not naturally occurring in large quantities on Earth. But humans have the power to harness nature in ways that seem Clarkean in their magical power. Scientists at the University of Massachusetts have figured out how to make electricity from water droplets in the air, by passing them through tiny-holed membranes, called nanopores. It's a nano-version of the process that makes lightning. Said one of the scientists of his vision, "Sometime in the future, we can get clean electricity literally wherever we go," because air humidity is continuous and everywhere. "I call it a sustainable, continuous, and ubiquitous powering solution." Moreover, the membranes can be made out of many things, including cellulose, which is to say, from organic

---

[490] Chandler, David, "Shining brightly," *MIT News*, October 26, 2011. https://bit.ly/46rlJHJ

[491] "In America climate hawks and Big Oil alike cheer geothermal energy," *The Economist*, March 14, 2023. https://bit.ly/3pmy0MG

plants.[492] We can see that, as with silicon, once we gain full understanding of a process, we can do it for so cheap, on such a mass scale, that we forget there was ever any such thing as a shortage. For investors, that will mean no shortage of upside.

INVESTMENT TAKEAWAYS

- Following the basic geopolitical wisdom—there are no final victories—investors will have to consider how much of the green framework will survive. During the Biden administration, the big pillar of green capitalism was the Inflation Reduction Act (IRA), the curiously named bill that was more about inflating green energy than reducing inflation. Yet within a year of its 2022 passage, Democratic senator Joe Manchin of West Virginia had threatened to seek its repeal. To be sure, Manchin had always been an outrider among Democrats, and yet another senator, John Hickenlooper, a Blue of good standing, said that the IRA has "obviously unraveled."[493] To be sure, plenty of federal spending programs shamble along, but few are as big as the IRA. And while some of its provisions, such as carbon capture, are popular with Republicans, others are not. So it's simply not clear, for how long or for how much, big subsidies to green capitalism will continue. Such uncertainty, of course, is a business confidence downer. And it takes confidence to plan ahead, and invest ahead. To be noticed—whether Democrats can bring Republicans on board for the building of an enduring green energy Framework.
- No matter what happens in Washington, DC, green energy is not going to disappear. It might not pass the Ten-Strike Test, but it

---

[492] Shankman, Sabrina, "Harnessing the same forces as lightning, new technology extracts electricity from humidity," *The Boston Globe*, May 26, 2023. https://bit.ly/3PxOBIa

[493] "What's next in the debt limit fight," *Punchbowl News*, April 27, 2023. https://bit.ly/3r6VOVC

has many strengths, and so it will coexist with carbon and nuclear. Green capitalists will have to adjust—or be adjusted—to this new reality. Most likely, in polarized, *duo*-ized America, Blue will have its energy framework, and Red will have its. Green energy will always be appealing to some, if for no other reason than the schismogenic joy of knowing that it's not "fossil fuel." We might even point to a snob factor here—okay, green energy might be more expensive, but it becomes a form of ethical conspicuous consumption. Plenty of good investments cater to conspicuous consumers. Of course, to say that rich people will want power from solar or wind is not the same thing as saying they may want to live near the power source. And so along with everything else in this split framework environment, issues of storage and transmission will have to be managed, and priced.

- Resources, wherever they are, will be valuable. Recognizing that the world might block them with WIINIMBY, Americans are once again prospecting for minerals here at home. In the words of *Science*, this is "a golden age for economic geology."[494] Yet if manganese, for instance, is poison, what does that suggest about other materials in the green energy supply chain? Investors should remember what happened to asbestos. A product once mandated in construction was later found to be toxic, and asbestos manufacturers were sued out of business. So Green Capitalists should be looking hard at liability shields as part of their hoped-for framework. Other investors might contemplate shorts.

- If we look around the world we see the climate-minded "West"—defined as North America (but not Mexico, and probably not red America), Europe (but not Russia), Japan and a few other Asian countries—is less than half the world's GDP, and less than 10 percent of the world's population. Hard to see how such a small base can have its way with the rest of world. Especially when the world

[494] Voosen, Paul, "Treasure Hunt," *Science*, June 1, 2023. https://bit.ly/44asLi2

is "decoupling into rival blocs—on geopolitics, supply chains, and the dollar. So once again, we can expect a multipolarity of energy.

- As we have seen, energy is abundant. But any energy we use is going to need to be Frameworked, because there's no energy source that can't be NIMBYd into nothingness. The world deserves an open debate, and competition, on energy, and it's entirely likely that we'll come up with more than one answer—solar in some places, nuclear in others, carbon in still others. That could lead to a healthy rivalry of paradigms, and so the investor will have to ponder each, mindful, of course, of arbitrage opportunities.

- Another way of thinking about the three silos of energy is to think of portfolio diversification. And that also has security implications, both at the national and personal level. The three silos of energy might be compared to the three strategic elements of the nuclear triad—bombers, rockets, and submarines. There's a robustness to having something important in triplicate. It's the same with an energy triad. The individual, as well as the nation, will be more secure—against all foes, foreign and domestic—if he or she has access to all three kinds of energy. Indeed, some, perhaps many, will pay a premium for the energy that comports with their vision of security. (The same thinking, by the way, will likely prop up the market for analog in a digital world, as people safeguard their memories and data with hard copies, the kind that can be safely stored in a filing cabinet or cellar.) Assuming people keep their healthy mistrust of centralized institutions, decentralized mechanisms—from the propane tank, to the home solar panel, to the long-lasting battery, to whatever other energy sources and tools— will likely sell well.

- Properly thought through, there could be two carbon industries, side by side. The first is the familiar process of carbon extraction— pull it up from the ground. The second could be carbon capture— pull it down from the air. In other words, carbon's ladder.

- We should keep in mind that there's so much money and enthusiasm in energy that innovation is a constant. So while we must ward off magical thinking, we should keep our minds open to mind-blowing possibilities. For instance, in 2023, scientists at the University of Maryland announced they had found a way to use chitin, a chemical found in the shells of crustaceans, as material for batteries.[495] It's possible that this organic breakthrough—including the possibility of vast crab plantations in the waters and seas—will obviate the need for noxious mining. If so, we'll be able to achieve green goals with less exotic and expensive inputs; actually, in fact, common and abundant inputs. In the history of innovation, this is familiar. We figured out how to make computers with silicon, the second-most abundant element on the planet, making up 28 percent of the earth's crust. Silicon is pretty much dirt, and thanks to human brains, it can be made into something surpassing gold. In the words of Marc Andreessen, "We are literally making sand think."[496]

- Tree planting will be a business in various ways. Even as the US contemplates planting more trees, China is actively de-foresting.[497] So if the world were to agree that trees have a solid value in carbon sinking, then there will be an ever larger market for carbon credits, including in the form of trees. In the meantime, as for the investment value of trees as an aesthetic improvement, in the shrewd words of social-media influencer Paul Graham, "Trees make towns look rich, and towns that look rich become rich."[498] Yes, for lots of reasons, trees are Directional.

---

[495] Stern, Ben, "Scientists discover lithium replacement that may revolutionize EV batteries: '99.7% efficient after over 400 hours of use,'" Yahoo News, July 25, 2023. https://bit.ly/3qXaJRT

[496] Andreessen, et al. "The Techno-Optimist Manifesto," October 16, 2023. https://bit.ly/3GnoVIy

[497] Global Forest Watch: China, https://bit.ly/472rUC4

[498] Graham, Paul (@paulg), X, July 20, 2023 https://bit.ly/3q1V97G

CHAPTER TWELVE
WATER IS WEALTH

A key theme of this book is that different systems will develop different economic strategies, different frameworks. Which we are free to like, or not like—to invest in, or not invest in. Yet now we come to a commonality of all economic development—water. If there's fresh water, there can be human life, as well as economic growth. If there isn't, there can't be. So water is worth fixing on, because even though each drop isn't worth much, it's what makes civilization.

In 2023, the population of the US reached 340 million, and the Census Bureau projects, by 2060, it will hit 400 million.[499] If anything, that projection seems low—it's a mobile world. But the one thing we can say for sure is that however many they are, all those people will be thirsty. So prudence, as well as the profit motive, requires that we think ahead, so that we don't end up like some desiccated place from *Dune*. With that in mind, let's consider the likely impact of the two contending dynamics in American history—Jeffersonian Liberty and the Hamiltonian Framework. Jeffersonianism means that the population will grow through immigration, and Hamiltonianism means that we must have orderly, can-do business plans. Those business plans will have to include, of course, more water. It's an age-old problem, albeit one with new solutions.

---

[499] International Data Base, United States Census, accessed June 4, 2023. https://bit.ly/431Gnv9

JAMES P. PINKERTON

MESOPOTAMIANS AS HAMILTONIANS

It's generally agreed that human civilization first emerged in Mesopotamia, somewhere around 4,000 BCE. We might add that "Mesopotamia" means "between rivers." And the presence of those two rivers, the Tigris and the Euphrates, gives us a clue as to why civilization flourished there—there was a lot of flowing water, which the locals were smart enough to channel into an irrigation system. In his monumental multi-volume *A Study of History*, Arnold Toynbee begins by detailing the "dynamic act" of the Sumerians, slogging into "jungle-swamps of the valley bottoms, never before pene-trated by man." Their hard work "succeeded beyond the most sanguine hopes in which the pioneers can ever have indulged." He added, "The wan-tonness of Nature was subdued by the works of Man; the formless swamp made way for a pattern of ditches and embankments and fields."[500] We can say—civilization begins with reclamation.

We might further say that Sumer pioneered the earliest Framework of Directional Investment. They had a goal—a stable agricultural society—and they organized themselves to achieve it. Admittedly, the workers were not always volunteers, nor were the benefits of increased productivity shared equally. Indeed, six millennia later, it's easy to criticize those who dug and dredged, disturbing wetlands. Yet those who would damn the past should be asked, what's the better alternative? Civilization is hard-won. As Camille Paglia asserts, "Everything great in Western culture has come from the quarrel with nature...rolling and milling of matter."[501]

The Sumerians were displaced by the Babylonians, who were even bet-ter organized—and so grew richer. "Such was the wealth which belonged to the ruler of Babylon," the Greek historian Herodotus wrote. And the source of that wealth? "The land...has but little rain...but the crop is ripened and the ear comes on by the help of watering from the river." The whole of

---

[500] Toynbee, Arnold, *A Study of History*, Abridgment of Volumes I-VI by D. C. Somervell (New York: Oxford University Press, 1946), 92.
[501] Paglia, Camille, *Sexual Personae: Art and Decadence from Nefertiti to Emily Dickinson* (New York: Vintage, 1991), 28.

Babylonian territory is "cut up into channels," he continued, some of them large enough for ships. The result of this hydrological sophistication was fatted farm yield increases, "two-hundred-fold for the average, and when it bears at its best it produces three-hundred-fold." For sure, Babylonian ag was a triumph. Indeed, the Babylonians were so good at moving water that their Hanging Gardens became one of the Seven Wonders of the Ancient World. (Talk about a tourist attraction.) Herodotus describes the wealth of Babylon's king, "There came in to him every day an *artab* full of silver coin"[502] That's about a half-ton of silver. Now of course, we needn't take the historian's word for all these details. Still, we can assume rulers reveled in a lot of money. Civilization is wealth creation.

Civilization also means law creation. The Code of Hammurabi, composed around 1750 BCE, is thick with rules regarding agriculture, irrigation, and land.[503] So we can further add, civilization is Framework creation. Indeed, as we think about land, we might wonder, what was the value of developed land in Babylon? The precise answer is lost in the mists of time, but arable land is worth vastly more than wilderness. So the more land reclaimed, the richer the kingdom.

Alas for Babylon, endless marauders and conquerors destroyed its wealth, and yet its successes tell us, civilization allows for Directional Investment, and Directional Investment makes for more civilization. And as an aside on good investments that stand the test of time, it's fun to note that the world's oldest still valid security was listed in Holland in 1634; the issuer was a water company, building and maintaining dikes.[504]

Beyond the Dutch and their works, there's probably not a city or country on the water, anywhere in the world, that hasn't physically altered some aspect of its border with water—building an embankment, filling in land,

---

[502] Herodotus, *The Histories*, Book One, Section 192. https://bit.ly/3NK1U6Z
[503] *The Code of Hammurabi King of Babylon*. Translated by Robert Francis Harper, 1904. https://bit.ly/431AhLd
[504] The security was issued by Hoogheemraadschap Lekdijk Bovendams. Today, after many reorganizations, the annual dividend is $16 a year. In 2000, the actual security sold at auction for $47,000. https://www.christies.com/en/lot/lot-1965498

draining marshes, channeling or re-channeling the flow. That's what civilizations do. They make the land more habitable for greater concentrations of people. To be sure, the vision of habitability is always evolving. Six thousand years after the Sumerians waded into the muck of Mesopotamia, many rich cities—from Boston to Berlin—are seeking to improve their "green infrastructure"; they are actively restoring wetlands, aka, muck.[505] The goal is, in its own way, Toynbee-esque—bringing nature back into the urban setting, including, for example, making once-polluted rivers safe for aquatic fun. All eco-ethical considerations aside, the monetary value of such restoration, for cities and property owners, is substantial. Whether it's building up or building down, water is Directional.

FRAMEWORKING RESOURCE DEVELOPMENT

As we move closer to home, we see the impact of Directed Investment in water infrastructure. Interestingly, for much of the twentieth century, the Democrats were the more Hamiltonian party of development. They had the idea that water projects—providing not just flood control and hydropower but also such valuables as better drainage for mosquito abatement—would allow for new economic development, new cities and towns and all the economic activity that went with. The 1948 Democratic platform, which helped President Harry Truman win a second term, highlighted the party's accomplishments during the New Deal—including the ultra-Hamiltonian Tennessee Valley Authority—and promised to do more, stating, "We pledge the continued full and unified regional development of the water, mineral, and other natural resources of the nation." The platform offered the Neo-Sumerian promise of "irrigation of arid land," adding a modern twist—"the development and transmission of electric energy."[506] In that

---

[505] Hockenos, Paul, "Let Them Swim," *New York Times*, July 10, 2023. https://bit.ly/459Es9h

[506] 1948 Democratic Party Platform, The American Presidency Project, July 12, 1948. https://bit.ly/431zz0u

same developmental spirit, the Democratic platform of 1960 pledged, "We will support and intensify the research effort to find an economical way to convert salt and brackish water." That is, desalination. That platform added a partisan dig at the rival party. "The Republicans discouraged this research, which holds untold possibilities for the whole world."[507]

This was the platform upon which John F. Kennedy based his victorious presidential campaign. We can add that while JFK's most famous words about the economy—"a rising tide lifts all the boats"—are remembered as being about tax cuts, they were actually said in praise of water development. Kennedy offered that tidal image on October 3, 1963, while dedicating a dam in Heber Springs, Arkansas. The new infrastructure, he said, would pay long-term dividends. "The full impact of it will be felt by the sense of recreation and industry and all the rest in five, ten, fifteen, or twenty years."[508] With a dam as a backdrop for this speech, it was easy for Kennedy to cite water imagery as he pitched further plans to boost economic growth, including tax cuts. Reducing tax rates is, for sure, a way to increase economic returns, but so, too, is increasing water infrastructure.

But then, beginning in the 1970s, the Democrats changed—they went green. Or, we might say, they went brown, the color of dry, in opposition to water projects. In 1977, President Jimmy Carter, in tune with thenfashionable "malaise" Malthusianism, sought to kill a slew of federal water projects.[509] Nowhere was the green anti-growth movement stronger than in California. For the ecology minded left, the state's phenomenal population growth over the previous century was a source of regret, even shame. The 1974 movie *Chinatown* put a retrospective Watergate-ish pall of corruption on the process of getting water for Southern California. Another touchstone of anti-growth thinking was the 1986 book *Cadillac Desert: The*

---

[507] 1960 Democratic Party Platform, The American Presidency Project, July 11, 1960. https://bit.ly/3JzwUUS

[508] John F. Kennedy, "Remarks in Heber Springs, Arkansas, at the Dedication of Greers Ferry Dam," October 3, 1963. https://bit.ly/3rs6JJp

[509] "Water Projects Compromise Reached," Congressional Quarterly, 1977. https://bit.ly/46otEoT

American West and Its Disappearing Water. Author Marc Reisner argued that additional infrastructure should be shunned, because it would mean additional people. He wrote, "When you added a couple of lanes to a freeway or built a new bridge, cars came out of nowhere to fill them. It was the same with water: the more you developed, the more growth occurred, and the faster demand grew. California was now hitched to a runaway locomotive."[510] And to think, it was the locomotive, and the railway, that connected California to the east coast, bringing gold prospected by '49ers to the east, and, in turn, making the Golden State secure. Yet in the minds of many, train imagery was now to be harnessed to de-growth. As we have seen, in this *e pluribus duo* country, people on the blue side of the duo hold to their views strongly. And yet there're also people on the red side, and they, too, have strong views—and rights.

WATER, WATER, NOWHERE

Toynbee's central idea is that history is a matter of "challenge and response." That is, when a civilization was confronted with a challenge—from channeling water to defending against invaders—the question arises, can the people summon up an effective response? If they can, the civilization continues to flourish. If they can't, it falls by the wayside. So with Toynbee in mind, let's move from California to its dry, thirsty, and challenged neighbor, Arizona. "Arid-zona" receives annual precipitation of just twelve inches a year, compared to a national average of thirty inches. In the meantime, more than a quarter of Arizona's water comes from the Colorado River. Its flow, tapped by seven states, is drying up.[511] Yet people have been moving to the Grand Canyon State. Its population didn't pass two million until 1972, and now, it's more than seven million.

---

[510] Reisner, Marc, *Cadillac Desert: The American West and Its Disappearing Water*, (New York: Viking, 1986), 360.

[511] Communications and Publishing, "Groundwater Flow to Colorado River May Decline By a Third Over Next 30 Years," U.S. Geological Survey, October 28, 2021. https://bit.ly/44ltPQm

A watershed came in 2023. Headline in *AZ Central*: "Arizona will halt new home approvals in parts of metro Phoenix as water supplies tighten."[512] Most notably, that decision put a dent in the Howard Hughes Corporation, the largest operator of planned communities in the US. In 2021, the company paid $600 million for 37,000 acres of land in the West Valley area, announcing plans to build 100,000 homes and 55 million square feet of commercial space.[513] We can add that many billions more in investments—in computer chips, electric vehicles, autonomous vehicles, plastics—are at risk if the city and region can't continue to develop, including building all-important affordable housing.[514] The Arizona law at issue, the Groundwater Management Act, dates back to 1980, those being the days of Carter-type "era of limits." The law requires that new developments show projections of adequate water for 100 years. That's the green "precautionary principle" at work, scanting the potential for innovation that transcends linear projection limits. We can ask ourselves, if the world contains 332 million cubic miles of water (97 percent of it salty) what are the chances that, over the next century, someone can't figure out how to get a few thousand cubic miles of fresh water to Arizona? We could do it easily, but some, for their own reasons, choose not to acknowledge the ease.

BORN IN BABYLONIA, MOVED TO ARIZONA

In "King Tut," Steve Martin's jokey 1978 novelty song, the titular character was born in Arizona, moved to Babylonia. Ha ha. But now we can reverse the sequence here, declaring that the far-thinking water work of Babylonians can now inform Arizonans. Here's a vision that would make

---

[512] Loomis, Brandon, "Arizona will halt new home approvals in parts of metro Phoenix as water supplies tighten," *AZ Central*, June 1, 2023. https://bit.ly/3NpGURz

[513] Walter-Warner, Holden, "Howard Hughes buys 37K acres to build 'city of the future'" *The Real Deal*, October 19, 2021. https://bit.ly/46Blhqv

[514] Boehm, Jessica, "Phoenix is emerging as the city of the future," *Axios*, June 21, 2023. https://bit.ly/3D6H8Zn

a lot of people a lot of money—lawns and gardens turn green, farmland becomes more productive, deserts bloom, wildfires are put out immediately. In general, there'd be more greenery and abundant life. Sound good? And along the way, there'd be plenty of money to be made in real estate. That is, the *other* kind of green. Many, many, billions, even trillions. Let's look. According to Redfin, at the end of 2022, the total value of home real estate in the US stood at $45.3 trillion.[515] Arizona represents about 2 percent of the national population, boasting a higher-than-median home price. So with a little ciphering, we can calculate that Arizona's homes are worth, in toto, about $1.36 trillion. That's a goodly sum, but a Directional Investor might start by asking, what if we could kick it up by 10 percent? That would add $136 billion to the wealth of homeowners. So how to do that value-adding? One way would be to make Arizona lusher and greener. As in, add water. And, of course, we mean fresh water, the kind we can drink and use for lawns, swimming pools and, crucially, fire extinguishing, thereby lowering fire insurance rates. So if we need more fresh water, let's think about desalination. The oceans are big, they won't notice.

In fact, the state had made some halting progress in that direction. In 2022, the state's then-governor, Doug Ducey, signed legislation to examine all possible water options for Arizona, including desalination.[516] The idea has continue to kick around in state politics, Republicans being mostly for it, albeit with few exact specifics, and Democrats being mostly against it.[517] So what's needed is a larger and more tangible vision that punches through the generality, a vision detailing all the good things that would come to Arizona with abundant water. Here we can pause to recall the wisdom of the Harvard Business School's Ted Levitt. Back in 1983, he published *The Marketing Imagination*, in which he argued that the key sales move was

[515] Katz, Lily, and Chen, Zhao, "U.S. Homeowners Have Lost $2.3 Trillion In Value Since June Peak," Redfin, February 22, 2023. https://bit.ly/3pkXwC9
[516] Medler, Robert, "Arizona Governor Signs Historic Bill That Makes an Unprecedented $1 Billion Investment to Secure Arizona's Water Future," Western Growers, July 7, 2022. https://bit.ly/478GGas
[517] Flavelle, Christopher, "Arizona, Low on Water, Weighs Taking It From the Sea. In Mexico." *New York Times*, June 10, 2023. https://bit.ly/3rB2Y4r

"tangibilizing the intangible." That is, making the prospect of product seem so real that the customer could practically taste it.[518] So if you haven't made the sale yet, that's because you haven't made it tangible enough. Arizona needs to tangibilize a future that's so green and lush that it has the modern-day equivalent of the Hanging Gardens, which all the world will flock to see, even buy.

Is it now feasible to desalinate sea water? To make this elixir of green? The answer is an emphatic *yes*. As the cost of desal has been falling rapidly, so, too, is its use in other countries. Israel gets more than half of its fresh water from desalination,[519] and for the United Arab Emirates, the percentage is 42.[520] But for the US, it's a mere 0.1 percent.[521] Yet Elon Musk said in 2023, desalinated water is "absurdly cheap." He followed up, saying, "Turning sea water into clean, drinkable water costs $2 to $5 for 1000 gallons. Less than half a penny per gallon is obviously absurdly cheap."[522] An Israeli company, IDE Technologies, estimates that it could build a desal plant for Arizona at a cost of $5 billion. That's not nothing, cost-wise, but the expense must be weighed against the betterment of Arizona, for which we've contingencied that $136 billion. We can add that bringing in water from the outside, as opposed to wells, oftentimes works to the advantage of a built-up area. Why? Because to drain away too much water from aquifers can cause subsidence, even sinkholes, which is ominous for structures.

So here's the deal for Arizona—use the projected 10 percent uptick in real estate prices with desal—that is, $136 billion—as collateral against which to raise the money needed to build the desal. That is, pay for the present with revenues and capital gains from the future. Companies do it all the time. They sell stock based on the hope of future income. States

[518] Levitt, Theodore, *The Marketing Imagination* (New York: The Free Press, 1983), 110.

[519] Jacobsen, Rowan, "Israel Proves the Desalination Era Is Here," *Scientific American*, July 29, 2016. https://bit.ly/3rBpkCX

[520] "Water Security Strategy 2036," UAE https://bit.ly/3O2FHjn

[521] "Desalination," U.S. Geological Survey, September 11, 2019. https://bit.ly/43BaFoK

[522] Musk, Elon (@elonmusk), X, May 7, 2023. https://bit.ly/470prbm

and localities do the same. They sell bonds based on projections of future revenue from taxes, fees, or tolls. So could Arizona, develop some sort of waterworking Hamiltonian combine? Desal is the sort of long play that would have made the Sumerians and Babylonians proud. Fresh water could restore agricultural abundance, make the forests more fireproof (and more useful for carbon capture), lower insurance rates, make everyone's lawn prettier, and perhaps their swimming pool fuller. All as part of making their homes more valuable. And increased value is what investment is all about.

Now it could be immediately objected that the $136 billion is diffused across hundreds of thousands of property owners, who may not be interested in any desal scheme. On the other hand, $136 billion is so much money that some environmental greens might decide that they'd rather have the financial green. In any case, developers are a much smaller group. They are already organized into trade associations and other combines. Indeed, this desal project could offer the opportunity to try out a new approach to politics, based on organizing people and firms on the basis of their own self-interest, aiming toward a kind of granular, crowd-based Framework. This we will detail in Chapter Sixteen.

Of course, there's one big problem—Arizona is landlocked. The oceanfront state to the west of it is California. And as we know, it's thick with NIMBY greens, even if, today, they are more like browns, opposing water projects. In the last few years, environmentalists have blocked a string of desalination plants from being built—and no doubt blocked even more from being contemplated.[523]

This blockage is discouraging, because not only does California need fresh water for its residents, but also for its farms. A *Washington Post*

---

[523] Johnson, Steven, "Manhattan Beach Says NO to Desal Plant Proposal," HealTheBay.org February 22, 2016. https://bit.ly/46WTGPv. See also, Meyer, Garth, "A winning nature – Stopping West Basin's desalination plant is the latest victory for environmentalist Craig Cadwallader," *Easy Rider News*, February 23, 2022, https://bit.ly/4a3viy3 and Becker, Rachel, "A salty dispute: California Coastal Commission unanimously rejects desalination plant," *Cal Matters*, May 12, 2022. https://bit.ly/44BEruM

headline from 2022 summed up agriculture's thirst, writing, "As it enters a third year, California's drought is strangling the farming industry." The story continued, "The scarcity of water and the now-exorbitant price for it have prompted many farmers to leave large tracts of land fallow, an alarming trend that is accelerating with each dry year."[524] No water = no farming = lost wealth.

Also, California could use fresh water to put out wildfires, which have tripled in the last three decades. Every year we see these fires, and in response, we see airplanes dropping creepy colored fire retardants on the fires. Are such chemicals, and such CO_2-belching airplane sorties, good for the environment? Of course not. Surely it would be better, and greener, to have fresh water handy—through pipelines or perhaps dropped from airships of some kind—to put the fires out. The economic damage to the state from a single year of wildfires, 2018, totaled $148.5 billion.[525] And oh, by the way, according to a UCLA study, the wildfires in a single year produced 127 million metric tons of greenhouse gas emissions, which was double the reductions that the state of California achieved from 2003 to 2019. In other words, one year of wildfire overwhelmed sixteen years of policy do-gooding on autos and barbecues.[526] Yet blue California has its own way of doing things. According to state official Michael Soller, California "recognizes the impact of climate change" and is spending billions of dollars to try to reduce the wildfire risk.[527] Doesn't seem to be money well spent. In fact, we might wonder, is California actually interested in putting out wildfires, or is it more interested in highlighting climate change as an issue…perhaps to further the ambitions of its governor? We might even further speculate that wildfires that burn out the interior of the state have

[524] Wilson, Scott, "As it enters a third year, California's drought is strangling the farming industry," *Washington Post*, March 21, 2022. https://wapo.st/44SXtfP

[525] Gedye, Grace, "How much do wildfires really cost California's economy?" *Cal Matters*, October 11, 2021. https://bit.ly/3K81OUF

[526] Mulkern, Anne C., "California's 2020 Wildfires Negated Years of Emission Cuts," *Scientific American*, October 18, 2022. https://bit.ly/44wYuus

[527] Eaglesham, Jean, "Insurers Are in the Hot Seat on Climate Change," *The Wall Street Journal*, July 13, 2023. https://bit.ly/3rs7wKs

the effect of depopulating the rural, mostly Republican, areas. For partisan Democrats, that's not the worst outcome. So yes, California should be interested in making fresh water, but most likely it won't be, at least no time soon.

If California won't help itself, it's not going to help Arizona. So now we might look at a map and notice that the Grand Canyon State has another neighbor to the south. That's Mexico, specifically, the state of Sonora, which abuts the Sea of Cortez, part of the Pacific Ocean. In fact, it's just sixty-four miles from the Arizona state line to the coastal town of Puerto Peñasco. So here's the possible deal—Arizona bargains with Sonora to build a desal plant in Mexico and then pipe the fresh water to Arizona. As we know, there's already a thriving cross-border trade between the two countries. And Mexico is already looking to sell electric power to the US, so it's not much of a leap to sell another kind of a utility, fresh water.[528] Would the deal with Sonora and Mexico be easy? Of course not. For instance, the *New York Times* worries of a possible pipeline, "It would flood the northern Gulf of California with waste brine, threatening one of Mexico's most productive fisheries. It would carve a freeway-sized corridor through a U.S. national monument and UNESCO site, established to protect a fragile desert ecosystem." The *Times* adds, "In addition to its ecological value, the land has spiritual significance for the Tohono O'odham Nation, whose people lived there for thousands of years before being displaced to a reservation east of the park."[529] We can see that this is the stuff of NIMBYism and WIINIMBYism, blown up to an international scale. So here's where that $136 billion could really come in handy. The mission is to tangibilize that new wealth for Sonorans and Mexicans, as well as Arizonans.

But if Mexico won't go for it, there are other possibilities. Arizona political figures have suggested, for example, that fresh water could be

---

[528] Udasin, Sharon, "Mexico is moving to power California and Arizona. But who will pay for it?" *The Hill*, March 28, 2023. https://bit.ly/3pVlNyS

[529] Flavelle, Christopher, "Arizona, Low on Water, Weighs Taking It From the Sea. In Mexico." *New York Times*, June 10, 2023. https://bit.ly/3rB2Y4r

piped in from the Midwest, perhaps the Great Lakes.[530] Another possibility is desalinating water from the Gulf of Mexico, piping it to Arizona via Texas and New Mexico. Yet of course, the Malthusians are resolved to "California-ize" the nation. They are seeking to block desal in Texas, fearing that it "could harm sensitive coastal ecosystems."[531] We might ask, in the minds of green legal brief writers, is there any such thing as an *insensitive* coastal ecosystem? For reasons described in previous chapters, it's likely that soon enough, Texas will take these matters into its own hands, in conjunction with Red Jeffersonia. But Arizona is a purple state. So it might have to choose its future direction. One vision is a greener, cooler, and more prosperous Arizona. The other vision is dry, dry, dry—nothing but thirst and sand and stagnation.

Both parties could embrace a new Framework for water, with liberty and money for all. That's Directional Investing at its best.

INVESTMENT TAKEAWAYS

- The story of civilization is the story of moving water to where it's needed. And the story, too, of wealth creation. With fresh water, there will be larger numbers of people (producers and consumers, both), greater agriculture, lusher forests, fewer wildfires—that's a lot of *cha-ching!* As a result, land prices will rise, insurance costs will fall, and growth will increase. *Cha-ching!* And if all that is counted, as it could be, as carbon capture, then even more *cha-ching!*

- If Arizona can make desal work, so can other dry states, including Nevada. Nevada knows from *cha-ching!* And we're only getting started on the prosperity that can come from curated geography.

---

[530] "Water for the West," Issues, Kari Lake for Senate, accessed July 10, 2023. https://bit.ly/44KkhyB

[531] Douglas, Erin, "EPA may try to block what could be the first seawater desalination plant built in Texas," *Texas Tribune*, September 22, 2022. https://bit.ly/3NqnBYo

CHAPTER THIRTEEN

FREEDOM TO CURE

T his chapter can be outlined simply: The *problem*, the *solution*, the *opportunity*. To solve the problem we'll see that once again, we need Jeffersonian Liberty and the Hamiltonian Framework. We should take the lesson from Nevada—a Framework can exist at the state level, not just the federal level. The states, and their rights to make their own rules, have the power to pull in billions, and as we shall see, maybe even trillions. We've quoted Jefferson on states' rights, now we can quote the more business minded Hamilton. "The State governments possess inherent advantages, which will ever give them an influence and ascendency over the National Government, and will for ever preclude the possibility of federal encroachments. That their liberties, indeed, can be subverted by the federal head, is repugnant to every rule of political calculation."[532] To be sure, the idea that the states are prior to the federal government on most matters is somewhat unfamiliar to many, but that's one reason why we study the past, and what's possible now—to gain actionable intel about new Directions for policy.

---

[532] Hamilton, Alexander, "Speech on the Compromises of the Constitution," Teaching American History, June 20, 1788. https://tinyurl.com/5cdxejrz

CAN'T BUY ME A CURE

On October 5, 2011, Apple co-founder and CEO Steve Jobs died of cancer. He was worth billions, and yet for all his money, he couldn't buy a cure, or even an effective treatment, and so he was dead at 56. Beyond the sadness of his early demise, in an economic sense, was a case of market failure—all that demand, but no supply. Yet the failure isn't just his inability to buy a cure, it's also America's inability to buy cures. We might consider this— in 2023, the National Health Expenditure of the US was $4.72 *trillion*— that's almost a fifth of our national output—and yet more than 600,000 Americans die of cancer each year.[533] This is more than a half-century after President Richard Nixon declared a national "war on cancer." Since then, we've won battles, but hardly the war.

Thinking about larger issues of public health, we can ask, how come all this money is being spent, even as overall American life expectancy has been flatlining? There are, to be sure, many causes, but one of them— especially pertinent to diseases such as cancer—is the Food and Drug Administration (FDA). It's a brake on progress. Indeed, it operates in defiance of technological progress, such that medicine is actually running in the opposite direction from Moore's Law.

EROOM'S LAW

Back in 2012, surveying the stagnation of pharmaceutical innovation, a trio of researchers coined "Eroom's Law," which is Moore's Law spelled backward. "The past 60 years have seen huge advances in many of the scientific, technological and managerial factors that should tend to raise the efficiency of commercial drug research and development (R&D)," they wrote. "Yet the number of new drugs approved per billion US dollars spent on R&D has halved roughly every nine years since 1950, falling around

---

[533] "Projected, National health expenditure data," CMS, accessed April 16, 2023. https://bit.ly/43YtHGB

80-fold in inflation-adjusted terms."[534] What happened? Why has digital tech gone one way, and medical tech gone the other way? The watershed was thalidomide, a drug used in the late 1950s and early 1960s to treat pregnant women's morning sickness—and was discovered to cause birth defects.[535] Thankfully, FDA never approved thalidomide in the US, and yet in the uproar over the drug, Congress felt the need to "do something." In 1962, its supposed "reform" legislation had the effect of deforming the industry. Egged on by a demagogic senator, Estes Kefauver of Tennessee, Congress went beyond trying to assure the safety of medicinal drugs, adding a new variable—efficacy, or "substantial evidence of effectiveness." At first blush, it might seem reasonable to stipulate efficacy, but the problem is proving it. Efficacious for whom? For you? For me? For that fellow behind the tree? People are different. During the debate, the American Medical Association (AMA) opposed the efficacy provision, arguing, "The only possible final determination as to the efficacy and ultimate use of a drug is the extensive clinical use of that drug by large numbers of the medical profession over a long period of time."[536] The tool for showing efficacy, the randomized controlled trials (RCT), was and is inherently narrow. It's simply too small to show whether or not a drug actually works in the larger world—and for whom. The best thing to do, the AMA advised, was to look and see what happened to real patients, in real time. But the Kefauver Amendment passed, and now the FDA would judge efficacy for a nation of several hundred million on the basis of data from a few hundred, at most a few thousand, people. Statistical samples, the equivalent of a snapshot public opinion poll, are a poor substitute for reality. Longtime healthcare observer Jeremy Shane points to more concerns: "The participants in a

---

[534] Scannell, Jack, et al.,"Diagnosing the decline in pharmaceutical R&D efficiency," *Nature*, March 1, 2012. https://www.nature.com/articles/nrd3681

[535] Interestingly, properly prescribed—*not* for pregnant women—thalidomide has proven effective against various maladies, including cancer.

[536] Greene, Jeremy, and Podolsky, Scott, "Reform, Regulation, and Pharmaceuticals—The Kefauver–Harris Amendments at 50," *New England Journal of Medicine*, October 18, 2012. https://www.ncbi.nlm.nih.gov/pmc/articles/PMC4101807/

clinical trial have to be a 'purified' sub-population, in the sense of not having taken prior drugs or not being on others currently that would have a confounding effect. This helps isolate if the drug can work in a particular setting, but it's unlikely to be the setting in which it's actually used post-approval. FDA now requires post-approval studies but these are seldom used to actually change how drugs are prescribed."

Because efficacy is such an evanescent concept, drug makers were stymied. And so the number of new drugs approved by FDA fell dramatically. In the ten years prior to Kefauver, 1951 to 1961, annual approvals averaged 303. Yet approvals fell to just sixty-seven the year after Kefauver passed. Most recently, in the decade 2013 to 2022, the average number of approvals was just 124.[537] It's Kefauver, of course, that's driving Eroom's Law—an approval plummet of 59 percent. As one retrospective on the efficacy provision put it, "The new burden of proof appeared to make the process of drug development both more expensive and much longer."[538] According to Deloitte, it now takes perhaps a decade, or more, and $2.3 billion, to bring a drug to market.[539] In fact, FDA drug approvals have devolved into a byzantine bureaucratic process, featuring lawyers, lobbyists, and "astroturfers" (fake grassroots campaigns).

Still, in keeping with the overall downward slant of Eroom's Law— seeking to know the unknowable, plus risk aversion, plus bureaucratic sclerosis—former Rep. Billy Tauzin of Louisiana once told me, "The FDA today would never approve *aspirin*." Of course, from a bureaucratic point of view, saying "no" is always the safest course. Economist Alex Tabarrok

---

[537] "Summary of NDA Approvals & Receipts, 1938 to the present," FDA. Accessed December 2, 2023. https://bit.ly/3pp9ZES

[538] Greene, Jeremy, and Podolsky, Scott, "Reform, Regulation, and Pharmaceuticals—The Kefauver–Harris Amendments at 50," *New England Journal of Medicine*, October 18, 2012. https://www.ncbi.nlm.nih.gov/pmc/articles/PMC4101807/

[539] Philippidis, Alex, "The Unbearable Cost of Drug Development: Deloitte Report Shows 15% Jump in R&D to $2.3 Billion," *Genetic Engineering & Biotechnology News*, February 28, 2023. https://bit.ly/3pg8nxf

adds a mordant point, "When the FDA fails to approve a good drug, people die but the bodies are buried in an invisible graveyard."[540]

THE DEADENING HAND

The FDA is the *main morte*, the dead hand, on the throat of medical innovation. That deadening effect is all the more glaring in the era of big data and artificial intelligence (AI). If personalized medicine means anything, it means that the drug that works for the person of Jones might not work for the person of Smith, but that's okay, because it's only Jones that needs it. In this big, diverse, country, it's foolish to use clinical trials as a way of seeking to know—more like pretending to know—what works for 340 million Americans, and, by extension, eight billion more around the world. If we're each diverse and unique, well, then, the regulatory system should allow for that. RCT are good enough to study the relatively simple variable of safety (although again, the subset is never the same as the set), and yet they offer only the wispy illusion of truth about efficacy. In the end, RCT can tell you what happened to participants in the trial, during the time that they were in the trial, and not much more. Any larger extrapolation—which, of course, is the FDA's supposed purpose—is a dodgy negotiation of truth. The philosopher-poet Paul Valéry considered situations in which pseudo-certainty replaces true knowledge. "A simple statement is bound to be untrue," he wrote, adding, "One that is not simple cannot be utilized." If the simple answer (as from RCT) is not true, and a non-simple answer can't be utilized, then the FDA is on a forlorn mission, in which the real victims are patients. We could even say that the mission of the FDA and its many supporters—including, it seems, Big Pharma, fond of a good cartel—is control, not cures.

The better answer is to use the drug on each willing patient. Direct application is, after all, the only way to know what's true for that patient. To

---

[540] Tabarrok, Alex, "Is the FDA Too Conservative or Too Aggressive?" *Marginal Revolution*, August 26, 2015. https://bit.ly/3XqVXiu

be sure, not everyone is interested in such experimentation, but then, not everyone has stage four colon cancer. For those that are desperately ill, it would be best to have close consultation with the doctor, to see what might work best. And here's where big data and AI come in, helping deliver better answers than an RCT, which, by definition, was long ago and far away. RCT is an artifact from an earlier age—the earnest but obsolete notion that a rough estimate of the greatest good for the greatest number is the best that medical science can do. It's the epitome of lowest common denominator thinking. That the FDA clings to RCT is proof that the agency prefers an old paradigm of rote simplification, as opposed to the new possibilities of nuanced, data-enhanced, problem-solving. Today, thanks to computerization and big data-fication, it's possible to actually see the results, in real time. It's that flowing data that should be guiding patients and their doctors, not a musty bureaucratic ruling.

As a coda to this account of institutional clot, we can add this—when there's real pressure on the FDA, it simply junks RCT and greenlights the drug, no questions asked. That's what happened with the COVID vaccines in 2020, and since.[541] There's no need, here, to go into the merits and demerits of COVID vaccines, but what does it tell us if the FDA's standard operating procedure is simply bypassed when authorities deem it expedient? It tells us that the SOP of RCT isn't necessary, after all. It tells us that authorities play favorites, that concerns over COVID rank much higher than concerns over cancer, and Alzheimer's, and just about every other disease. From that we might conclude that advocates for curing other diseases might need to hire better lobbyists (that's always the sly pitch of direction-minded Washingtonians). Or, much better, we might conclude that the whole RCT contraption for efficacy was always a bad idea, and by now, compared to what's possible, it's a *really* bad idea. Curiously, the Biden administration had a chance to do just that—to make the leap forward to a better medical paradigm—and chose not to.

---

[541] "FDA Takes Key Action in Fight Against COVID-19 By Issuing Emergency Use Authorization for First COVID-19 Vaccine," FDA, December 11, 2020. https://bit.ly/3XnDAuZ

THE MOON SHOT MISSED ITS SHOT

Joe Biden's son Beau died of cancer in 2015. He was only forty-six. Ever since, the elder Biden has said America needs a John F. Kennedy-esque "moon shot" to cure cancer—and who can argue? Yet when the moment came, President Biden missed his shot. In 2021, the Biden administration declared its intention to win, finally, the war on cancer. The administration proposed the Advanced Research Projects Agency for Health—ARPA-H—the name being an homage to DARPA, the renowned Defense Advanced Research Projects Agency that, as we saw in Chapter Nine, actually pushes products into existence. So an ARPA-H, done right, would have had the power to skip past hurdles, including, of course, the FDA. Not surprisingly, the idea of doing things differently didn't sit well with the sentries of the status quo, at the FDA and elsewhere in Big Health. So with nary a peep of protest from the asleep Bidenites, ARPA-H was whittled down just an adjunct to the National Institutes of Health (NIH). Whereas once it had been hoped that ARPA-H would be headquartered in some tech-friendly place such as California or Massachusetts, there to embrace a culture of innovation, ARPA-H was reeled back inside the Beltway, the better for NIH to keep track of it, there to imbibe the culture of same old, same old risk-aversion.[542] Indeed, the FDA's authority over ARPA-H is written into the enabling.[543] As one close-in observer said of the misbegotten new entity, "The contrast with DARPA couldn't be greater."[544] Moon Shot: *Missed.*

[542] "HHS Secretary Becerra Establishes ARPA-H within NIH, Names Adam H. Russell, D.Phil. Acting Deputy Director," Department of Health and Human Services, March 25, 2022. https://bit.ly/3XoDTpm. See also: Kaiser, Jocelyn, "Biden's new biomedical agency fails to gain independence from NIH," *Science*, March 31, 2022. https://bit.ly/3pmaejY

[543] "An Act to establish the Advanced Research Projects Agency-Health, and for other purposes," 117th Congress, June 23, 2022. https://www.congress.gov/bill/117th-congress/house-bill/5585/text

[544] Bushak, Lecia, "ARPA-H is officially established. Now what?" *Medical Marketing and Media*, June 6, 2022. https://bit.ly/3pqvpS8

SOFTWARE IS EATING THE WORLD: LET IT EAT DISEASE

At the opposite end of Eroom's Law, of course, is Moore's Law. Perhaps Moore's Law has slowed down. After decades of shrinkage, we can't make transistors smaller than single electrons—but if so, it seems likely that AI will speed things up. In any case, over a decade ago, Silicon Valley mogul Marc Andreessen observed, "software is eating the world."[545] That is, software was virtualizing hardware, and everything else that's hard. And now we can say, AI is eating software. From a medical point of view, this is an exciting prospect, because it offers the prospect of further accelerating the digital design of new drugs, by predicting, for example, every possible protein fold or mutation. To be sure, there's no guarantee that such *in silico* pioneering will succeed, but tech's track record tantalizes. In the meantime, we know this much—in this AI-ized future, there will be a terrible mismatch between what's possible and what's actual. That is, AI can maybe develop a new candidate drug every second. And yet the FDA—one-half Naderite, the other half "captured" by Big Pharma—typically takes many years to decide what's efficacious and thus what's approved.

There's another interesting possibility for AI, which is already, of course, being explored. That is, AI can be used, not just to design new drugs, but to evaluate old drugs, and even old substances, with an eye toward new uses. In the past, it was mostly serendipity that led scientists to discover, for instance, that grubby mold could be made into penicillin, or that the rat poison warfarin could be a lifesaver on strokes. More recently, curiosity and desperation over COVID led to a surge of interest in various "populist" treatments, including vitamin D, zinc, and such controversial compounds as hydroxychloroquine and ivermectin. Do these treatments work? As is inevitable with personalized medicine, the answer could be as variable as human anatomy and human psychology. And yet people have long been experimenting, sometimes finding success. (It's called science.) Now with AI, we'll be able to find out even faster.

---

[545] Andreessen, Marc, "Why Software Is Eating the World," a16z, August 20, 2011. https://a16z.com/2011/08/20/why-software-is-eating-the-world/

Importantly, AI isn't just the province of some costly and remote supercomputer. Thanks to the cloud, AI will soon be universally available. Which is to say, millions of people could be involved in the search for new compounds and cures. It's been estimated that humanity has made, found, or used an estimated 50 million unique chemicals. Moreover, a novel substance is either isolated or synthesized every 2.6 seconds.[546] So we see the prospect of the ultimate in crowdsourcing. As an aside, we can see that our two friends, Hamilton and Jefferson, are in the middle of a new kind of application. The centralized Hamiltonianism of super computing is now being spread out, and, in keeping with the Jeffersonian dream of property ownership, widely distributed. Is there the potential for medical mayhem? You bet. But that's true of everything people do, inside government, as well as outside government. For our purposes here, we can simply observe that AI has the potential to transcend RCT and the FDA.

Okay, so that's a good theory—AI will *eat* old-time regulation. But just because the rationale of the FDA is eaten away doesn't mean that the institution itself will go away. It could survive as a fully funded zombie husk, complete with its dead-handed regulatory authority. So how to get past the FDA? We can consider two possibilities, one at the federal level, and the other at the state level.

HIGH-TECH HEALTH

Suppose the President of the United States decided to create a High Trajectory Health Agency (HTHA), focused on AI-based drug approvals. That is, bypassing the FDA, on the grounds that the older agency is simply not relevant to *in silico* drug discovery. After all, AI can make a unique drug for each unique patient—which is to say, all of us—so there's no need for the FDA's cumbersome RCT method, any more than we need cathode ray tubes for today's computers. So why not make a second, high-tech,

---

[546] Madrigal, Alexis, "Humans Have Made, Found or Used Over 50 Million Unique Chemicals," *Wired*, September 9, 2009. https://bit.ly/3PsRx93

path to drug approval? HTHA could be established by legislation, of course, but HTHA could be brought into existence, a lot quicker, by presidential executive order. Can the president do that? Why, yes. We know that to be true because presidents have done it in the past. By executive order. Here's a partial list of hugely consequential actions US presidents have taken by executive order: the Emancipation Proclamation in 1862; the creation of Export-Import Bank in 1934; the integration of the armed forces in 1948; the launching of the Peace Corps in 1961; the creation of the Federal Energy Office in 1973, which wielded vast powers over the price and allocation of energy, and grew to become the Department of Energy; the Deferred Action for Childhood Arrivals (DACA) in 2012. As of this writing, in all of US history going back to President Washington, there have been a total of nearly 16,000 executive orders.[547] And yes, Biden could have established ARPA-H that way. To be sure, any agency, or policy, that one president can create by the stroke of a pen, a subsequent president can un-create by the stroke of a pen. So we're back to a critical issue of the Hamiltonian Framework. If it is to survive, it must be popular. So the maintenance of popularity becomes a key task—which suggests the Framework has to work. But before it can be maintained, of course, it has to be created.

Let's think about what might happen if a president were to create a High-Tech Health Agency. HTHA would be charged with working with Big Tech (and every other sized tech) to facilitate approval of AI-driven drugs. It would then, be, therefore, an entire new pathway to drug approval, using the power of big data to measure efficacy in the most efficacious way possible—by seeing if a drug actually helps a patient. Needless to say, HTHA would immediately gain the attention of billionaires, as well as their trillion-dollar corporations. The corporations might be immortal, but their executives and shareholders are not, at least as far as we know. Indeed, given Tech's fascination with longevity and transhumanism, we

<hr/>

[547] Howell, William, and Lewis, David, "Agencies by Presidential Design," University of Chicago, 2001. https://bit.ly/3Py3ydm. The authors found that no fewer than forty-three federal agencies were created by presidential executive order from 1946-1995, and another 240 by other kinds of executive fiat.

might surmise that there's already a substantial underground economy of medicines and treatments. That is, billionaires could already be working on their own personal life-extension plans, relying on nodes that stretch from Palo Alto to the Alcor Life Extension Foundation in Arizona to China to the Dark Web. Much of this activity might never wish to be brought to light. Yet it's likely that many Techsters would be very interested in seeing some new, legal, fusion between the best tech and the best medicine, conducted by licensed doctors in licensed hospitals, eliminating, through transparency, the danger of bad treatment—and blackmail. Notably, Eric Schmidt, the former CEO of Google, spent millions to gain influence, legally, in the Biden White House's Office of Science and Technology Policy. Schmidt believes, for instance, that "5G and quantum computing are poised to enable new growth in AI capabilities, while AI stands to transform the biological sciences, producing significant technological breakthroughs and turning the biotechnology sector into one of the primary drivers of overall economic competitiveness."[548] Who can argue with any that?

Earlier, we made the point that imagining precedes investing, and nowhere is that more true than in the blue-sky world of billions in personal wealth and trillions in corporate capital. In other words, an HTHA would hit the sweet spot. If approval was made immediate for "accredited patients," investment would increase it a hundred-fold. And so the nearly $5 trillion that the US spends every year on health—and trillions more around the world—would find a new hub of innovation—a medical Las Vegas on the San Francisco Bay.

If the better health plan were thought through properly and presented wisely, the general public would be pleased to know that drugs developed via algorithm would be not only better, but cheaper, because computer time is cheaper than years of RCT waiting and the FDA's wheedling and special pleading.

---

[548] Thompson, Alex, "A Google billionaire's fingerprints are all over Biden's science office," *Politico*, March 28, 2022. https://bit.ly/3Ds97CI

So we might wonder, who would oppose HTHA? For sure the Naderites and Luddites would oppose it, but of course, they oppose *everything*. Perhaps, too, Big Pharma companies would be nays, as they've grown comfortable with the cartel-like FDA, which often blocks newbies. And yet some pharma, at least, would see the value of a dual pathway to drug approval. And then there are the trial lawyers; HTHA would have to include some sort of safe-harbor provision to protect against their predations. So now, would Democrats oppose HTHA, knowing that its work was lighting up innovation in blue places, such as California or Massachusetts? And what of Republicans, who think of themselves as the natural home of liberty minded deregulators? The bet would be that HTHA, created by Executive Order, would be seen so quickly as a good idea that it would be permanentized by legislation and law.

We can add, the prospect of shaking up that near $5 trillion in US health expenditures—and the reality that there's a lot more capital than that, financial and intellectual, to be roused—puts the NIH in perspective. Obviously, the $50 billion a year that the NIH spends makes a great contribution to biological and medical knowledge. And yet as we have seen, Eroom's Law is overriding much of the NIH's potential benefit to actual human health. Moreover, in the wake of the backlash against Anthony Fauci and COVID, many on the right argue that the NIH has gone so woke and censorious as to have lost much of its effectiveness.[549] And those right-wing critics have been joined by some in the middle and on the left—or however one might peg, say, Robert F. Kennedy, Jr., Whatever the budgetary fate of the Hamiltonian NIH, it seems that the *real* capital for medical innovation will come when and if there's a Jeffersonian breakthrough—the liberation of innovation.

---

[549] Schumaker, Erin, "Covid changed Newt Gingrich's mind about health research funding," *Politico*, July 20, 2023. https://bit.ly/46TNvwH

TAKIN' IT TO THE STATES: A HEALTH FREEDOM ZONE

As we've observed, one of the key trends to trend-spot is federalism—the states asserting their own power. But now we can think more actively, about trend-shaping federalism. That is, actively encouraging the states to assert their power—and in changing laws at the state level, forcing a change in national health outcomes.

There's ample recent precedent for this idea of states leveraging policy. In February 2004, Gavin Newsom, then the mayor of San Francisco, started issuing marriage licenses to same-sex couples. Immediately, legal questions surrounded Newsom's actions. Were these marriage licenses valid? It's worth recalling that just in 2000, California had voted, in a statewide referendum, to ban same-sex marriages. Yet nobody was coming to arrest Newsom or those same-sex couples. In fact, one news report from back then quoted a San Francisco city official, who observed, "Couples are coming from as far away as New York and Minnesota to be married here."[550] Now *that's* economic development, same as Nevada engineered its economic development on the basis of divorce and gambling. So in addition to all the other issues surrounding same-sex marriage, we can see the germ of an enterprise zone for legalized choices. In March 2004, the California Supreme Court halted San Francisco's weddings and nullified those that had been performed. Yet still, the point had been made. The djinni was loosed. Thanks to Newsom's initiative, San Francisco had reaffirmed its status as the most pro-gay city in the nation, at a time when most of the country was moving in a pro-gay direction. And in the meantime, nothing bad happened to Newsom. Which is to say, in front-running gay marriage, Newsom had not taken any sort of risk. Indeed, three years later, he was re-elected as mayor with more than 73 percent of the vote. Then in 2010, a California judge nullified the 2000 referendum on gay marriage, a nullification that was upheld by the US Supreme Court in 2013.

---

[550] "Gays rush to San Francisco to wed," BBC, February 15, 2004. https://bit.ly/3NqEsKH

So California was back in the lucrative, once again legal, business of being a gay marriage mecca.

Yet as happened to Las Vegas and Nevada on gambling, the gay marriage niche enjoyed by San Francisco and California was eroded by the legalization of gay marriage in many states, and then nationally in 2015, after the Supreme Court's ruling in the case of *Obergefell v. Hodges*. In the meantime, Newsom was well rewarded. After two terms as lieutenant governor, he was elected governor of California in 2018, and re-elected in 2022, emerging, as we have already seen, as an important national figure.[551] So any other ambitious pol, in either party—for or against gay marriage—would have to look at Newsom's record and conclude that there's a big reward for shaping a trend.

The investment implications of legalized gay marriage were not small, but the investment implications of legally accelerated medical innovation are enormous. There's that nearly $5 trillion to think about, as well as all the additional money that would come flooding into the sector if there were more actual cures to be bought. So let's ask, in addition to a hypothetical federal HTHA that might be based in California, what if California, or some other state, "did a Newsom" to the FDA? That is, if they flouted federal authority, started a fight, and ultimately prevailed. We can note that there's a little of this already going on. As we saw in Chapter Six, Oregon has decriminalized hard drugs. Does anyone think that anyone in Oregon is inspecting heroin or LSD for safety, let alone efficacy? In addition, well more than half of the nation's population lives in states where recreational marijuana is fully legal, even if weed is still illegal under federal law. Cannabidiol (CBD) is even more widely available. Once again, these drugs are illegal under federal law. And yet Uncle Sam is mostly choosing to look the other way. It's a Constitution thing—state law says one thing, federal law says another—and nobody has sorted it out. And maybe they never will. But in the meantime, Oregon is its own sort of enterprise zone. So

---

[551] Mason, Melanie, "When Gavin Newsom issued marriage licenses in San Francisco, his party was furious. Now, it's a campaign ad," *Los Angeles Times*, May 15, 2018. https://bit.ly/44hwp9H

now let's ask, if hard drugs are tolerated, why shouldn't cancer drugs be tolerated? Why does the FDA worry about pharmaceuticals, but not psychedelics? To be sure, it's hard to see a pharma company being willing to operate in the same sort of gray zone as a meth dealer in Portland. After all, even small pharma companies have millions on the line, to say nothing of their hope for billions. Yet at this same time, few of us know the passion of medical visionaries and their magnificent obsessions. So maybe we should let them decide how they wish to operate. Maybe a state should open up a window of opportunity for medical innovation, just to see what happens.

So that's the idea. Just as Nevada took unilateral action on gambling, just as San Francisco did it on gay marriage, just as Oregon declared itself to be a laboratory of chemistry, so now here's the opportunity for some other state to declare itself to be an FDA-free zone. And then, of course, it must use state power to create a Framework. That is, a legal and political structure that would enable a pharma company that plays the long game to set up shop in a state, operating legally within that state, even if federal law still applied to other states. This distinction, *intra*state v. *inter*state, was established back in the 1970s, when Southwest Airlines argued, successfully, that it was exempt from federal regulation because it only operated within the State of Texas.[552] So what state might be interested in this approach for medical drugs? It's hard to know. Let's start with blue states. On the one hand, Blue is higher tech and would have more upside. On the other hand, Blue is typically deregulatory on lifestyle and regulatory on everything else. So let's leave it as an open question to Blue. Now to Red. Idaho is next door to Oregon. The Gem State—a partisan ruby if there ever was one—already sees itself as a citadel on another kind of deregulation, guns. A state law back in 2014 was said to effectively "nullify" federal gun legislation, and it was updated in 2021. The Idaho Firearm and Firearm Accessories and Components Protection Act reads, in part:

---

[552] "Courting Success," southwest50.com, accessed June 19, 2023. https://bit. ly/3OwZlWt

"No federal executive order, agency order, treaty, law, statute, rule, or regulation issued, enacted, or promulgated on or after the effective date of this act will be knowingly and willfully ordered to be enforced by any official, agent, or employee of an Idaho government entity if contrary to the provisions of section 11, article I of the constitution of the state of Idaho."[553]

In other words, Idaho is doing its best to insulate itself, and its gun owners, from federal firearms regulation. So would it do the same for pharma? Idaho's powers haven't fully been tested in court, and yet we can say that there's a distinct libertarian-ish, anti-federal government trend. Just in the years 2021 to 2023, conservative Federalist Society-type litigants scored four victories before the Supreme Court, each one vindicating individuals and states peeling back federal power.[554] In each instance, the general argument was that federal regulators had overreached. After all, the basic statute—the legislation voted on by Congress and signed by the president—is relatively straightforward. The issue comes in the delegation of authority from Congress to "alphabet" regulatory agencies. Thus the question—is a regulation constitutional? If it is, it must be obeyed (unless Congress changes its mind). But if it is not constitutional, then a court can and should throw it out.

This brings us to the whole issue of the administrative state, and whether it abides by Congressional intent or goes off on its own tangent. That's the issue to be raised about the FDA. Are all its regulations constitutional? Or have the bureaucrats overreached? Overall, the question of delegation, proper or improper, is just about the hottest issue in governance, and most conservatives agree that the administrative state has overreached. That doesn't mean conservatives will win—unless, of course,

[553] Boldin, Michael, "New Idaho law effectively nullifies future federal gun control," Tenth Amendment Center, March 21, 2014 https://bit.ly/3DqCyVQ. See also: "Idaho Statutes, Section 18-3315B," Idaho Legislature. https://bit.ly/43BI4zu
[554] One case, *Alabama Realtors*, against CDC and HHS; another, *National Federation of Independent Businesses*, against OSHA; and two cases, *West Virginia* and *Sackett*, against the Environmental Protection Agency.

there's a six-to-three conservative majority on the Supreme Court, as there has been in the early 2020s.

Yet as we saw earlier, when Republicans are in the White House, Democrats have been just as eager to challenge central authority, albeit on different issues. But we can see, if the right is challenging federal authority on some issues, and the left is challenging the federal authority on other issues, then there aren't many issues that going unchallenged. Indeed, maybe left and right are both on to something. Maybe it's just the case that the federal government is now one of those forlorn middle of the road institutions, such as the department store or broadcast TV. So one trend to spot is the weakening of national authority, and one to shape is its further weakening.

Returning to the FDA, we might ask, do liberals want to see the FDA regulate marijuana? Put pot, at least new strains of it, through all the hoops of RCT? If not, then maybe left and right can agree that the FDA should play a much smaller role in the regulation of *any* drug. That seems like a plausible compromise, and that would leave both sides free to pursue their dreams. Can every assertion made here be disputed? Of course. That's the point about constitutional law, or any law. That's what lawyers do, they dispute. The key is to have some smart ones on the side of state-based medical innovation.

In fact, the states are in motion, pursuing arguments that weren't made a decade ago. One states' rights trend-shaper in the Biden era has been the Lone Star State's Republican governor Greg Abbott. Opposed to the Biden administration policies on the border, and mobilizing Texas to do more itself, Abbott declared in July 2023, "Texas has the sovereign authority to defend our border, under the U.S. Constitution and the Texas Constitution." And he added a curt, "We will see you in court, Mr. President."[555] In the meantime, Abbott can point to his own Texas Constitution, which declares, up front, in Article One, Section One, "Texas is a free and independent State, subject only to the Constitution

---

[555] Abbott, Greg (@GregAbbott_TX), X, July 21, 2023. https://bit.ly/44ZUm63

of the United States, and the maintenance of our free institutions and the perpetuity of the Union depend upon the preservation of the right of local self-government, unimpaired to all the States."[556]

So if we take the language of Idaho, and the language of Texas, we can see a strong case for autonomy from federal government overreach. So why not attach that sense of state sovereignty to the cause of better health? Specifically, FDA-free medical experimentation and innovation? So here's the deal. A governor declares a health emergency and so suspends FDA rules, at least some of them, at least for a time. That is, the governor creates, in effect, an enterprise zone—call it, maybe, a Health Freedom Zone (HFZ). Anything goes in the HFZ. Long COVID treatment, cancer treatment, any kind of treatment—and it's all legally protected, as to contracts, property, and safety, by state authorities—up to an including, of course, keeping the feds out. It would be, in an almost literal sense, one hundred flowers blooming, and it could unite a wide spectrum of supporters.

It would be, in a sense, reminiscent of the way that gay marriage bloomed in San Francisco. To be sure, such an HFZ would end up in court. And yet here we can recall that it's no cinch that the federal government would win, at least not in the long run. As Newsom proved in his city, once an idea whose time has come bursts out, opposition, once seemingly formidable, has a way of evaporating. And so that would be the bet, now, with HFZ. After all, FDA rules are not self-executing. If FDA enforcers were to reach into an HFZ in, say, Idaho, they would have to deal with a local culture, and a jury pool, made up, substantially, of nullifiers. As a sidebar example, we recall, from Chapter One, how, in the last century, moviemakers fled the regulatory strictures of the east coast to come to outlaw-friendly California. And we can recall, in this century, the buccaneering success of Uber. Not every company has the stomach to do what moviemakers, or Uber, did, but history shows that if they can make a big play work, business history—and investment outcomes—are changed. Fortune favors the bold.

---

[556] Texas Constitution, tlc.texas.gov. https://bit.ly/3rKRtY9

We can think of other variations on this theme of power to the states. For instance, a state, knowing that the feds are looking the other way on recreational drugs, might choose to legally define pharma drugs as "fun" drugs. Or as foods, or as supplements, which are less regulated—or as some new category that doesn't fit an existing regulatory template. Yes, yes, this would all up in court—and so the question would be, whose court? We might also consider that as with other kinds of American political diversity, diversity on pharma drugs would eventually go bimodal. That is, there'd be a red solution and a blue solution. For Blue, that would likely mean the FDA as it is. To borrow a phrase, "If you like your FDA, you can keep it." But for Red, the "FDA" might be nothing more than a series of informational, voluntary dashboards—that is, digital clearinghouses of information about a drug or a disease, such as, for instance, the current COVID website, c19early.org.

Would an HFZ attract quacks? Sure. But many would say that we have quacks under the current system, and they are all the worse because they have the power to spend, to censor, and to police. And others would say, "If I have a terminal disease, I have nothing to lose by taking my chances on something new." More importantly than the quacks, an HFZ would also attract visionaries of all kinds—from transhumanists and immortalists to venture capitalists. It would be, in a word, a Las Vegas times ten—or times a hundred.

Yes, of course, there'd be political issues to sort out, as the Hamiltonian Framework were developed and perfected. Patients are not a powerful voting bloc now—they should be, but they aren't—but we can consider how to fix that in Chapter Sixteen. For now we can close by recalling the electric vision of Supreme Court Justice Louis Brandeis. Let's make full use of the power of the states as "laboratories of democracy," and to do so, "We must let our minds be bold."

INVESTMENT TAKEAWAYS

- Politicians like to say that "we spend too much" on healthcare, and yet the actions of the American people bely that notion. About half of the nearly $5 trillion that the U.S, spends comes from government—Medicare, Medicaid, the VA, and similar payers—and the other half from private insurance and out-of-pocket spending.[557] So what's going on? The simplest answer is that healthcare is what economists call a "superior good." As income and affluence rise, people consume more of superior goods. Superior goods include such obvious luxuries as caviar and yachts—and yet much of healthcare, too, can be considered a superior good. For many, frequent doctor-trips and treatments are a prized luxury. So as incomes rise in the future, so will healthcare expenditures.

- Still, it's possible to change the composition of overall expenditures, by making medical progress. As capitalist-turned-philanthropist Michael Milken observed in 2010, "When I was a child in the early 1950s, economists estimated that by the year 2000, treating polio would cost the United States $100 billion annually. Today's polio immunization programs cost one thousand times less than that and have virtually eliminated the disease. Thanks to medical research on all diseases and growing awareness of prevention, especially nutrition, we live longer, more active lives with fewer years of disability." And it's also possible to improve the overall economy with better health. As Milken also wrote, "Improvements in life expectancy added approximately $3.2 trillion per year to America's wealth over the three decades beginning in 1970."[558] Yes, that's monetizable medical progress with a larger social payoff. If we wished, we get even more. Healthy people are

---

[557] National Health Expenditures, Centers for Disease Control and Prevention, accessed June 24, 2023. https://bit.ly/3PxKr31
[558] Milken, Michael, "Health Reform," *Milken Institute Review*, First Quarter 2010. https://bit.ly/3CS30HH

less expensive than sick people. A cure is less expensive than care. It's cheaper to beat than to treat.

- Americans spend money to be healthy And if they can't, or won't, be healthy, they will still pay to be treated. That's a bellringer for investors. And the loudest bellringer is a genuine cure. That will come from new technology. So we just need, one way or another, to get the FDA out of the way.

- The paradox of the status quo—low-velocity regulation and politics, high-velocity money. As was the case with Hollywood or Uber, once the dead hand is lifted, things speed up, and soon, the thing is unstoppable. Investors can choose to either spot that trend, or help shape the trend.

- In addition to funding the obvious entrepreneurial plays of an HFZ, we mustn't forget the ancillary plays of an investment zone, such as real estate—what top-quality health complex is without fancy hotels nearby?—construction, and services for both patients and staff.

CHAPTER FOURTEEN
MEATSPACE AND CYBERSPACE

FROM PROTAGORAS TO NAISBITT

Twenty-five hundred years ago, the Greek philosopher Protagoras declared, "Man is the measure of all things: of the things that are, that they are, of the things that are not, that they are not." If that's still true, then man, woman (and perhaps other categories, tbd) will be the measure of all things, small and big.

Speaking of small and big, the philosopher Pascal opined that humankind is suspended between two infinities—the infinitely large and the infinitely small. Yet be it micro, macro, or in between, *we* are the measure. That is, it will always be about us—what we see, make, judge, and value. That's certainly the way to bet; if we're wrong, and AI, or something else, kills us all, well, then, it won't matter. But unless or until we're deleted, we will continue to be the arbiter.

Moreover, for as long as we're corporeal beings, with bodies and bodily needs, it'll behoove us to think in terms of our two friends from politics, Jeffersonian Liberty and the Hamiltonian Framework. These, separately and together, will enable us to flourish. So let's look at the infinitely small, and the infinitely large, in turn.

The internet, of course, is a tribute to both Jeffersonianism and Hamiltonianism. It was created by the federal government, and yet then mostly libertarians took it ran with it, creating something worth many trillions—and with a social and cultural impact going far beyond mere money. And yet the net has been, in various ways, Frameworked by the feds. And so it goes—a Jeffersonian burst, followed by Hamiltonian consolidation, followed by another Jeffersonian burst. Yet through these oscillations, *Homo sapiens* stand tall. That is, us and our Protagoran metric. What do *we* think? What do *we* like? Whenever a net tycoon, no matter successful, loses sight of the human factor, said tycoon becomes less successful. What they say about a television screen is also true of a computer or smartphone screen—people like to watch people. Preferably, real people, doing real things. Movie director Christopher Nolan refuses to use computer generated imagery (CGI) in his films. Similarly, Tom Cruise insists on doing his own stunts, without benefit of digital trickery, thus keeping human scale—it's really him. As one film reviewer put it in 2023, "Cruise is an analog star fighting the good fight against CGI unreality."[559] It's no accident that Nolan and Cruise are among the most successful figures in Hollywood.

Same with the internet. If it's about *people*, people will log in, and if it's not, they won't. That's where avatars have gone wrong. Sites such as Second Life were fun—for about two seconds. Perhaps someday, avatars will be their own audience group. Avatars might well prefer to watch other avatars, but so long as we, here in "meatspace," are the audience, we will insist on watching "meatpuppets" perform.

Mark Zuckerberg started out grasping this Protagoran point. Back in 2004, he named his new venture TheFacebook (later, of course, just Facebook), and everyone got it. It was about faces—pretty, ugly, whatever—and the people attached to them. Yet then Zuckerberg started thinking less about faces; in 2014, he spent $2 billion to buy Oculus VR, a maker of virtual reality goggles. Zuckerberg's hope was that someday, wearing goggles would be as normal as wearing eyeglasses—never mind that the much smaller Google glasses had already failed. Heedless of that

[559] Schager, Nick, "Tom Cruise's Stunts Are as Spectacular as You Hoped in New 'Mission: Impossible,'" *Daily Beast*, July 8, 2023. https://bit.ly/3DaogZd

warning, Zuck declared in 2017, "We want to get a billion people in virtual reality."[560] When a tech Master of the Universe talks in such bold terms, we have to listen, but we don't have to do as he says. Still, following his plan, Zuck made the big switch. He snuffed out part of his highly valued brand—Facebook, the company, became Meta, as in metaverse. Bad move. Despite enormous expenditures, Meta simply could not make virtual reality and the metaverse a success. Critics compared it to a ghostly mall food court populated by ghosts and zombies. In 2022, *Coindesk* reported that Decentraland, on which Meta had spent $1.3 billion, had just thirty-eight daily active users.[561] So it was People 1, Zuck 0. Protagoras rules.

Obviously, Meta in its VR incarnation was flunking the Ten-Strike Test. VR was not ten times better than IRL—in real life. In his Ahabian quest into the Great Tiny Way, Zuckerberg sheared off, from late 2021 to 2022, two-thirds of the value of his company. Zuck had forgotten, or never truly knew, the most important trend identified by futurist John Naisbitt. Writing in 1982, two years before Zuck was born, Naisbitt preached, the higher the tech, the more human it had be: "High tech/high touch is a formula I use to describe the way we have responded to technology. What happens is that whenever new technology is introduced into society, there must be a counterbalancing human response—that is, high touch—or the technology is rejected. The more high tech, the more high touch."[562]

Happily for shareholders, bu 2023, Zuck had woken up from his virtual fever dream. He shifted to AI, and Meta stock recovered. A young person—Zuckerberg was born in 1984—can make serious miscalculations and still have the energy to bounce back. We can further look to Zuck's launching of Threads as a rival to Twitter, purchased by Elon Musk in 2022. For the first time in a long time, Zuck was getting genuinely positive

---

[560] Gartenberg, Chaim, "Mark Zuckerberg: 'We want to get a billion people in virtual reality,'" *The Verge*, October 11, 2017. https://bit.ly/3r4qjvn

[561] Thompson, Cam, "It's Lonely in the Metaverse: DappRadar Data Suggests Decentraland Has 38 'Daily Active' Users in $1.3B Ecosystem," *Coindesk*, October 7, 2022. https://bit.ly/3NnGXNX

[562] Naisbitt, John, *Megatrends: Ten New Directions Transforming Our Lives* (New York: Warner Books, 1982), 39.

coverage, as left-leaning reporters cheered him on against the Dreaded Musk. "A Twitter copycat worth rooting for" trilled Bloomberg News. *Axios* depicted Zuck with a halo.[563] Zuck was playing to people once again, including their tribal partisanship—Democrats being increasingly hostile to anything Musk. "Twitter Is a Far-Right Social Network" headlined *The Atlantic*, and a crescendo of further accusations were to follow.[564]

MUSK V. ZUCK

Still, Musk has, shall we say, a strong track record. He renamed Twitter as X, in keeping with his long-held vision of a single "everything app." In the meantime, he laid off several thousand leftists and do-nothings, while adding new features such as Grok AI— pleasing both conservatives and Robert Heinlein fans. In fact, for all the death-of-Twitter/X discourse, the site was still central to the planetary conversation. In late 2023, Tyler Cowen sparked a punditry counter-trend when he wrote of "The Robustness of Twitter."[565] Meanwhile, Threads lost momentum. Perhaps it has suffered from "the innovator's dilemma," as Meta's existing properties, Facebook and Instagram, resist yielding turf to the newbie.[566]

Whatever the outcome of Musk v. Zuck (as well as the many other X rivals/wannabes) it's likely that Naisbittian *touch*—including political resonances— will matter as much as *tech*.

---

[563] Counts, Aisha, "A Twitter copycat worth rooting for." Bloomberg Tech Daily, July 6, 2023. https://bit.ly/3rgnuHs. (Bloomberg later changed the headline). See also: Fischer, Sarah, and Fried, Ina, "Zuck's Threads Halo," *Axios*, July 7, 2023. https://bit.ly/3NKxyAb

[564] Warzel, Charlie, "Twitter Is a Far-Right Social Network," *The Atlantic*, May 23, 2023. https://bit.ly/3pgof2N

[565] Cowen, Tyler, "The robustness of Twitter," *Marginal Revolution*, December 10, 2023. https://tinyurl.com/54dd6xr5

[566] Clayton Christensen's 1997 book, *The Innovator's Dilemma: When New Technologies Cause Great Firms to Fail,* explains why companies are often reluctant to deploy their best technology.

SEEING OTHER WORLDS

Eventually, someone will do a better job with goggles, virtual reality, and the metaverse. For instance, Apple debuted its Vision Pro headset in 2023. Mindful of "touch," the company took care to make sure that others could see the eyes, at least, of users. It's possible that goggles and glasses will evolve toward miniaturization such that they disappear—becoming implants, or pills, or some sort of cloud ambience. It's also possible that someday we'll live inside the metaverse—it might beat dying. Yet it's *also* possible that as Silicon Valley keeps pushing to make everything analog into digital, it will keep bumping up against limits. As one Silicon Valley veteran, Roger McNamee, said of the Tech Lords, "They've assumed that everything that they touch is going to work. And in reality, it's not."[567] No renaissance, no golden age, no *belle époque*, lasts forever.

AI: THE TREND IS YOUR FRIEND—OR ELSE

Ever since *Frankenstein*, imaginative writers have anticipated that our technology will turn on us. But perhaps no author has made the point about computers as vividly as Harlan Ellison, author of the 1967 short story, "I Have No Mouth and I Must Scream." In that tale, a computer takes over and kills all of humanity except for five unlucky people, who are kept alive so the machine can enjoy torturing them. *Forever.* The wrathful machine says to one of its victims, "Hate, let me tell you how much I've come to hate you since I began to live. There are 387.44 million miles of wafer thin printed circuits that fill my complex. If the word hate was engraved on every nanoangstrom of those hundreds of millions of miles it would not equal one one-billionth of the hate I feel for humans at this micro-instant. For you. Hate. Hate."[568]

---

[567] DeVynck, Gerritt, "The age of the Silicon Valley 'moonshot' is over," *Washington Post*, March 2, 2023. https://bit.ly/3NLvYiG
[568] Ellison, Harlan, *I Have No Mouth and I Must Scream*, (New York: Pyramid Books, 1967), 33.

Okay, so there's the downside of AI. Now let's talk about the upside. For sure, AI passes the Ten-Strike Test, and so in the first six months after Chat GPT burst on the scene in late 2022, it was estimated that tech moguls had added $150 billion to their wealth.[569] As numerous other AIs come online, trillions more will be added.

Indeed, there's good reason to hope that AI will add to the wealth of all. Sam Altman, the chief driver of Open AI, speculates of his opus, "What if we're able to cure every disease? That would be a huge victory on its own. ... What if every person a hundred years from now is a hundred times richer?"[570] A hundred times richer sure sounds good, even if it takes us into political challenges.

PROTAGORAN POINTS

If Protagoran thinking prevails, that means humans will have survived. And if humans survive, that means politics survives, including political challenges, of which we can name five:

First, AI will not transcend the human-ness of its origins. If it was made by people, it will always have people in its DNA. These makers are humans of a certain type, clustered in Northern California, around Seattle, and in New York City. So even amidst the transcendence of the tech, personal opinions—including wokeness—will be in the mix. Such biases will please some and displease others, and so it's inevitable that various ideological niches will be left open, to be filled, perhaps, by rivals such as Grok.

Second, AI will further reflect the complexity of its makers in their dealings with each other. Including, as a future b-school case study, the soap opera over OpenAI. Its CEO, Sam Altman, was fired and rehired within days in late 2023. More broadly, there's the diversity of opinion as

---

[569] Pringle, Eleanor, "Mark Zuckerberg has got $39 billion richer during the A.I. boom. He's not alone—the world's über wealthy have made a killing," *Fortune,* June 20, 2023. https://bit.ly/3JUVMqr

[570] Weiss, Bari, "Is AI the End of the World? Or the Dawn of a New One?" *Free Press,* May 1, 2023. https://bit.ly/440GPuG

to what AI should be. One 2023 survey identified five schools of thought: "Euphoric true believers"; "Commercial profiteers"; "Curious creators"; "Alarmist activists" and "Global governistas."[571] Amidst this Cambrian explosion of tech, soon enough there will be even more species, and with them, new political expressions.

Third, some sort of governance system will emerge. This author has suggested the US Constitution as a starting point.[572] Admittedly, that document says nothing about tech, but it says a lot about how we should proceed on anything: with enumerated rights, checks and balances, due process, and federalism. That last concept includes a state's right to make its own choices, laboratories-of-democracy-style, separate from the federal government. To be sure, the Constitution doesn't give us an answer to international questions; to cite one potential concern, SoftBank CEO Masayoshi Son was quoted saying that with AI, his firm will "rule the world."[573] (Insert ironic sci-fi plot twist.). Yet nearly two-and-a-half centuries of successful constitutional governance in the US should give Americans confidence that they can grapple successfully with whatever comes next.

Fourth, the creative destruction to come. We're starting to grasp how much wealth is going to be created, but how much will be destroyed? Some suggest that up to 80 percent of current jobs will be disrupted.[574] Dramatic as that number sounds, history tells us that we can, over time, handle it. In 1800, some 75 percent of the American workforce worked in agriculture. Then mechanization—most notably, the McCormick Reaper—surged, and so did productivity. So today, the percentage of Americans working on

[571] Sonnenfeld, Jeffrey, "Meet the Five Schools of Thought Dominating the Conversation about AI," Yale School of Management, June 30, 2023. https://tinyurl.com/m3mj6ekb

[572] Pinkerton, James, "Constitutional Intelligence," *The American Conservative,* September 11, 2023. https://tinyurl.com/2jcttwb7

[573] Maxwell, Thomas, "SoftBank CEO Masayoshi Son thinks his firm will 'rule the world' thanks to its AI investments," *Business Insider,* June 22, 2023. https://bit.ly/42XDuLR

[574] Eloundou, Tina, et al.,"GPTs are GPTs: An Early Look at the Labor Market Impact Potential of Large Language Models," Working Paper, University of Pennsylvania, August 22, 2023. https://tinyurl.com/4r8dutjv

farms is less than two.[575] And yet today we eat better (or at least more) than ever. The optimists were right. As agriculture mechanized, fewer hands were needed on the farm, and so they migrated to the cities—first working in factories, and then, as the generations went by, in offices. There's good reason to think that the same sort of positive transition—including all the issues involving creativity and copyrights—could happen with AI. If it generates the kind of economic surplus many expect, there will be abundance for the taking, as opposed to the working.

Fifth, what happens if we do achieve material abundance. The 1960s TV show *Star Trek*—still deeply influential in all its spinoffs and cultural motifs—envisions the abundance of replicator-based technology producing a new sense of honor and purpose. On the other hand, Isaac Asimov's 1956 novel *The Naked Sun* imagines everybody so rich that population growth has collapsed; people would rather live with ten thousand servant-robots than with other people—and when they do meet, murder most foul. There are, of course, a zillion other scenarios—perhaps even a multiverse worth.

INVESTMENT TAKEAWAYS

- In the eternal spirit of making the trend your friend, we can observe that the usual pattern is that an industry resists regulation, and yet once it comes, the industry realizes that it's not so bad. In fact, sometimes businesses decide that regulation can be used to its own advantage and so they themselves concoct the regulatory scheme.[576] So this might suggest the inevitability, if not necessarily

---

[575] Ruggles, Steven, "The Decline of Intergenerational Coresidence in the United States, 1850 to 2000," *American Sociological Review*, December 2007, https://bit.ly/3ppLXJK

[576] Gabriel Kolko's 1963 book, *The Triumph of Conservatism: A Reinterpretation of American History 1900-1916*, argues business forces created and then immediately "captured" the Federal Trade Commission. The phenomenon of "regulatory capture" is a constant in US history.

the desirability, of a federal regulatory body for AI. Already in 2023, Congress was mulling a Digital Platform Commission.[577] Yet the twist will come as *e pluribus duo* plays out. Red will never trust Blue, and vice versa. So it's more likely that there will be two regulatory systems, one red and one blue. This will open up abundant opportunities for experimentation and, of course, arbitrage.

- To use a term from both computers and television, someone will counter-program the predominant AIs. If Fox News is any kind of precedent, the AI that claims the "fair and balanced" realm will have a lot of valuable territory to itself.

- If Red does go its own way, it will need more tech brains than it has now. If AI tech comes from Blue, Red will be an open book to Blue. For its own sake, Red is going to have to declare its "AI-ndepedence" from Blue. It will need its own AI capacity; the sort of Protagoran ability to measure everything according to its own red rules. We can recall our consideration of a math-intense "800 U" in Chapter Eight—it's that level of brain capacity that Red will need.

---

[577] "Digital Platform Commission Act of 2023," Congress.gov, https://bit.ly/3rWApyu

CHAPTER FIFTEEN
TO BOLDLY INVEST...

THE SEARCH FOR A SPACE FRAMEWORK

I n the 1950 Hollywood movie *Destination Moon*, an American tycoon finances a manned trip to the Moon and back—with himself as the commander of the mission. And yet the film, coauthored by libertarian sci-fi icon Robert Heinlein, assumes that if the private sector can prove the concept of space travel, then the public sector, Uncle Sam, will step in to bear the cost of future spacefaring. In other words, free enterprise builds it, and Uncle Space, grateful for the gain in technology and mindful of defense needs, buys it. Seven decades later, with the success of Elon Musk and SpaceX—his best customers being NASA and the Pentagon—we're seeing something akin to the movie's scenario.

Indeed, we're seeing the emergence of something exciting—a new Hamiltonian Framework. We've already considered how the Framework delivered for past transportation systems, such as trains and cars, albeit not forever. So now to this new Framework for space, the stakes are, of course, galactic.

Space travel was the dream of libertarian-minded Jeffersonians—interested in freedom and adventure—benefiting greatly from Hamiltonian institutions, including universities and the military. Heinlein, for instance, wrote many tales of independent "spacepreneurs," and yet for a long time, he was part of a statist system (he graduated from Annapolis in 1929, then served in the Navy for five years). For most of his life, he lived in Southern California, then much dependent on defense-related tech and aerospace. In fact, during the Cold War, Hamiltonians ran the show, funding NASA and its many successes, culminating in the 1969 moon landing. But perhaps not surprisingly, after that high, NASA slumped. The Japanese have a word for that: *shenshoubyou*, victory disease.

Yet then a new mission for space emerged—commercial space launches for private satellites. However, the nascent industry found itself in a bureaucratic tangle of Parkinsonian proportions. By one reckoning, a total of seventeen federal agencies had at least some jurisdiction over space launches.[578] The result, of course, was a spaceflight and investment-smothering pile of poo.

Along came a young Republican Congressman from Georgia, Newt Gingrich. He was that rarity among practicing politicians—a visionary. In 1984, he published *Window of Opportunity*, a book calling for, among other grand goals, vastly expanded space operations. But how to get there, if NASA was plateaued, and commercial space stymied? Gingrich teamed up with a Democratic lawmaker from Hawaii, Rep. Daniel Akaka and the bipartisan partners went to work, steering a reform bill through both the Democratic-controlled House and the Republican-controlled Senate. The fruit of their labor was the Commercial Space Launch Act (CSLA) of 1984. That bill built upon some canny moves already made by the Reagan administration. The Reaganites, supportive of the private sector and also mindful of the military implications of space, recognized the risk of the smelly status quo. So as a solution, they designated the Department of Transportation (DOT) as the lead agency on commercial space. This might sound like mere bureaucratic box shuffling, but in point of fact, it was a shrewd move. The Secretary of Transportation is usually one of the more nimble members of a president's Cabinet. Back then, the Secretary

---

[578] "Origins of the Commercial Space Industry," Federal Aviation Administration, accessed July 1, 2023. https://bit.ly/477E9O7

was Elizabeth Dole, wife of Bob Dole and a future senator herself. Then CSLA formalized the lead of DOT on space launches, specifically entrusting the Office of the Secretary with authority. That office, of course, is always thick with political appointees, who could be expected to heed presidential intent. For his part, President Reagan made that intent clear. Signing the bill on October 30, 1984, he declared,

> *"One of the important objectives of my administration has been, and will continue to be, the encouragement of the private sector in commercial space endeavors."*[579]

Such language is important, because officials, lobbyists, litigators, and judges pay close attention to presidential word choices. And oh yes, entrepreneurs and investors notice, too. Even more important was the actual language of the statute, 51 U.S.C. Ch 509. It uses the words "promote" and "facilitate" in regard to the space-launch industry ten times each, and "encourage" fifteen times. So that's thirty-five usages of an encouraging Directional word. CSLA was the foundation of a Hamiltonian Framework for space. In the '80s, launching was slow—this is, after all, difficult technology to ramp up. By 1990, the number of American launches reached ten. By 2022, it was up to seventy-eight.[580] Much of that success, of course, comes from falling launch costs. Compared to 1981, a launch today is thirty times cheaper. We can add that this cost crash has been exactly what Alexander Hamilton had in mind. The government Frameworks the activity, entrepreneurs get the message—and go for it. Today, worldwide, the commercial space business is valued at $500 billion, with most of that

---

[579] *Administration of Ronald Reagan,* (Washington DC: Government Printing Office) p. 1688

[580] "U.S. commercial space launches from 1990 to 2021," Statista, accessed, July 15, 2023 https://bit.ly/3XY6tyg. See also, Klotz, Irene, "New Record Set In 2022 For Orbital Launch Activity," *Aviation Week,* January 3, 2023. https://tinyurl.com/yc7rxvt3

action clustered in the US And projections go north from there, by 2040, Citibank prophesies, to $1 trillion.[581]

"TO INFINITY, AND BEYOND!"

Those, of course, are the words of the *Toy Story* character Buzz Lightyear. But assuming we don't blow ourselves up before we get a beachhead in space, that's actually not such a bad prediction. Jeff Bezos, no slouch at looking ahead, prophesies a "trillion" people living in space, including "1,000 Mozarts and 1,000 Einsteins."[582] So how much will the output of all of them be worth? How much money will be spent to get there? How much wealth will be generated? We could ask the most narrowly numbers-minded, least-visionary finance guy, "What's the net present value of a future investment vehicle in which trillions of people live in space?" The number, whatever it might be, is Heinleinian. In addition to founding Amazon, Bezos is also the founder of a space company, Blue Origin, the name of which bespeaks the Protagoran roots of the spacer impulse. It's *humans* who provide the impetus, the *raison d'être* for settlements off Earth.

Movement, as a form of change, is life itself. The story of humans moving around the planet has been a stirring—sometimes inspiring, sometimes heartbreaking—saga for hundreds of thousands of years. To put that another way, the idea of packing up and picking up is hardwired into us, evolutionarily. And so now, with space, comes the prospect of moving on a scale a bigger, farther, and longer. Even people who aren't Bezos can think big space thoughts.

The lyrical romance of space travel, of course, is reinforced by a grounded assessment of the risks to this single "spaceship earth." Even before he was the first to envision atomic weaponry in 1914, H.G. Wells

[581] "A New Age for Space: Citi GPS report," Citibank, September 20, 2022. http://citi.us/46PEhl4
[582] Powell, Corey, "Jeff Bezos foresees a trillion people living in millions of space colonies. Here's what he's doing to get the ball rolling," NBC News, May 15, 2019. https://bit.ly/43s5mIb

had speculated about the entropic heat-death of the planet, or about Martians invading.[583] As we know, there's never been a shortage of planet ending scenarios, from asteroid strikes to pandemics, from ice ages to sea level rises—and now, of course, AI. If there's a chance that any of these doomsdays could come true, then it's a good idea for humans to diversify their locational portfolio. "Something will happen to Earth eventually, it's just a question of time," says the Mars-minded Musk. "Eventually the sun will expand and destroy all life on Earth, so we do need to move at some point, or at least be a multi-planet species. You have to ask the question: do we want to be a space-flying civilization and a multi-planet species or not?"[584] And the answer of many, of course, is that we do.

By now we're in a realm infinitely beyond bottom-line investment calculations. Yes, there are plenty of purely numbers minded space investors, but it's a safe bet that plenty more have a high destinarian vision. What's the value of guaranteeing the survival of the human species? More proximately, what's the value of making sure that one's own children, or grandchildren, are survivors? Huge. Off-the-charts huge. No-point-in-bothering-with-the-calculations huge. People are going to Just Do It.

We can add another point. Humans often do things for reasons of vision or passion—things that make, in the short run, no sense at all. And yet over the long run, they do make sense. Some new invention emerges (oftentimes mothered by necessity) and so the passion project proves to be a win-win—a win for higher aspirations, as well as a win for the bottom line. People have explored and traveled around the Earth for a multi-mix of reasons—curiosity, for the lust of conquest, for the sake of trade, to evangelize and minister to others, to find religious refuge—or just to be alone. These reasons are so complex that it's not possible to sort them all out. And that's okay, we don't have to. But here's one point we can make. People have gone to do one thing, and ended up doing another thing. The socio-cultural economic model has changed many times over the centuries, and

---

[583] Wells, H.G., *The World Set Free*, 1914. https://bit.ly/3NZdb2j
[584] Khalaf, Roula, "Elon Musk: aren't you entertained?" *The Financial Times*, October 7, 2022. https://bit.ly/3Xns5nn

yet the cumulation of wealth has been colossal. Compared to the fifteenth century, the beginning of the Terrestrial Age of Exploration, the GDP of the world has increased by a factor of at least 250.[585] So we can better see that the future value of the Extraterrestrial Age is well beyond our current capacity to quantify.

Yet even so, the long run is a series of short runs, and somebody has to provide the logic, and pay the bills, each step of the way.

THE SHORT RUNS

As we've looked at past Frameworks, such as trains and cars, we've noted that they decay over time. And so it could be with the Space Framework— it's under attack. Today, space launches enjoy a substantial carveout from the strictures of the National Environmental Policy Act, which requires the burdensome environmental impact statements that have been the bane of so many industries, including green energy. Yet thanks to CSLA, space rocketry enjoys a partial workaround. It can get its NEPA/EIS approval from the Federal Aviation Administration, which is, by design, a lighter touch. For instance, SpaceX got its permit back in 2014, and has launched on that ever since.[586] Yet an April 2023 SpaceX launch at its site in Bolsa Chica, Texas, caused a firestorm. Okay, not actually a firestorm, but dust and debris were scattered around for miles. In fact, the legal firestorm has been real enough, as green groups sued SpaceX, citing the damaging environmental impact of its launch. It was a lawsuit made all the more delicious, of course, since greens (blues) can double-barrel their distaste for Musk

---

[585] Maddison Database, https://bit.ly/3Kkj34W.
[586] "SpaceX Texas Launch Site Environmental Impact Statement," Federal Aviation Administration, accessed July 10, 2023. https://bit.ly/3XK9MbY

(red).[587] For his part, Musk said that a requirement for a new EIS "would set us back for quite some time." He added that were he hit with a new EIS requirement, he might have to move his launch operation out of Texas, to the more legally secure facility at Cape Canaveral. Interestingly, in 2023, Florida enacted a law limiting the liability of space flight companies.[588]

It's probably only a matter of time before the Greens and NIMBYs are joined by the WIINIMBYs, bringing left and right together in oppositionalism. Might this enlarged coalition win? Might they able to slow, or even stop, space launches? That depends on strength of the Framework. And here we can ask, will the national government continue to offer a Framework to Musk and other spacers? And if not, what will the state of Texas do? Or any other space-minded state? Will there be a pro-launch Red to stick together and oppose an anti-launch Blue? Let's suppose, for a moment, that the space Framework is broken, and Musk, and the rest, are chased out of the US altogether. Will they be able to somewhere else to launch? To Mexico? We can note that for reasons of physics, the best place to launch into space is from the equator. So now we can spin the globe and look for some possible equatorial locale. On the list—Ecuador (of course), Indonesia, the Maldives, and Kenya. We can also see that oceans account for most of the equator's circumference. So maybe, in the future, space launches could lift off from a floating barge, or from some optimized outcrop of guano rock or carbon-captured landfill. We can add such micro-political places as Sealand, or some other man-made platform. They've never been able to work as viable, recognized, But maybe one day they'll find recognition for a newfound space-purpose.

We can add that the Framework would be all the more valuable—and need to be all the stronger—if we were ever to build a *space elevator*. That's

---

[587] *Center for Biological Diversity et al. v. Federal Aviation Administration and Space X.* United States District Court for the District of Columbia, June 30, 2023. https://bit.ly/3rbAPRo. See also: Rabie, Passant, "SpaceX Wants Environmental Lawsuit Against Its Starship Rocket Dismissed," *Gizmodo,* July 5, 2023. https://bit.ly/3NLlzCj

[588] Kuhr, Jack, "Florida Limits Spaceflight Liabilities to Attract Launch Businesses," *Space Payload,* May 31, 2023. https://bit.ly/3NOXYAN

an idea that's been around since the nineteenth century. A cable could be extended from earth to a satellite in geostationary orbit, 25,000 miles out. The cable would be akin to an elevator cable, in this case, held taut by the pull-pull interplay of gravity, pulling inward, and centrifugal force, pulling outward. Cargo could then be winched up, from Earth to space—at a fraction of the cost of a rocket launch.[589] As with just about everything else, the technology needs to be improved, but we can say this much: The "ground floor" of the space elevator would be the prince of ports, a thousand Shanghais. (And if the cable were to be made of carbon nanotubes— assuming something better doesn't come along—it would make good use of a lot of captured carbon.)

Yet to even think about putting a 25,000-mile string into space is to be reminded that the elevator would need international Frameworking. And we mustn't underestimate the potential pushback on any big space idea. Even in our time, when the permanent extraterrestrial population is zero, critics worry about a spaceward "secession of the successful." That is, the fear that plutocrats will exit the planet, leaving victims behind. Asks one critic, "Are they just gearing up to wash their hands of the planet and leave the rest of us to clean up? By pushing outward while ignoring the problems it causes back on the home turf, are they effectively creating a galactic upper class that rests on the backs of the earthbound? Even if that's not literally the plan, it may be the ultimate outcome."[590] To be sure, the most Promethean might read such words and be all the more inclined to damn the torpedoes and go full speed into space. And yet a moment's reflection tells us that it will be a long time before anyone can truly sever the surly bonds of Earth. Why? For one thing, it will be a long time before spaceniks can defend themselves against weapons and predators from Earth. No one's space-business model includes defense against missiles, vandals, and pirates. So again we come back to the distinction between

---

[589] Cohen, Stephen, "Space Elevators Are Less Sci-Fi Than You Think," *Scientific American*, November 25, 2022. https://bit.ly/3XTe5C0

[590] Zimmerman, Jess, "What if the mega-rich just want rocket ships to escape the Earth they destroy?" *Guardian*, September 16, 2015. https://bit.ly/44FlkzE

Nevada and Hong Kong. Nevada was, and still is, a gambling enterprise zone enjoying the politico-military protection of the United States. Hong Kong was, and is not now, an overall enterprise zone. To be sure, money is still being made in Hong Kong, but the Chinese communists could grab the money, and its makers, anytime. A good Framework is both free *and* protected. Spacepreneurs will have to figure that out. Will such protections be national? International? Or intergalactic?

In the meantime, let's consider some of the moneymaking possibilities of space:

Space Junk. The issue of miscellaneous flotsam and jetsam from human activity in space—even a tiny piece that came off a spacecraft can destroy another spacecraft—is looming large, threatening to ruin the magnificent space industry. In the words of space scholar Julia Hudson, "Mankind's productive use of the low Earth orbit, from 400-2,000km in altitude, is at risk from increasing counts of debris objects and derelict satellites, which pose collision risks to active spacecraft." She adds, "Of particular concern to space agencies and industry is the Kessler Syndrome, which is the term for a hypothetical collapse scenario in which collisions between debris and satellites cause more debris, causing a destructive cascade that leaves the orbital environment unusable."[591] So what we're seeing with this space pollution, is a "Tragedy of the Commons"-type collective action problem. It's in everyone's interest to see that the problem is fixed, but it's expensive, and likely futile, to seek to fix the problem on one's own. That is, if one country wants to clean up space junk, while other countries don't care— or even see some competitive advantage in dispersing, even weaponizing, junk—then the cleanup effort will fail. So here's a case where some sort of international understanding, even a Framework, will be needed. And it's a truth universally acknowledged that a problem for someone is an opportunity for someone else. Here on earth, smart people have figured out better mousetraps. Up there, some smarty can figure out a better space-junk trap.

---

[591] Hudson, Julia, "KESSYM: A stochastic orbital debris model for evaluation of Kessler Syndrome risks and mitigations," *Journal of Student Research*, February 28, 2023. https://bit.ly/46WIR12

Space Tourism. It's estimated that only around 600 humans have ever been to space—that's a pretty exclusive club. And exclusive clubs can charge astronomical rates. Space jaunts are already sort of a business, and as jaunts become tours, who can say what will happen in zero-g-ville. The only thing we know is that people will pay. We can add a further dimension to space wanderlust—it's the human dimension in space that makes space interesting. Just as the metaverse isn't interesting without identifiably real people in it, so the universe isn't so interesting if it's just R2-D2 flying around. If the adventure is just watching something happen on a screen, then it might as well be the inner metaverse.

Not many space adventures happen without people measuring all things. No matter where in the galaxy the saga is spun, it's the closeup, or the kiss, or the fight, that seals the deal with the audience. In this case, the audience is all the people of the world who might wish to go to space, or cheer for others as they go to space. They want to know what happens to the hero, or the villain. They don't care about the algorithm. Indeed, the real limit on human space travel, including colonization, is not financial cost, but human health—as we'll get to.

Space Defense, Part One. Donald Trump established the US Space Force (USSF) in 2019. Interestingly, that was one Trump idea that Joe Biden didn't undo. Which suggests that the USSF is on its way to institutional permanence. It already spends $30 billion a year, which is surely enough to attract Directional attention. Many will argue, of course, that space defense is best managed with machines, because, after all, crewed flight is vastly more expensive. And while they have a point, their logic flunks the Protagoran point—people didn't go to all the trouble of figuring out how to go space just so that robots could go to space. They went to that trouble so that they themselves could go to space, including as warfighters. Moreover, as space weapons inevitably develop planet killing capabilities, earthbound leaders are unlikely to entrust the fate of the planet to machines. Nobody wants HAL 9000 deciding our fate. Yes, of course, any space force will make heavy use of machines, and robots, and holograms, and whatever else, to do the scut work. But there will always be a space warrior in the picture, somewhere. And that means that USSF—on its own or in tandem with other space forces—will likely lead on the key issue confronting all humans in space. Namely, the reality that spending much time in outer space is devastating to the human body. The combination of zero-g and radiation means that bones soften, eyes bulge, IQ goes down, and the risk of cancer shoots up. All manner of fixes and shields will be suggested and attempted, but it seems most likely that, in the long run, determined space-venturers will begin to develop some new human biological capacity for resilience in space. Through gene-editing or some kind of cyborg-ization, we'll develop *Homo sapiens astronauta.*

To put it mildly, this bio-transformation will be controversial, piled as it will be, atop all other space-troversies. Will we be creating half-lived freaks? Frankensteins? Marcher Lords? Will they be doomed *Untermenschen*, as in *Blade Runner*, or will they be pampered *Übermenschen* as in the 2013 movie, *Elysium*? With space, the issues that need to be Frameworked stretch to infinity and beyond. And yet if we can achieve some sort of order-and-progress system, earthbound humans, too, could have a lot to look forward to. How so? If we figure out the biological rules needed for good health in space, we will likely also figure out the rules for better health and longevity on Earth. That's been the happy health-spinoff story of past military technology. Penicillin and other antibiotics were a collateral benefit of World War II.

Space Defense, Part Two. Presumably everyone agrees that we should defend Earth against Armageddon, or "Deep Impact." Here, we might take note of NASA's $324 million Double Asteroid Redirection Test (DART). In 2022, DART, having traveled 6.8 million miles, hit its 500-foot-wide target, the asteroid Dimorphos, deflecting it from its course. Dimorphos itself was no threat to earth, and yet the DART strike proved the concept of deflecting calamity. "All of us have a responsibility to protect our home planet...it's the only one we have," said NASA Administrator Bill Nelson, who added, "This mission shows that NASA is trying to be ready for whatever the universe throws at us. ...This is a watershed moment for planetary defense and all of humanity."[592] So we see that good Hamiltonianism is good survivalism. And that's good for stocks, especially space-defense stocks.

Space-Based Solar Power (SBSP). Let the US Department of Energy explain the idea: "On earth, solar power is greatly reduced by night, cloud cover, atmosphere and seasonality. Some 30 percent of all incoming solar radiation never makes it to ground level. In space the sun is always shining, the tilt of the Earth doesn't prevent the collection of power and there's no atmosphere to reduce the intensity of the sun's rays. This makes putting solar panels into space a tempting possibility." The DOE then explains how it could work. "Self-assembling satellites are launched into space, along with reflectors and a microwave or laser power transmitter. Reflectors or inflatable mirrors spread over a vast swath of space, directing solar radiation onto solar panels. These panels convert solar power into either a microwave or a laser, and beam uninterrupted power down to Earth. On Earth, power-receiving stations collect the beam and add it to the electric grid. The two most commonly discussed designs for SBSP are a large, deeper space microwave transmitting satellite and a smaller, nearer laser transmitting satellite."[593] Since 173,000 terawatts of solar energy strike Earth continuously—more than 10,000 times what the world uses—it's easy to see that a relatively small solar panel array up in space could satisfy the world's energy needs. To put it mildly, the political issues surrounding SBSP would be daunting. For instance, it would be necessary to convince the planet's WIINIMBYs that the energy beam coming down from space wasn't some sort of death ray. Yet as we have also seen, green capitalists are so intent on solar energy that they are willing to rethink existing environmental restrictions as they eye a Framework. So they might be the energetic force that makes the sale on this energy source.

Space Mining. A single asteroid, 16 Psyche, about 200 million miles away, is thought to be the core of a former planet. It consists mostly of

---

[592] Bardan, Roxana, "NASA Confirms DART Mission Impact Changed Asteroid's Motion in Space," NASA, October 11, 2022. https://bit.ly/3phuX8K

[593] "Space-Based Solar Power," Department of Energy, March 6, 2014. https://bit.ly/44LomCq

iron and nickel, possessing a hypothetical current value of $10,000 qua-drillion.[594] Such googol numbers have enticed many entrants into the field, including Planetary Resources. Founded in 2009, it had raised $50 million by 2016—and found itself out of business by 2020. The problem has been that those pursuing the Heinleinian coolness of space mining have lost sight of the practical difficulty. We can note, further, that were metals mined in galactic levels of abundance ever brought back to Earth, the terrestrial price would surely fall, perhaps undercutting the economic viability of the extraterrestrial operation. To be sure, some day it will be possible to use extraterrestrial materials to feed extraterrestrial industries with little or no spillover back to earth. That might be awhile but the prospect of industries in space, possibly leaving Earth to be nothing but leafy and green, will always have the imaginative casting their glance asteroidally. Yet for all the joy of space, we must now consider a killjoy.

THE DEAD-HAND FRAMEWORK

In the 1979 sci-fi movie *Alien*, spacefarers abroad the dark ship *Nostromo*, come across a crashed spaceship on a lost planet. It's a scary sight—and it gets worse from there. Shifting from reel to real, space fans might say that the Outer Space Treaty (OST) is its own hulking horror story. Written in 1967, at a time when people still believed the United Nations would usher in the Brotherhood of Man, the US, and 113 other countries, have ratified the OST. Which is unfortunate, because it's a kind of space communism, or at least communalism. It reads in part, "The exploration and use of outer space, including the moon and other celestial bodies, shall be carried out for the benefit and in the interests of all countries, irrespective of their degree of economic or scientific development, and shall be the province of all mankind." If space were a John Lennon song, it might be possible

---

[594] Kizer Whitt, Kelly, "Asteroid Psyche: $10,000 quadrillion or rubble pile?" *EarthSky*, June 16, 2021. https://earthsky.org/space/asteroid-psyche-metal-or-rubble-pile/

to "Imagine" that such world federalist rhetoric could be translated into practical political economy and business plans. But as Lennon himself discovered at the end of his life in 1980, Earth isn't always such a nice place. So why should space be different? The OST is as workable as the UN General Assembly. *Not*.

There have been some clever legal work-arounds on the OST. For instance, one clause forbids "national appropriation." Okay, the work-rounders say, "national" speaks to what a nation can't do, not to what a corporation can do.[595] That's a reasonable argument, but of course, the adjudication depends on the judge. The pro-space business Trump administration attempted to fix the OST with the Artemis Accords. That agreement, signed in 2020, states, "The Signatories note that the utilization of space resources can benefit humankind by providing critical support for safe and sustainable operations." That's useful language, but then the Accords take much of it back, declaring that any space mining operation "should be executed in a manner that complies with the Outer Space Treaty." And furthermore, that space mining should be "safe and sustainable."[596] With language such as that, we could even have a NEPA/EIS regime in space—some galactic EPA could wrap the universe in red tape. In addition to the US, two-dozen countries have signed the Artemis Accords, including such space-minded nations as India, Israel, Japan, and the United Arab Emirates. Once again on a space matter, the Biden administration— influenced by Blue Hamiltonians—has kept continuity with the Trump administration on Artemis.[597] However, Artemis signatories do not include China and Russia. Moreover, the Accords are not an international treaty. All this means that nobody really knows what the future legal status of space assets will be. For the time being, of course, powerful countries are pretty

---

[595] "Treaty on Principles Governing the Activities of States in the Exploration and Use of Outer Space, including the Moon and Other Celestial Bodies," United Nations, 1967. https://tinyurl.com/bdh2vync

[596] "The Artemis Accords," NASA, 2020. https://tinyurl.com/25ck9tfy

[597] Bardan, Roxana, "NASA Welcomes Spain as 25th Artemis Accords Signatory," NASA, May 30, 2023. https://bit.ly/3rqKfIM

much doing whatever they want, and yet history shows that wild wests are eventually enclosed in some sort of legal regime. Space is infinitely large, and yet the area around Earth is not. Eventually, a Framework, or perhaps Frameworks, will be put in place.

As a last point on our prospects in space, we might recall the work of the British naturalist D'Arcy Wentworth Thompson (1860-1948). One of his key tenets is that growth creates form, but form limits growth. That is, growth fills out a form, but after that, the form limits growth. Among the examples Thompson cites is the shell, which enables growth of the organism, but then confines it.[598] In that spirit, we can say that for us, Earth is a shell—a gloriously life-giving and wonderful shell, of course, but still, a shell. And now, a small shell at that, compared to the human prospect in space. Which is to say, to continue flourishing, we will need to go outside our form, off the Earth. One needn't be a doomsdayer to nonetheless see that our luck on this planet will one day run out. So best for us to be in two, or more, places at once.

We can add that in space, Directional Investment is at its most, well, Directional. How to invest successfully to spread outward, to the point where human survival is safely compartmentalized and distributed, and human potential maximized to Bezosian dimensions? That will be the sort of astral transcendence that effectively blends the self-interest of investment with the altruism of humanity's betterment.

INVESTMENT TAKEAWAYS

- According to a 2023 report in *Payload Space,* "Seattle, Austin, and Denver are just a few promising emergent space hubs readying for the next space age. Startup clusters have also sprouted in places like Long Beach, Phoenix, Northern Virginia, New Mexico, and

---

[598] Thompson, D'Arcy Wentworth, *On Growth and Form,* 1917. https://bit. ly/3Q2HXKn

Florida."[599] We can note that some of these places are blue, and others are red. It's possible, of course, that there will be a blue cluster, and a red cluster.

- All the biological work done to help humans survive and flourish in space will, as noted, feed back to Earth. That is, someone will take the smarts and use them to revive dinosaurs, create new life forms, and on and on from there. So there will be many new products in the bio-bazaar.

- As everything is up for grabs in space, all manner of astro-political solutions will likely be essayed. Some players will wish to go it alone in space, while others will seek legal structures. Most likely, the challenge of insurance will weigh heavily. Insurance is based on calculating risk, and so insurers, eager to find some benchmark for their numbers, will grope toward the assurance of some kind of Framework. And that suggests, in turn, urgent politics on an international scale. Which is to say, diplomacy. It's interesting to note that the most famous diplomats of Western history—Machiavelli, Talleyrand, Metternich, Kissinger—have all shared a right-of-center outlook, what's called "conservative realism." That's the sort of worldview that goes well with investment. But is past prologue? Or will the future be more liberal, even progressive, as imagined in *Star Trek*? The fate of commercial empires could depend on who is funding, and electing, future space leaders. With such questions in mind, we'll next look at Directional Politics.

---

[599] Sorenson, Aaron, "Seattle, Denver, Austin Vie to be 'Silicon Valley of Space,'" *Payload Space*, July 7, 2023. https://bit.ly/46QjduQ

CHAPTER SIXTEEN

DIRECTIONAL POLITICS

In previous chapters, we've considered the Direction of investments—trends to be *spotted*, and trends to be *shaped*. The shaping, of course, comes from politics. And now, in this concluding chapter, we'll look at how politics itself can be shaped, with an eye toward shaping positive investment Frameworks. If Frameworks can be Directed by politics, and we can Direct politics, we've got it made.

MONEY IN POLITICS

The usual discussion of "money in politics" concerns donations to candidates. One credible estimate of the amount of money spent on the 2020 election put the total at $14.4 billion.[600] For sure, that's a lot of money. But let's keep in mind, that $14.4 billion was a mere 1/1500 of US gross domestic product that year. If we want to see where the real money in politics resides, we must look to the economy itself—that is, to the GDP. It was more than $21 trillion in 2020, and risen since. That's how much money is leverageable in every election.

---

[600] Evers-Hillstrom, Karl, "Most expensive ever: 2020 election cost $14.4 billion," Open Secrets, February 11, 2021. https://bit.ly/3CVe06V

In November 2020, about 159 million people voted for president. And how much money was shifted because of 2020 presidential election results? To cite just one inflection, investments in green energy did much better under President Biden. Indeed, if we divide the $21 trillion GDP in 2020 by the 159 million people who voted, we get a "valuation" of each vote being "worth" about $132,000. And that's just for annual GDP. As a further metric, we can recall that the total amount of wealth in the US is around $150 trillion. And the total amount of *potential* wealth, waiting to be unleashed with the right policies, is vastly greater still. What's the future value of the economy? Highly variable. Will the US grow by 2 percent per year in the next twenty years, as it has for past twenty years? Or will it do better? Grow 4 percent? Or 6 percent? Or with AI, can it grow all the way up to the projection made by Open AI's Sam Altman—a 100-fold increase in wealth? That's the *real* money in politics, the wealth shaped by politics for better and for worse.

We should hasten to say, of course, that an individual's vote cannot be directly monetized. It's not legal to pay someone to vote, or not vote. And that's as it should be. However, people have always been free to vote their self-interest, and that self-interest, expressed by voters and the politicians who seek their votes, oftentimes seem, well, transactional. Some campaign messages come pretty close to saying "vote yourself money," and they are fully legal. In the meantime, the amount of wealth that's in play should get us thinking—thinking about leverage. And so, in pursuit of leverage, let's think about reengineering politics.

If your side wins an election, it can be good for you as an investor. If, that is, the candidate gets elected with a mandate to do positive things. Indeed, there's confusion built into the current system, starting with the word "side," as in, political party. It can be argued that the two major parties, Democratic and Republican, have become so barnacled and baroque that they are incapable of delivering a "pure play" on an investment. In homage to Peter Lynch, we could say that they suffer from "revealed diworseification." That is, we've discovered that the parties have their fingers in so many pies that they no longer act coherently on key polices. In some sense, this is at should be. The American people are, after all, diverse—which means deeply divided. Reflecting that status quo, the parties are simply not configured to get big things done.

In previous chapters, we've considered some big-delta, big-alpha ideas, including desalinated water, medical cures, and accelerated space exploration. Each is a good idea, each would poll well, and yet none of them are anywhere near the top of the national agenda. To be sure, there are plenty of competing issues, and yet it's the American way to politick, legally and peacefully, to move an issue up to higher prominence. So that's what we should do. Indeed, it takes an enormous commitment to building a favorable Framework for good goals—and we should do that, too.

Some might ask, which of the two political parties, Democrat or Republican, is more supportive, *and* competent enough, *and* focused enough, to build one or more Frameworks? Many will say Republicans are more instinctively in favor of business-minded projects—they are certainly more anti-green—and yet one could scan the headlines and look in vain for evidence that any of the goals we've discussed are top GOP priorities. Others might say that Blue Hamiltonian Democrats are more serious-minded, technologically literate, and realistic about getting things done. However, those aren't the only Democrats. So there's no chance, here, to resolve the question of partisan optimality. As Peter Lynch would say, it's best to *notice* that which we do and don't like, and draw our own conclusions.

Still, let's drill down on one particular topic: desalination. In Arizona, Republicans were cautiously in favor of desal, and yet it was hardly a top issue for them in 2022. And in any case, the Democrat won the governorship that year. To actually get the Arizona desal project built will take enormous amounts of what physicists call activation energy. Activation energy, guided by a clear vision, is what creates Frameworks.

Here's the point of this chapter: *If investors can join with voters in common cause, it's likely that one party will be with them—maybe even both parties.* That's how Frameworks have worked in the past; in the nineteenth century, both parties were pro-railroad. In that spirit today, if the voters of

Arizona got together and said, "Hey, we *really* want this water project," at least one of the parties would be happy to rush to the front and lead the par. Politicians, of either party or any party, have their own priorities, but as Illinois senator Everett Dirksen quipped of his political kind, "When they feel the heat, they see the light." Democracy can work. The challenge is making sure the message is unmistakably clear—in more than one election, if need be. In a political environment filled with multiplicities of media, staying on message, with oomph, is an enormous challenge.

Let's fix all this, so that voters can find good issues, and wield their power on behalf of them. As an aside, if voters can wield their voting power, then the familiar definition of "money in politics" will matter less. Politicians know that if they have the votes, they don't need so much money, at least not for their campaigns. In fact, if voters wield their power for the sake of Frameworks, then we'll be on our way to mobilizing the real money in politics...which is, of course, the GDP of the US, and beyond that, all the foreign capital that would come here for the sake of a good investment in, for example, a Health Freedom Zone. So for the health and freedom of all of us, let's find a way to harness people power to Framework objectives. Let voters hear the message, "turn your vote into money." Not in a crooked or corrupt way, of course, but in a Frameworked way. A Framework that makes not only Black Swans, but also, Golden Geese.

UNLEASHING THE BUNDLE: FROM SPAC TO SPOT

Investors are a relatively weak force in society, which is interesting, because they are so numerous. According to Gallup, 61 percent of American adults say they own stock—that's about 150 million voters, or potential voters.[601] Now of course, the number of people who really think about their investments, or vote with them in mind, is smaller. Still, whatever the actual

---

[601] Jones, Jeffrey, "What Percentage of Americans Own Stock?" Gallup, May 24, 2023. https://bit.ly/3NLvucm

number might be, it's big. So why the political weakness? Three reasons come to mind:

First, many investors are so focused, or so quantitative, that they are oblivious to larger political trends—or to larger anything. Also, they might lack, shall we say, the optimum personality for politics. To be sure, they might have political opinions, even strong political opinions, and yet passionate intensity often cuts against effectiveness.

Second, speaking of passion, capitalism produces its own set of disconnects and detours. Back in 1976, Daniel Bell suggested the coming difficulty, observing that corporations built on cold calculus were, at the same time, promoting "pleasure, instant joy, relaxing and letting go."[602] Here's how that can play out in politics. People get rich from business, and then they—or more likely, their heirs—are seduced by demonstrative, performative and Anti-Directional styles.

Third, investors are divided between the two parties. Republicans still get the rap as being the "party of the rich," and yet after the 2022 elections, of the ten most affluent Congressional districts in the US, Democrats held nine. Lots of Blue Hamiltonians. At the same time, Republicans, Red Jeffersonians, represent the majority of the House districts below the national median income.[603] So both parties have constituents that are indifferent, perhaps even hostile, to "big business," or maybe anything big.

So neither party can be described as a pure play for investors. In addition to being diworseified, the parties are bundled with all the other interests and interest groups that fill out American life. So maybe we should think about unbundling investor interests from these encrusted status quo conglomerations. Maybe we need to hack the status quo, in the sense of reinventing it.

So does that argue an unapologetic "Investors Party"? One never says never, but the first-past-the-post electoral system in the US makes it much more plausible to argue for an assertive investors faction within each party.

---

[602] Bell, Daniel, *Cultural Contradictions,* 72.
[603] Kight, Stef, "Dramatic realignment swings working-class districts toward GOP," *Axios,* April 16, 2023. https://bit.ly/42YGQOy

If that were to work, whichever party wins, investors would be okay. In any case, there should definitely be *something*, because the two parties need a jolt. Only Frameworks will unleash the can-do spirit we need to do big things, both popular and profitable. We can note that this sort of reconfiguration happens all the time in business. The very idea of the corporation, going back thousands of years, solved the problem of the mortality of the individual. So the person might fade away, but the corporation would not. (The Catholic Church is a nonprofit corporation.) Then the joint stock corporation solved the problem of raising capital. Most recently, investors have attempted to solve red tape problems created by the Securities and Exchange Commission by turning to the SPAC, or Special Purpose Acquisition Company, to ease business deals. So in this problem-solving spirit, we need a SPOT, a Special Political Operations Team. A SPOT could operate within the Republican Party, the Democratic Party—or any party. Of course, SPOT would have to pass the Ten-Strike Test—is it 10x better than the old paradigm? Interestingly enough, reinventing political techniques can yield dramatically better results. We know that because at one level, electoral politics is a numbers game—he/she with the most votes wins. And that reminds us to think of another numbers game that's been reinvented, with 10x results.

LESSONS FROM *MONEYBALL*

"If you challenge conventional wisdom, you will find ways to do things much better than they are currently done." So said Bill James, who was first the iconoclast, and then the guru, of baseball statistics.[604] Those words, of course, could have been said by anyone looking to squeeze more value out of an existing system. But let's stay with baseball. It's always been a game for number crunchers (the first box score was recorded in 1845). Indeed, anyone who goes a ballgame knows that more than a few fans will sit there

---

[604] Quoted in Lewis, Michael, *Moneyball: the Art of Winning an Unfair Game,* (Waterville, Maine: Thorndike Press, 2003), 177.

in the stands, barely watching the game as they cipher up statistics—for purposes of gambling, maybe, but more likely, just geekery. Indeed, just about all baseball fans revel in statistics, especially the "glamorous" stats, such as home runs and strikeouts. Yet going back to the 1940s, keen brains could see that the sexiest numbers and the winningest numbers were two different things. Allan Roth, statistician for the Brooklyn Dodgers, figured out that the glam-stats were not the ones that best indicated who was going to win the most games. Instead, Roth focused on more mundane statistics, such as on base percentage, or harder to compute stats, such as hits with men on base, that better correlated with game victories. Roth's key insight was profound and obvious at the same time—the fundamental statistic in baseball is the run. Get more runs in each game, win each game. We can pause over that statement and observe, the team that gets more runs can be weaker in every other statistical measure, and yet, if it ekes out the most runs, it wins. In the Roth-ian vision, superstars and superstats are nice to have, but winning the game is the must-have. It's that quality of insight that helps explain why the Dodgers have been so successful as a team, and further explains why, decades after his death, Roth is a revered figure in baseball. In the admiring summation of stat-king Bill James, "He was the guy who began it all."

About Roth and his boss at the Dodgers, the visionary executive Branch Rickey, it's been written, "Rickey and Roth's fundamental contribution to the advancement of baseball statistics comes from their conceptual revisionism, their willingness to strip the game down to its basic unit, the run, and reconstruct its statistics accordingly."[605] Building on this incisive thinking, Bill James began publishing his own take on baseball statistics, which blossomed into the Society for American Baseball Research (SABR). What's now called Sabermetrics has undergirded the

---

[605] John Thorn and Pete Palmer, *The Hidden Game of Baseball*, quoted in Society for American Baseball Research, accessed April 30, 2023. https://sabr.org/bioproj/person/allan-roth/. Rickey made many other contributions to baseball, including the batting helmet, the modern farm team system, and, of course, the racial integration of the game.

intellectual revolution in Major League Baseball itself, in the person of Billy Beane, who managed the Oakland Athletics to glory at the turn of the century. Beane was made even more famous by Michael Lewis' 2003 book *Moneyball*, and then, eight years later, in the Brad Pitt movie. And if the A's are nothing special these days, that's because all MLB teams use Rothian SABR/*Moneyball* metrics. As we observed in Chapter Ten, there's good reason to guard a good idea as a trade secret.

In any case, we can all study this history, applying lessons to other realms. For instance, the cautionary point that Lewis makes about the evaluation of ball players is a warning to anyone seeking to assay an asset, human or otherwise—be sure you're measuring the key performance indicator. Lewis writes, "If gross miscalculations of a person's value could occur on a baseball field, before a live audience of thirty thousand, and a television audience of millions more, what did that say about the measurement of performance in other lines of work? If professional baseball players could be over- or undervalued, who couldn't?" Those are challenging questions, full of implications for any numbers-based undertaking. How do you properly evaluate the inputs you need to maximize what you need, be it runs, or dollars, or votes. Lewis continues, "Bad as they may have been, the statistics used to evaluate baseball players were probably far more accurate than anything used to measure the value of people who didn't play baseball for a living."[606] So there's a "fog of baseball," such that even shrewd veterans can make a gross miscalculation. But of course, all humans can be in a fog, and anything they do is subject to gross miscalculation. So that's why we need hard metrics, to keep it real. Mistakes will still be made, but at least we can data-crunch our way to a fix.

No wonder politics is a mess. It's that much bigger, and foggier, than baseball. But if Roth, Rickey, James, and Beane could strip baseball down to its essentials and figure out a better way for baseball, we can do the same for politics. We don't need to change the rules, we just have to be smarter. Specifically, we need to address the four obstacles that hobble American

---

[606] Lewis, Michael, *Moneyball*, 134.

politics: first, the *inefficiency* of campaigning; second, the *superfluity* of the media; third, the *uncertainty* of the voters; and fourth, the *unaccountability* of politicians.

CAMPAIGN INEFFICIENCY

As was the case with pre-Sabermetrics baseball, political candidates and their campaigns tend to focus on statistics that seem important, but actually aren't all that important. That is, campaigns think of money raised, and polls, of course, and measures of media reach, such as retweets, likes, or gross ratings points for TV advertising. In addition, candidates and consultants love to think about "momentum" and "buzz." We might pause over that metric that might seem to be the "hardest," the opinion poll. Upon close examination, even it isn't so good. A poll is, at best, a snapshot. And what is it a snapshot of? It's a snapshot of the people polled. We can usefully compare a poll to a similar statistical construct, the Randomized Controlled Trial for pharma drugs. As we have seen, RCT is a distinctly dubious way of knowing whether or not a drug works. Indeed, in both cases, polling and RCT as it interplays with the FDA, there's a considerable behind-the-scenes negotiation of truth.

Back to politics. If we start with murky metrics, add on dubious assumptions, and sprinkle money on top, we're not likely to get a good result. Indeed, we've seen some gross miscalculations, even by smart moneymen. For instance, Michael Bloomberg spent some $1.25 billion, in his 2020 bid for the Democratic presidential nomination, and got of course, bupkis.[607] And in 2022, Citadel's Ken Griffin donated $50 million to an Illinois Republican gubernatorial hopeful, Richard Irvin, who did all the usual candidate-y things, such as running TV ads. And yet Irvin lost badly, coming in third in the GOP primary, garnering a meager 119,000 votes.

---

[607] Tindera, Michela, "Here's Where Mike Bloomberg, The Biggest Spender In The 2020 Election, Has Donated This Year," *Forbes*, November 5, 2021. https://bit.ly/3Px9jrE

Griffin's $50 million "investment" worked out to $420 a vote.[608] To lose. So what's going on? We could cite many more reasons, including, of course, the problem of weak candidates—also, that campaign consultants have a curious attachment to the status quo. This is an industry ripe for reinvention.

To get us started, we can recall the Drucker Test: *If we weren't doing this now, would we start?* If the honest answer is, "No," then we have to start thinking about a change. As our guide to change in electoral politics, we can borrow from Allan Roth's axiom about the run in baseball and say, for politics, the fundamental unit is the vote. If we stay focused on votes, we can see that the costly superstructure of political campaigning is extrinsic. What's intrinsic, and needs to be honed in on, is the actual process of getting voters to the voting booth—or, of course, these days, with absentee and mail-in voting, getting the voting booth to the voter. Just as Roth wanted more runs, we want more votes. Let's keep it that simple.

With simplicity in mind, let's apply the Drucker Test to campaign operations. But first let's preface with the realization that most voters, in both parties, have already resolved how they're going to vote. This is the base we hear so much about—those voters who vote in every election, or almost every election, always, or almost always, for the same party. Probably 80 percent of voters in the US count as base voters, roughly split between the two parties. So if a base voter is one of "ours," SPOT's challenge is to push the probability that he or she actually votes for our candidate to the highest possible level—ideally, to 100 percent. Just as winning baseball teams strive to clear the bases by getting all their on-base players to home plate for the runs, so, too, we wish to "clear the bases" by getting all our voters to vote.

So how, exactly, to get all our peeps to the polls? This effort might entail any degree of "white glove" treatments for the voter, such as nudges, reminders, peer pressure. We can add gamification (voters who build up a "streak" of right votes could be even more honored) and non-fungible

[608] Pearson, Rick, "Billionaire Ken Griffin has now given $50 million to Richard Irvin's campaign for governor," *The Chicago Tribune*, June 1, 2022. https://bit.ly/43WOBFP

tokens (an NFT needn't have any monetary value—for voters, it could be fun and helpful to favored candidates, and that's good enough) as tools for motivation and enthusiasm.[609] The idea is to create a wave of enthusiasm, and have it crest at the election. In fact, we've already seen something of a dry run for this. In 2021, an army of activist investors, informed by free-for-all platforms such as Reddit, and powered by low-cost or no-cost trading platforms such as Robinhood, chose to drive up the stock price of video game retailer GameStop. The stock was worth less than a dollar in 2019, and yet the activists thought it was undervalued, so they bid it up to as high as $347 in January 2021.[610] At the time, this author wrote of the political potential, "Anyone who can build an online group might also be able to build an online *bloc of voters*. To be sure, politicians and parties have been assembling voter blocs for eons and yet there's always a new and better way, based on some emerging issue." I added, "There's always some new emerging technology, such as, most recently, handheld apps. Can Redditors—or users of other platforms, including the newer newbies—figure out a better way to build a vote-minded platform or ecosystem?[611] Thanks to digital technology, blocs can scale. Once the initial investment is made, the marginal cost of going from one voter to a million—or 100 million voters—isn't so daunting.

When we speak of SPOT organizing blocs of votes, focusing on getting out the vote (GOTV) some might say this approach recalls the old Tammany Hall-type political machines of New York or Chicago. Indeed, those political machines were all about GOTV. In those days, campaigns were inexpensive, because there wasn't much media—and certainly no TV—on which to spend money. So campaigns focused on speeches and

---

[609] Pinkerton, James, "If a Non-Fungible Token Is Worth $69 Million to an Artist, How Much is NFT Worth to Politics?" *Daily Caller*, March 18, 2021. https://bit.ly/3KkJmrL

[610] Malz, Allan, "The GameStop Episode: What Happened and What Does It Mean?" *Cato Journal*, Fall 2021. https://bit.ly/3Nq0GMQ

[611] Pinkerton, James, "Just as Politics Has Come to GameStop, So GameStop Activism Will Come to Politics," *Breitbart*, February 20, 2021. https://bit.ly/3XoYObU

parades, and most of all, they focused on getting their people to the polls. The system worked. The political machines won elections. And by winning, they supported the framework of their choice—solidaristic, albeit corrupt, ethnic and partisan power. This is not the Framework to which we aspire today, but we are reminded of what we already knew—the best way to make something work is to make it automatic. Once we convince voters to support a Framework of good things—things that will be good for all of us—we want support for it be automatic. Perhaps the electoral equivalent of a crypto smart contract.

As we muse on the impact of new technology on electioneering, it's worth recalling that the old political machines faded with the coming of television. With TV, along with suburbanization, voters could get ideas about politics from a source other than the local ward heeler. And so the granular relationship between the voter and the vote-broker broke down as people were mass-marketed by mass media. So if TV transcended the old political machine, it's fitting that the new political machine will transcend TV.

MEDIA SUPERFLUITY

There's one familiar aspect of campaigning that we've left out—the media. That's not a slap at our friends in the Fourth Estate. It's just an observation that as we focus on the core thing—voting—we realize that we don't need to focus on what's non-core. This is Occam's Razor in full swing. It's the voter's granular relationship—now helped along by digital—with our candidate that matters to us. The voter's non-granular relationship to the media does not matter. Pols can win an election without media, but they can't win it without the most votes. If pols have the votes, they don't need the media. Of course, some will insist that the media is vital to the electoral process. After all, they are delivering news, affecting opinion, carrying advertising. And yes, the media does all those gerunding things— delivering, affecting, carrying—and yet that doesn't make them vital to a campaign. After all, it's perfectly possible to consume a lot of media and not vote—or to vote for the wrong party or candidate. Indeed, it can be argued that mainlining cable news makes most elections boring. That is, if the big contest is the presidential election, then elections for lesser offices—where even an attuned voter might not know the names of the candidates—seem dull. Even worse, national campaigns, including media razzle-dazzle, might generate more heat that is actually needed. That is, to turn a turbine, water must rise to 212 degrees Fahrenheit to make steam— and then it's best to stop there, heat-wise. More heat doesn't turn the turbine any faster, it just causes trouble for the system. This, by the way, is a big problem with nuclear reactors. The temperature of the radioactive core is a couple thousand degrees, and so disposing of that excess heat is a systemic challenge that can break down and melt down. In political terms, too much heat can distort party primaries, rewarding extremists who are less likely to be electable in a general election. And our goal, of course, is to win the election with a rational, or at least amenable, pro-Framework candidate. For all these reasons, it behooves us to disintermediate the media from our GOTV operation. People, journalists, and pundits can do as they please, but our campaign wishes to build a tight relationship with actual voters. Voters are the signal, the media is the noise. The pursuit of that clear channel signal means direct candidate-to-voter contact…which, of course, is cheaper than TV advertising.

VOTER UNCERTAINTY

There's another thing wrong with the current media environment. Let's visualize—a citizen is watching TV, surfing past a news channel or a news show, and gets an idea about taking some political action. Yet now the voter confronts a curious gap, or bifurcation. That is, there's one screen from which to passively consume media, and there's another screen upon which to actively do something. The person watches TV, which is one screen, gets stirred up and then has to go to another screen (smart phone/laptop/

desktop) to "like," post a comment, give money, and perhaps even register to vote or apply for an absentee ballot. We can call this split the "two-screen dilemma" because it violates the instinctive parsimony of human behavior. We all want to simplify, streamline, and generally do less work. And so that means one screen. Smart user experience (UX) operators understand that, and they give people what they want. That's why social media can be so frictionless, and that's why people are "spoiled." Folks have come to expect that a single screen—or, more recently, a voice assistant—can run everything in their home and maybe even their life.

So why is politics, bifurcated as it is, UX-wise, such as lagging indicator? Why is it so far behind the curve of tech capability? In large part, it's a matter of legacy. One legacy is cable TV, a dinosaur of 1970s non-interactive technology that shambles on, even as it sheds subscribers. A second legacy is the media's self-conception. Across the left-right spectrum, outlets see themselves as covering the news—and perhaps even making news—but they don't see themselves as being actual electioneers. That self-conception sounds reasonable, until we remember that our purpose is not to understand the media, but rather, to win elections. Winning elections requires a Razor-meets-SABR willingness to think new thoughts.

As part of that new thought process, we might recall an old acronym from marketing: AIDA—*Attention, Interest, Decision, Action*. The whole point of a good system is that it makes AIDA easy. A well-designed UX is "sticky," encouraging the customer to stay within the ecosystem. AIDA is what makes Amazon so powerful. You look for the product, click on it, and it's ordered. Instant gratification! It's this instantaneity that makes e-commerce such a success. And it's also the key to consumer relationship management (CRM) software, of the kind used nowadays by just about every business. So it should be a SPOT project to develop VRM—voter relationship management. Of course, right now, even if we had VRM, there's the problem that the voter's attention is split between those two screens. In politics today, the first two letters of AIDA, "Attention" and "Interest," go to the TV screen, and the second two letters, "Decision" and "Action," go to the internet screen. Bifurcated, even fractured, is the opposite of efficient.

So instead of two screens, we need one screen. One screen to rule them all. Or at least, to win elections. One screen where the citizen can be warmed up (but not overheated) to vote. And thanks to nuanced digital technology, including AI, SPOT will stay with the voter every step of the way, all through the AIDA sequence. But mindful of our ultimate purpose here, let's call it the Direction app.

Okay, but why would a voter go to this one-screened Direction app? What content would appear on it? Here's the voter magnet—the app would talk about the big issues of Frameworks, including, for example, a Health Freedom Zone for medical cures. That's a compelling topic, for sure. And so the Direction app would have to be advertised as the place to find out about an HFZ. With a well-crafted pitch—*vote yourself health*—it's not so hard to see a voter pledging to support HFZ, and pledging to support candidates who support HFZ. Utilizing the granularity of digital, it would be easy to share, with permission, the news of this pledge-taking, and so build an online community.

Still, HFZ is not the sort of topic that would grab voters' attention every day, or even on a second day. But here's the point. The Directional app wouldn't need the voter to come back every day, or even on the second day. Unlike TV or other media, SPOT doesn't need chronic couch potatoes, watching and clicking hour after hour, week after week, paying the cable bill, imbibing advertising. Instead, it needs voters. And voting is (or should be) a once-per-election thing. So the app doesn't need to entertain on an ongoing basis, it just needs the voter to vote that one time. If the voter checks that box, as it were, everyone's happy and the Framework is secure. Earlier, we pointed to the GameStop wave of 2021. That's what Directionalists should want in every election—a burst of energy that gets everyone doing one thing—voting. So SPOT could stage parties, physical or virtual, where each voter shows off his or her marked ballot, and is duly rewarded with psychic benefits. We trust the voters, of course, but it's always good to verify.

The Directional app aims for an electoral harmonic convergence— the right voters, hearing the right message, at the right time, all coming together in the right place. We can say that this is the DARPA approach to politics. Just as the Framework stays with the investor project every step of the way, so SPOT stays with the voter every step till the election. In the meantime, of course, the voter goes about life, but the SPOT is always there—as a bot buddy, a crypto nudger, an AI assistant—with just one mission ... assuring that the voter votes.

POLITICIANS' UNACCOUNTABILITY

Okay, with SPOT in place, we now turn our attention to politicians. They all promise to do, in general, what's right and good. So how now to make sure they follow through with the specifics of an HFZ, or some other good, such as a High-Tech Health Agency? Here, SPOT marks the X—that is, the crossroads where voters' desires and politicians' ambitions intersect. As we've seen, SPOT "blocs" the votes, electing the politician. And in return, the politician promises to enact HFZ.

But is it that simple? After all, politicians are not always accountable. In fact, sometimes, they are downright *un*accountable. So let's zero in on accountability. Here's a good way. We make our Ask as specific as possible. In fact, we boil it down it a pledge. A pledge for an HFZ, or anything else Framework-wise. Pledges work. The proof comes from activist-macher Grover Norquist. Back in the 1980s, Norquist developed the No Tax-Increase Pledge, offering any candidate a fifty-five-word vehicle to make visible his or her opposition to tax increases. At least in Republican circles, that's a strong message. But then, once in office, how to hold them to their promise? As Norquist says, "Politicians often run for office saying they won't raise taxes, but then quickly turn their backs on the taxpayer. *The idea of the Pledge is simple enough: Make them put their no-new-taxes rhetoric in writing.*"[612] More than 80 percent of Republicans in the Senate and House have taken the pledge, and it's fair to say that "The Pledge," as it's

---

[612] "About the Pledge," Americans for Tax Reform, accessed, May 20, 2023. https://www.atr.org/about-the-pledge/

known, has profoundly shaped Republican thinking on taxes for the past three decades. To be sure, that's Republicans, but one can say that other ideas, too, have developed their own sorts of pledges. For instance, it's hard to find a Democrat who hasn't pledged allegiance to Planned Parenthood.

Of course, pledges have been broken—the most notorious pledge-breaker being, perhaps, George H.W. Bush, who signed the tax pledge as a presidential candidate in 1987 and broke it in the White House in 1990. And look what happened to him. He lost calamitously two years later—indeed, his popular-total fell by seventeen points. It can't be said that all that decline was due to breaking The Pledge, but ticking off the tax-minded, and the truth-minded, was certainly a negative. And the fact that Republicans since have mostly abided by The Pledge is testament to its power. Taking an oath is a powerful statement. So is breaking an oath. So if pols take an oath, they will be loath to break it. Some will say, of course, that pledges are a straitjacket on elected officials. To which Norquist on the right, and Planned Parenthood on the left, would say in response, that's exactly why pledges are so good.

To state the matter positively, once politicians are inspired with a message, they can be very articulate and persuasive. For instance, look at Abraham Lincoln. In the middle of the nineteenth century, the arguments for and against slavery were fast and furious. And yet in 1858, Lincoln summed up the abolitionist argument in a snappy line: "As I would not be a slave, so I would not be a master."[613] There in a snap—the anti-slavery argument, fourteen words. In our time, we don't have to be Lincoln to still be pithy.

In pursuit of the right political coalition to build and sustain our Frameworks, we've spotted four concerns: campaign inefficiency, media superfluity, voter uncertainty, and politicians' unaccountability. Now, with SPOT, we can shape the solution. If we build our Framework, good things will come.

---

[613] Abraham Lincoln, fragment, *Collected Works of Abraham Lincoln. Volume 2.* August 1, 1858. https://bit.ly/3plDSWw

INVESTMENT TAKEAWAYS

- If the goal is Directional Politics, aiming at economic transformation, one opportunity along the way is developing the tools needed. We've mentioned two of those needed tools— SPOT (Special Political Operations Team) and VRM (Voter Relationship Management). Who's going to build those? Toolmaking is money-making.

- A SPOT, for example, could exist within a marketplace—an electronic dashboard, listing SPOTs available as a means of getting things done. It could actually be a three-way market with SPOTs, Directional Investors, and blocs of voters. All in the marketplace at the same time—*first*, Directional Investors looking to build Frameworks; *second*, vote-blocs looking for something to vote for and wondering what the reward for them might be; *third*, SPOTs looking for a gig.

- VRM could have five layers of revenue: *first*, from parties or SPOTs; *second*, from individual campaigns; *third*, from proponents of specific projects; *fourth*, ancillary advertising and promotion; and *fifth*, gamification and other kinds of deepened involvement.

- SPOT and VRM offer a new vista of participation—new business models galore, with ample ability to accommodate future tech evolutions, such as AI. In the meantime, SPOT and VRM also starve out much of the exiting political media, because there will be less need to write articles and launch press campaigns on behalf of an idea. It will be simpler to simply vote for it. So there are some shorts, as well as longs. Directional Investing will always rely on honest persuasion and earned good will, but there'll be no need to flog the same arguments, endlessly. Better to win the election and start doing it. By this campaign reckoning, the media are simply middlemen, no longer needed.

THE SEVEN PILLARS OF DIRECTIONAL WISDOM

T his book has argued that investors, and all of us, need liberty, because only liberty makes room for our diversity. And yet at the same time, we need order, because our persons and property need predictability. There's a tension between liberty and order, but there's also an energy. The preceding pages have outlined ways of putting the two concepts together, building Frameworks for growth, jobs, national strength, human better-ment—and, yes, greater investment returns.

Let's sum up. In the ninth chapter of the Book of Proverbs, we are told, "Wisdom hath builded her house, she hath hewn out her seven pillars." That number, seven, seems like a good number for pillars of wisdom. So in that proverbial spirit, here goes:

1. The bigger the delta, the bigger the alpha. Big returns come from big things. Making money any legal and ethical way is fine, but it's also true that fortune favors the bold.

2. Directional Investing is the realization that cultural and political trends drive investments, and that those trends can be *shaped*, not just *spotted*.

3. Imagining precedes investing, and yet historical perspective helps. History is a series of case studies, all of which offer lessons about what works, and what doesn't work. Knowing that the trend is the friend, the investor will wish to spot trends and ride them upward. The trend might, for example, be an S-Curve. But where, on the S-Curve? The steep part? Or the flat part? It pays to be able to notice the difference.

4. Nobody makes money without some sort of a Framework to protect investment. The best Frameworks are legal, productive, and popular.

5. Wherever investment goes—inner or outer—the Protagoran reality holds that man, and woman, will be the measure of everything. If humans are making it and paying for it, humans will be the star of it.

6. Life is future-oriented, and so people are naturally optimists. Show them a path to a better life, backing up the vision with facts, figures, integrity, and a little pizzazz, and they will happily trod that upward path. They will leave the details to leaders—but only if they trust them.

7. Since a Framework of Directional Investing depends on public support, it pays, literally, to tend to politics. And since voters, too, care about money, wealth, and other good things, the Directional Investor has a good story to tell.

A few lines later in Proverbs we are told, "Forsake the foolish, and live; and go in the way of understanding." For the sake of life, civilization—and money—that's a good Direction.

ABOUT THE AUTHOR

James P. Pinkerton is a veteran of two White Houses, three presidential transitions, and six presidential campaigns. He worked at Fox News for twenty years, as a columnist for Newsday for fifteen years, and has published widely, from *The New York Times* to *Foreign Affairs*, from *National Review* to *The American Conservative*.